Pro .NET 4 Parallel Programming in C#

Adam Freeman

Apress®

Pro .NET 4 Parallel Programming in C#

ISBN-13 (pbk): 978-1-4302-2967-4

ISBN-13 (electronic): 978-1-4302-2968-1

Printed and bound in the United States of America 9 8 7 6 5 4 3 2 1

Trademarked names may appear in this book. Rather than use a trademark symbol with every occurrence of a trademarked name, we use the names only in an editorial fashion and to the benefit of the trademark owner, with no intention of infringement of the trademark.

President and Publisher: Paul Manning
Lead Editor: Ewan Buckingham
Technical Reviewer: André van Meulebrouck
Editorial Board: Clay Andres, Steve Anglin, Mark Beckner, Ewan Buckingham, Gary Cornell, Jonathan Gennick, Jonathan Hassell, Michelle Lowman, Matthew Moodie, Duncan Parkes, Jeffrey Pepper, Frank Pohlmann, Douglas Pundick, Ben Renow-Clarke, Dominic Shakeshaft, Matt Wade, Tom Welsh
Coordinating Editor: Anne Collett
Copy Editor: Heather Lang
Production Support: Patrick Cunningham
Indexer: BIM Indexing & Proofreading Services
Artist: April Milne
Cover Designer: Anna Ishchenko

Distributed to the book trade worldwide by Springer-Verlag New York, Inc., 233 Spring Street, 6th Floor, New York, NY 10013. Phone 1-800-SPRINGER, fax 201-348-4505, e-mail orders-ny@springer-sbm.com, or visit www.springeronline.com.

For information on translations, please e-mail rights@apress.com, or visit www.apress.com.

Apress and friends of ED books may be purchased in bulk for academic, corporate, or promotional use. eBook versions and licenses are also available for most titles. For more information, reference our Special Bulk Sales–eBook Licensing web page at www.apress.com/info/bulksales.

The information in this book is distributed on an "as is" basis, without warranty. Although every precaution has been taken in the preparation of this work, neither the author(s) nor Apress shall have any liability to any person or entity with respect to any loss or damage caused or alleged to be caused directly or indirectly by the information contained in this work.

The source code for this book is available to readers at www.apress.com. You will need to answer questions pertaining to this book in order to successfully download the code.

For my wife Jacqui Griffyth and her chickens

Contents at a Glance

Contents

About the Author

■**Adam Freeman** is an experienced IT professional who has held senior positions in a range of companies, most recently chief technology officer and chief operating officer of a global bank. He has written several of books on Java and .NET and has a long-term interest in all things parallel.

About the Technical Reviewer

■**André van Meulebrouck** has an interest in functional programming and the functional approach to parallel computing. He has written white papers and articles on functional programming and theoretical computer science and is a beta tester for F#, which is Microsoft's new functional programming language. He lives in southern California and works as a .NET developer.

Acknowledgments

I would like to thank everyone at Apress for working so hard to bring this book to print. In particular, I would like to thank Anne Collett for keeping things on track and Ewan Buckingham for commissioning and editing the book. I would also like to thank Heather Lang and André van Meulebrouck whose respective efforts as copy editor and technical reviewer made this book far better than it would have been without them.

■ ■ ■

CHAPTER 1

Introducing Parallel Programming

When I started programming in the mid-1990s, Java was the hot new language. One of the most talked-about features was its support for parallel programming—the ability for an application to do more than one task simultaneously. I was very excited; I worked in a research lab, and I finally had a way to use the four CPUs in the Sun server that I had managed to get in a moment of budget madness.

Having a four-CPU machine was a big—no, huge—deal in those days. It cost $150,000 and designed for use in a data center, and I made the machine into a desktop computer by adding a couple of monitors and shoe-horning it into my tiny office. On a summer's day, the office temperature reached 95 degrees, and I got dizzy from dehydration. But I was in geek heaven—cool hardware, cool language, and cool project.

When I started to actually write parallel code, I hit a brick wall; my code didn't behave the way I wanted. Everything would suddenly stop, or I'd get bad results or tie up all of the CPUs so badly that I would have to reboot the machine. A reboot took up to an hour, which was far from ideal when giving demonstrations.

So, like many other people before me, I embarked on a long and painful learning process to figure out how to get things right.

A lot has changed over the years. Sun has been sold; a computer with ten times the power of my old Sun server can be bought at the local mall for $500, and there are rules against making a sauna out of an office, even in the name of geek glory.

One thing that has remained the same is the gulf between the knowledge and skills required to write single-threaded versus parallel code. Languages have evolved to make the programmer's life easier for writing regular programs, but little has changed for parallel programming—until now, of course. Microsoft has added features to C#, the .NET Framework, and Visual Studio 2010 that take a big step toward pairing a modern programming language with a modern approach to parallel programming.

Introducing .NET Parallel Programming

This book is about the parallel programming features of .NET 4, specifically the Task Parallel Library (TPL), Parallel LINQ, and the legion of support classes that make writing parallel programs with C# simpler and easier than ever before.

I have been writing parallel programs on and off since I had that overheated office, about 15 years in all. I can honestly say that the TPL is the single most impressive, useful, and well thought out enhancement in all that time.

With the widespread use of multiprocessor and multicore computers, parallel programming has gone mainstream. Or it would have, if the tools and skills required had been easier to use and acquire.

Microsoft has responded to the need for a better way to write parallel programs with the enhancements to the .NET framework I describe in this book.

.NET has had support for parallel programming since version 1.0, now referred to as classic threading, but it was hard to use and made you think too much about managing the parallel aspects of your program, which detracts from focusing on what needs to be done.

The new .NET parallel programming features are built on top of the classic threading support. The difference between the TPL and classic threading becomes apparent when you consider the basic programming unit each uses. In the classic model, the programmer uses threads. Threads are the engine of execution, and you are responsible for creating them, assigning work to them, and managing their existence. In the classic approach, you create a little army to execute your program, give all the soldiers their orders, and keep an eye on them to make sure they do as they were told. By contrast, the basic unit of the TPL is the task, which describes something you want done. You create tasks for each activity you want performed, and the TPL takes care of creating threads and dealing with them as they undertake the work in your tasks. The TPL is task-oriented, while the classic threading model is worker-oriented.

Tasks let you focus primarily on what problem you want to solve instead of on the mechanics of how it will get done. If you have tried parallel programming with classic threads and given up, you will find the new features have a refreshing and enabling approach. You can use the new features without having to know anything about the classic features. You'll also find that the new features are much better thought out and easier to use.

As I said, the classic threading model is still there, but the TPL takes care of it for you. Threads are created and used to execute one or more of your tasks, all without you having to pay attention to the details of how it happens. The process is very cool and makes parallel programming much more pleasant and productive.

What's in This Book (and What Is Not)

If you want to know how to write parallel programs using C#, this is the book for you. This focused, hands-on book shows you the classes and features, how to use them, and the kinds of problems they can be used to solve. Lots of fully worked code samples are included, as well as lists of methods and properties and pointers and warnings for topics that have potential traps.

This book contains a lot of code. I believe that the best way to learn how to use a feature is to see it used. You'll often see a chain of examples that only have minor differences, and I make no apology for this similarity. When you want to remind yourself of a specific class or technique, you will want to see it being used fully, without having to piece together fragments of examples from different sections and chapters. For the same reason, the examples tend to be trivial, often adding a series of numeric values or calculating integer powers. The point is always to show you how to use something in the TPL, not for me to demonstrate that I can write large applications. Seeing small, simple, frequent, repetitive code, and more code, is how programmers learn best.

I have avoided writing about the theory behind the new features, and I'm pretty liberal in my use of terms. Parallel programming is an active area of academic research, and the new .NET parallel features incorporate some recent innovations and ideas. But this is a book about programming, and my guess is that you have picked up this book because you, like me, want to know how to program as quickly and as effectively as possible. I love the research; I find it interesting and respect the people who do it, but this book is not the place for it.

Similarly, I don't cover the classic threading model except in a couple of advanced sections explaining how you can control the way that the TPL interacts with the underlying threads used to perform your work. Some good books are available on the classic model, but given that the whole point of the TPL is to abstract away from the details, I am comfortable leaving that material to other authors.

Understanding the Benefits (and Pitfalls) of Parallel Programming

Parallel computing is, at heart, a performance play. The work that a program performs is broken up into pieces, which are performed by multiple cores, processors, or computers. Some of those pieces of work will be performed at the same time, that is, in *parallel*, or *concurrently*, which is where the two key terms for this kind of programming arise. Writing the code that breaks up and arranges for parallel computing is called *parallel programming*.

If you have a multicore or multi-processor machine, spreading the pieces of work across them can reduce the amount of time to complete the work overall. The key phrase here is can reduce; there are some caveats that you should be aware of as you read this book.

Considering Overhead

Parallel execution doesn't come for free. There are overhead costs associated with setting up and managing parallel programming features. If you have only a small amount of work to perform, the overhead can outweigh the performance benefit.

Coordinating Data

If your pieces of work share common data or need to work in a concerted manner, you will need to provide coordination. I explain this is detail in Chapters 3 and 4, but as a general rule, the more coordination that is required, the poorer the performance of your parallel program. If the pieces of work can be performed in complete isolation from one another, you don't have to worry. But such situations are uncommon, and mostly, you will have to take care to ensure that coordination is used to get the results you desire.

Applying coordination is not hard, but applying just the right amount is a trick that comes with forethought and experience. Too much coordination compromises the performance of your parallel program; too little gets you unexpected results.

Scaling Applications

Adding a second core or CPU might increase the performance of your parallel program, but it is unlikely to double it. Likewise, a four-core machine is not going to execute your parallel program four times as quickly— in part because of the overhead and coordination described in the previous sections. However, the design of the computer hardware also limits its ability to scale. You can expect a significant improvement in performance, but it won't be 100 percent per additional core, and there will almost certainly be a point at which adding additional cores or CPUs doesn't improve the performance at all.

Deciding When to Go Parallel

My advice for assessing if a problem can be parallelized successfully is to just give it a try and measure the results. If a problem is difficult to write a parallel solution for, you will find out pretty quickly. If the problem can be parallelized but is affected by one or more of the caveats in the previous section, you can make an informed decision as to whether to use the parallel version or stick with the sequential implementation. Either way, you'll have increased your exposure to, and experience with, parallel programming.

The key is measurement. Don't just assume that a parallel solution will give you better performance and move on. Aside from the caveats I mentioned, you may well find that your first attempt can stand to be improved, and unless you measure, measure and measure again, you won't know what's going on. See Chapter 7 for details of how to use the `Stopwatch` class as a simple and effective measurement tool.

Deciding When to Stay Sequential

It may seem odd to emphasize the value of sequential execution in a book about parallel programming, but effective parallel programmers know when to leave well enough alone. Some problems are inherently sequential in nature—there are no pieces of work that can be performed concurrently. Some problems require so much coordination that the overhead incurred by parallel execution cancels out the performance gains. Some problems come with a mass of legacy code that would require too much rewriting to integrate with parallel code.

One of the most important times to consider sequential execution is when something is wrong with your parallel code and you can't work out why. There are some new parallel features in the Visual Studio 2010 debugger that can be very helpful in tracking down bugs (see Chapter 7), but sometimes you need to go back to the basics to make sure that you are able to code a solution that works at all.

Getting Prepared for This Book

You should already know how to write C# code and use Visual Studio to create, compile, and run .NET applications in C#. You need Visual Studio 2010 and .NET 4 for this book. The edition of Visual Studio you have doesn't matter except in Chapter 8, which uses the Concurrency Visualizer and some debugger features that are only available with the commercial editions. All of the examples in this book are available for download as Visual Studio solutions; you can get them from the Source Code page at `www.Apress.com`.

Understanding the Structure of This Book

The first several chapters of this book focus on introducing and using the basic unit of the TPL, the `Task` class. There is a lot to take in, especially in Chapter 2, but stick with it, and you will start to make sense of it all. When you get to Chapters 3 and 4, I hope you will start to see how these features can be of use to you in your programming.

Chapter 5 focuses on parallel loops, which are replacements for the standard `for` and `foreach` loops, except that loop iterations are processed in parallel. This is like "parallel programming light," but I have put it after the `Task` class chapters, because to get the most from these useful loops, you need to understand something of what is happening behind the scenes.

Chapter 6 looks at Parallel Language Integrated Query (PLINQ), which is a parallel-enabled version of LINQ to Objects. If you are a LINQ programmer (and if not, why not?), you will love this chapter. PLINQ is a happy marriage of the performance of parallelism and the flexibility and ingenuity of LINQ.

In Chapter 7, I give a very brief overview of the tools available to help you measure the performance of your parallel code and track down bugs. Parallel programming adds some unique problems to debugging, but the new Visual Studio 2010 parallel debugger features go a long way to addressing them.

The final chapter, Chapter 8, contains some sample implementations of common parallel algorithms. In many cases, especially when you are starting with parallel programming, you will find that what you are looking for—or at least something that you can use as a starting point—is contained in this chapter. If nothing else, you should look at these examples to understand how the new parallel features of .NET can be combined to create powerful algorithms with surprisingly little code.

Getting the Example Code

You can get the source code for all of the examples from the Apress web site. There is a different Visual Studio solution for each chapter and each listing is contained in a separate project. Figure 1-1 shows you how this appears in Visual Studio 2010.

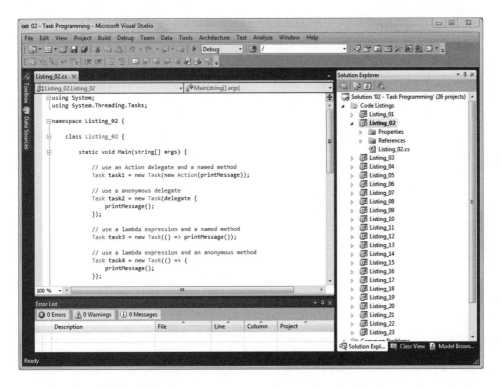

Figure 1-1. The example code for Chapter 2 in Visual Studio 2010

To run a listing, right-click the project in the Solution Explorer window, and select Set As Startup Project, as shown in Figure 1-2. Once you have selected the project you want, press Ctrl+F5 to compile and run the code.

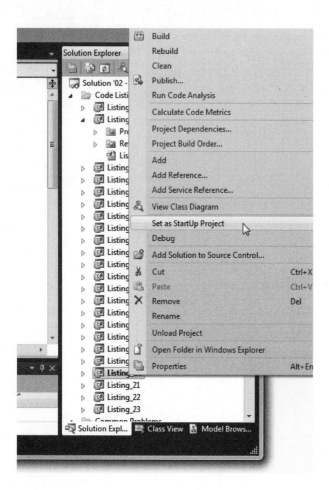

Figure 1-2. Selecting the startup project

Summary

It should be clear that I am very enthusiastic about the new .NET parallel programming features—enthusiastic enough to write this book and to say that I have huge respect for the team that created them. These well-designed and well-implemented features will, I am sure, change the way that parallel programming is perceived by mainstream programmers and do much to drive up the utilization of all of those multicore machines out there.

CHAPTER 2

■ ■ ■

Task Programming

Listing 2-1. Hello Task

```
using System;
using System.Threading.Tasks;

namespace Listing_01 {

    class Listing_01 {

        static void Main(string[] args) {

            Task.Factory.StartNew(() => {
                Console.WriteLine("Hello World");
            });

            // wait for input before exiting
            Console.WriteLine("Main method complete. Press enter to finish.");
            Console.ReadLine();
        }
    }
}
```

Hello Task

Do you feel different? Did your brain pop at the versatility, utility and general flexibility of the new task programming model? Probably not, but don't be disappointed. Listing 2-1 shows how to start a simple task, but it doesn't begin to illustrate the power of the Task Programming Library.

This chapter shows you the basics. If you have used .NET classic threads, you will see that standardizing the building blocks for creating and managing tasks can drastically reduce the amount of code you have to write to create a parallel application. If you are new to parallel programming, then you should take the time to read through each of the sections – these are techniques that you will use in every program that you write.

We will start with the Task class, which is at the heart of the Task Programming Library (TPL). I'll show you how to use the new standardization features to create and start different types of Task, cancel them, wait for them to complete, and read their results, as well as how to deal with exceptions.

To start, take a quick look at the first code listing; it includes some key building blocks that you'll see throughout this book and use in your own code. Look at the imported namespace:

```
using System.Threading.Tasks;
```

This namespace is one that we will be spending a lot of time with, and you will see it in almost all of the examples in this book; it contains the key classes for parallel programming. Another important namespace is System.Threading, which you may recognize as the home of the classic .NET threading classes. This namespace contains classes we'll use when we come to coordinate the work of several tasks in Chapter 4.

The most important part of the first listing is the following:

```
Task.Factory.StartNew(() => {
    Console.WriteLine("Hello World");
});
```

This is your first sight of the System.Threading.Tasks.Task class, the fundamental class for parallel programming. We use the static Task.Factory.StartNew() method to create a simple Task whose body prints a message to the console. This is the simplest way to create a task that requires no input data and produces no result. You'll learn how to create and start more complicated tasks in the following sections.

And that is our first (simple) parallel program. Running the program produces the following result:

```
Main method complete. Press enter to finish.

Hello World
```

Creating and Starting Tasks

To create the simplest of Tasks, you only need to have a task body, that is, a delegate or action that represents the workload you want performed in parallel. The Task in Listing 2-1 has a simple body, where the workload consisted of printing a message to the console. We defined the Task body using a lambda expression, which is the form we will use most often throughout this book. Table 2-1 summarizes the different ways that you can use Tasks and the listings in this section that demonstrate them.

Table 2-1. *Getting Started with Tasks*

Problem	Solution	Listing
Create and start a simple task	Call the static `Task.Factory.StartNew()` method with an `Action` delegate as an argument.	2-1
	Create a new `Task` with an `Action` delegate as an argument. Call `Start()` on the `Task` instance.	2-2
Provide state to a task	Create a new `Task` with an `Action<object>` delegate and an object as constructor arguments.	2-3 and 2-4
Get a result from a task	Create a new `Task<T>`, where T is the type of the result you want, and use an `Action` or `Action<object>` delegate as a constructor argument. Use the `return` keyword in the task body to create the result in the task. Read the result by calling the blocking `Task.Result` property.	2-5
	Call the static `Task.Factory.StartNew<T>()` method (where T is the type of the result you want) with an `Action` or `Action<object>` delegate as an argument. Use the `return` keyword in the task body to create the result in the task. Read the result by calling the blocking `Task.Result` property.	2-6

Creating Simple Tasks

To perform a simple `Task`, create a new instance of the `Task` class, passing in a `System.Action` delegate that represents the workload that you want performed as a constructor argument. You can explicitly create the `Action` delegate so that it refers to a named method, use an anonymous function, or use a lambda function. Once you have created an instance of `Task`, call the `Start()` method, and your `Task` is then passed to the *task scheduler*, which is responsible for assigning threads to perform the work. We look at the task scheduler in detail in Chapter 4. Listing 2-2 shows the different ways of creating and starting simple tasks.

Simple `Tasks`, while often useful, are limited by their lack of data input and result output. The TPL provides ways for you to create `Tasks` with both inputs and outputs, and I'll show you all of the options available in the following sections.

Listing 2-2. *Four Ways to Create Basic Tasks*

```
using System;
using System.Threading.Tasks;

namespace Listing_02 {

    class Listing_02 {

        static void Main(string[] args) {
```

```
// use an Action delegate and a named method
Task task1 = new Task(new Action(printMessage));

// use a anonymous delegate
Task task2 = new Task(delegate {
    printMessage();
});

// use a lambda expression and a named method
Task task3 = new Task(() => printMessage());

// use a lambda expression and an anonymous method
Task task4 = new Task(() => {
    printMessage();
});

task1.Start();
task2.Start();
task3.Start();
task4.Start();

// wait for input before exiting
Console.WriteLine("Main method complete. Press enter to finish.");
Console.ReadLine();
        }

        static void printMessage() {
            Console.WriteLine("Hello World");
        }
    }
}
```

Running the code in Listing 2-2 gives the obvious result of calling the `printMessage()` method four times, as follows:

```
Main method complete. Press enter to finish.

Hello World

Hello World

Hello World

Hello World
```

Listing 2-1 uses the `Task.Factory.StartNew()` method to create and start a `Task`. There is little difference between the approaches shown in Listing 2-2 and the `Factory.StartNew()` method, but Microsoft recommends using `Factory.StartNew()` for simple, short-lived tasks.

> ▦ **Tip** You can't Start() a Task that has already run. If you need to repeat the work performed by a Task that has completed, you must create another Task instance with the same workload.

Setting Task State

You can supply the state for a Task by passing in an instance of **System.Action<object>** and an object representing your state as the command line arguments. Setting the Task state lets you have Tasks perform similar workloads on different data. For example, imagine that we want our four Tasks from the previous example to print out different messages to the console so that we know which technique printed which message. We create instances of **Action<object>** to set the message that we wanted each task to print out and use them as we create the Tasks. Listing 2-3 shows how to do this.

Listing 2-3. Adding Task State

```
using System;
using System.Threading.Tasks;

namespace Listing_03 {

    class Listing_03 {

        static void Main(string[] args) {

            // use an Action delegate and a named method
            Task task1 = new Task(new Action<object>(printMessage),
                "First task");

            // use a anonymous delegate
            Task task2 = new Task(delegate (object obj) {
                printMessage(obj);
            }, "Second Task");

            // use a lambda expression and a named method
            // note that parameters to a lambda don't need
            // to be quoted if there is only one parameter
            Task task3 = new Task((obj) => printMessage(obj), "Third task");

            // use a lambda expression and an anonymous method
            Task task4 = new Task((obj) => {
                printMessage(obj);
            }, "Fourth task");

            task1.Start();
            task2.Start();
            task3.Start();
            task4.Start();
```

```
        // wait for input before exiting
        Console.WriteLine("Main method complete. Press enter to finish.");
        Console.ReadLine();
    }

    static void printMessage(object message) {
        Console.WriteLine("Message: {0}", message);
    }
  }
}
```

The example may not seem that useful until we pick one technique for creating Tasks and then use the state feature to create several at once. Listing 2-4 shows how to get the same effect as in Listing 2-3 but in a much clearer and more concise manner. Now, we are able to create several Tasks, each of which has the same code statements in the body, but which operates on different state data.

Listing 2-4. Creating Several Tasks Using Task State

```
using System;
using System.Threading.Tasks;

namespace Listing_04 {

    class Listing_04 {

        static void Main(string[] args) {

            string[] messages = { "First task", "Second task",
                "Third task", "Fourth task" };

            foreach (string msg in messages) {
                Task myTask = new Task(obj => printMessage((string)obj), msg);
                myTask.Start();
            }

            // wait for input before exiting
            Console.WriteLine("Main method complete. Press enter to finish.");
            Console.ReadLine();
        }

        static void printMessage(string message) {
            Console.WriteLine("Message: {0}", message);
        }
    }
}
```

Notice that we explicitly cast the state data to a string so that we can call the printMessage() method in the lambda expression in Listing 2-4. The only way to pass state to a Task constructor is using Action<object>, so you must convert or cast explicitly if you need to access the members of a specific type. Running the code in Listing 2-4 produces the following results:

Main method complete. Press enter to finish.

Message: Second task

Message: Fourth task

Message: First task

Message: Third task

The order in which the messages print out when you run the code may be different to the order shown in these results. The task scheduler decides how to allocate threads to perform **Task**s and the order can vary.

Getting a Result

To get a result from a **Task**, create instances of **Task<T>**, where T is the type of the result that will be produced and **return** an instance of that type in your **Task** body. To read the result, you call the **Result** property of the **Task** you created.

It is simple and easy to do. Listing 2-5 shows two **Tasks** that return results, one that uses state and one that doesn't.

Listing 2-5. Getting Results from a Task

```
using System;
using System.Threading.Tasks;

namespace Listing_05 {

    class Listing_05 {

        static void Main(string[] args) {

            // create the task
            Task<int> task1 = new Task<int>(() => {
                int sum = 0;
                for (int i = 0; i < 100; i++) {
                    sum += i;
                }
                return sum;
            });

            // start the task
            task1.Start();

            // write out the result
            Console.WriteLine("Result 1: {0}", task1.Result);
            // create the task using state
```

```
        Task<int> task2 = new Task<int>(obj => {
            int sum = 0;
            int max = (int)obj;
            for (int i = 0; i < max; i++) {
                sum += i;
            }
            return sum;
        }, 100);

        // start the task
        task2.Start();

        // write out the result
        Console.WriteLine("Result 2: {0}", task2.Result);

        // wait for input before exiting
        Console.WriteLine("Main method complete. Press enter to finish.");
        Console.ReadLine();
    }
  }
}
```

Reading the Result property waits until the Task it has been called on has completed. In Listing 2-5, this means that the second Task will not be started until the first has completed, because we call the Result property on the first Task before creating and starting the second Task.

In Listing 2-1, we are able to create and start a new Task using the static Task.Factory.StartNew() method. Task.Factory also includes the StartNew<T> method, which will create and start a Task<T> in a single step as shown by Listing 2-6.

Listing 2-6. Getting a Result with the Task Factory

```
using System;
using System.Threading.Tasks;

namespace Listing_06 {

    class Listing_06 {

        static void Main(string[] args) {

            // create the task
            Task<int> task1 = Task.Factory.StartNew<int>(() => {
                int sum = 0;
                for (int i = 0; i < 100; i++) {
                    sum += i;
                }
                return sum;
            });
```

```
        // write out the result
        Console.WriteLine("Result 1: {0}", task1.Result);

        // wait for input before exiting
        Console.WriteLine("Main method complete. Press enter to finish.");
        Console.ReadLine();
    }
  }
}
```

Specifying Task Creation Options

Some of the constructor overloads for `Task` allow values from the `System.Threading.Tasks.TaskCreationOptions` enumeration to be specified. We will discuss the classes these options relate to later in this book, but they are listed in Table 2-2 just for completeness.

Table 2-2. Members of the TaskCreationOptions Enumeration

Member	Description
None	Uses the default task creation options
PreferFairness	A request to the task scheduler to schedule tasks as fairly as possible (See Chapter 4 for more information about the task scheduler.)
LongRunning	Specifies that the task will be long running, which is a hint to the task scheduler (See Chapter 4 for more information about the task scheduler.)
AttachedToParent	Specifies that a child task is attached to a parent in the task hierarchy (See Chapter 4 for more information about the child and parent tasks.)

Identifying Tasks

The `Task.CurrentId` property returns a unique `int` that identifies the current `Task`. This property will return `null` if it is called outside of a `Task` body.

Cancelling Tasks

One of the new areas of standardization in the TPL is cancelling tasks. This may seem like an odd thing to regard as useful, especially if you are accustomed to writing your own cancellation code using classic .NET threads. The new approach makes parallel code simpler and more consistent and reduces the risk of encountering some of the most commonly encountered problems when performing a cancellation, as you will see when we discuss putting a thread to sleep later in this chapter.

Creating a Task that you can cancel is a four-step process:

1. Create a new instance of System.Threading.CancellationTokenSource:

   ```
   CancellationTokenSource tokenSource = new CancellationTokenSource
   ```

2. Call the CancellationTokenSource.Token property to get a System.Threading.CancellationToken:

   ```
   CancellationToken token = tokenSource.Token;
   ```

3. Create a new Task or Task<T> using an Action or Action<object> delegate and the CancellationToken from step 2 as constructor arguments:

   ```
   Task task1 = new Task(new Action(myMethod), token);
   ```

4. Call the Start() method on your Task or Task<T> as you would normally.

To cancel a Task, simply call the Cancel() method on the CancellationTokenSource created in step 1. Task cancellation is *cooperative*, which means that the .NET Framework doesn't force your tasks to finish; you have to monitor the CancellationToken you used to create your task and stop your task when you detect that a cancellation has been requested. Passing the cancellation token to the Task constructor allows the .NET Framework to avoid starting tasks that rely on tokens that have already been cancelled. Table 2-3 provides a quick summary of the different mechanisms available for cancelling tasks, each of which I describe in the following sections.

Table 2-3. Canceling Tasks

Problem	Solution	Listing
Create a cancellable task.	Get a System.Threading.CancellationToken by creating a new instance of System.Threading.CancellationTokenSource and accessing the Token property. Use the token as a constructor argument to the Task class.	2-7
Cancel a task.	Call the Cancel() method on CancellationTokenSource.	2-7
Cancel several tasks.	Use a single CancellationToken in the constructor of several Tasks, and call the Cancel() method on the CancellationTokenSource.	2-10
Monitor several tokens.	Create a composite cancellation source by calling the CancellationTokenSource.CreateLinkedTokenSource() method.	2-11
Poll for task cancellation.	Check the isCancellationRequested property of CancellationToken each time your task body loop iterates. If this property returns true, release any resources you have been using and throw an instance of OperationCanceledException.	2-7
Poll for task cancellation.	Call the Token.ThrowIfCancellationRequested() method to check for cancellation, and throw an instance of OperationCanceledException in a single code statement.	2-8

Problem	Solution	Listing
Use a delegate for task cancellation.	Pass an `Action` delegate to the `Token.Register()` method. The delegate will be invoked when the `CancellationTokenSource.Cancel()` method is called.	2-8
Use a wait handle for task cancellation.	Call the `Token.WaitHandle.WaitOne()` method to block the calling thread until the `CancellationTokenSource.Cancel()` method is called.	2-9
Determine if a task was cancelled.	Read the `Task.IsCancelled` property, which returns `true` if the `Task` was cancelled.	2-12

Monitoring Cancellation by Polling

Many task bodies contain loops to iteratively process data. You can use the loop iterations to check if your task has been cancelled by polling the `IsCancellationRequested` property of the `CancellationToken` class. If the property returns `true`, you need to break out of the loop and release any resources you are holding (network connections, transaction containers, etc.)

You must also throw an instance of `System.Threading.OperationCanceledException` in your task body; this is how you acknowledge the cancellation, and if you forget, the status of your task will not be set correctly. The following code fragment shows the basic anatomy of a task body loop that polls for cancellation:

```
while (true) {
    if (token.IsCancellationRequested) {
        // tidy up and release resources
        throw new OperationCanceledException(token);
    } else {
        // do a unit of work
    }
}
```

If you don't have any resources to release, you can simplify your code by calling the `CancellationToken.ThrowIfCancellationRequested()` method, which will perform the cancellation check and throw the exception in one step. This changes the loop anatomy as follows:

```
while (true) {
    token.ThrowIfCancellationRequested();
    // do a unit of work
    }
}
```

Listing 2-7 demonstrates creating a cancellable task and polling to check for cancellation.

Listing 2-7. Cancelling a Task

```csharp
using System;
using System.Threading;
using System.Threading.Tasks;

namespace Listing_07 {

    class Listing_07 {

        static void Main(string[] args) {

            // create the cancellation token source
            CancellationTokenSource tokenSource
                = new CancellationTokenSource();

            // create the cancellation token
            CancellationToken token = tokenSource.Token;

            // create the task
            Task task = new Task(() => {
                for (int i = 0; i < int.MaxValue; i++) {
                    if (token.IsCancellationRequested) {
                        Console.WriteLine("Task cancel detected");
                        throw new OperationCanceledException(token);
                    } else {
                        Console.WriteLine("Int value {0}", i);
                    }
                }
            }, token);

            // wait for input before we start the task
            Console.WriteLine("Press enter to start task");
            Console.WriteLine("Press enter again to cancel task");
            Console.ReadLine();

            // start the task
            task.Start();

            // read a line from the console.
            Console.ReadLine();

            // cancel the task
            Console.WriteLine("Cancelling task");
            tokenSource.Cancel();
```

```
        // wait for input before exiting
        Console.WriteLine("Main method complete. Press enter to finish.");
        Console.ReadLine();
      }
    }
}
```

Monitoring Cancellation with a Delegate

You can register a delegate with a CancellationToken, which will be invoked when the
CancellationTokenSource.Cancel() method is called. You can use this as an alternative to the method
shown in Listing 2-7 for checking cancellation, which can be useful if your task relies on other
asynchronous operations, such as I/O reads. You can also use the delegate feature to be notified when a
cancellation happens; this can be useful in UI applications. Listing 2-8 shows how the delegate feature
can be used.

Listing 2-8. Monitoring Cancellation with a Delegate

```
using System;
using System.Threading;
using System.Threading.Tasks;

namespace Listing_08 {
    class Listing_08 {
        static void Main(string[] args) {

            // create the cancellation token source
            CancellationTokenSource tokenSource
                = new CancellationTokenSource();

            // create the cancellation token
            CancellationToken token = tokenSource.Token;

            // create the task
            Task task = new Task(() => {
                for (int i = 0; i < int.MaxValue; i++) {
                    if (token.IsCancellationRequested) {
                        Console.WriteLine("Task cancel detected");
                        throw new OperationCanceledException(token);
                    } else {
                        Console.WriteLine("Int value {0}", i);
                    }
                }
            }, token);

            // register a cancellation delegate
            token.Register(() => {
                Console.WriteLine(">>>>>> Delegate Invoked\n");
            });
```

```
        // wait for input before we start the task
        Console.WriteLine("Press enter to start task");
        Console.WriteLine("Press enter again to cancel task");
        Console.ReadLine();

        // start the task
        task.Start();

        // read a line from the console.
        Console.ReadLine();

        // cancel the task
        Console.WriteLine("Cancelling task");
        tokenSource.Cancel();

        // wait for input before exiting
        Console.WriteLine("Main method complete. Press enter to finish.");
        Console.ReadLine();
      }
   }
}
```

Listing 2-8 is very similar to Listing 2-7, with the addition of the cancellation delegate registered using the `Register()` method of the `CancellationToken` class, which is shown in the bold code in the listing. The `Register()` method takes an instance of `Action` or `Action<object>`. The latter allows you provide a state object to your delegate in much the same manner as you would when passing state to a task delegate. When the `Task` is cancelled, the `Action` you have specified is performed. In the case of Listing 2-8, this is to print out a simple message.

Monitoring Cancellation with a Wait Handle

The third way to monitor task cancellation is to call the `WaitOne()` method of the `CancellationToken.WaitHandle` property. I cover wait handles in depth later in this book, but for this chapter, it is enough to know that when you call the `WaitOne()` method it blocks until the `Cancel()` method is called on the `CancellationTokenSource` that was used to create the token whose wait handle you are using.

Listing 2-9 demonstrates the use of the wait handle for cancellation monitoring. Two `Tasks` are created, one of which (`task2`) calls the `WaitOne()` method, which blocks until the first `Task` is cancelled.

Listing 2-9. Cancelation Monitoring with a Wait Handle

```
using System;
using System.Threading;
using System.Threading.Tasks;

namespace Listing_09 {
    class Listing_09 {
        static void Main(string[] args) {
```

```
// create the cancellation token source
CancellationTokenSource tokenSource
    = new CancellationTokenSource();

// create the cancellation token
CancellationToken token = tokenSource.Token;

// create the task
Task task1 = new Task(() => {
    for (int i = 0; i < int.MaxValue; i++) {
        if (token.IsCancellationRequested) {
            Console.WriteLine("Task cancel detected");
            throw new OperationCanceledException(token);
        } else {
            Console.WriteLine("Int value {0}", i);
        }
    }
}, token);

// create a second task that will use the wait handle
Task task2 = new Task(() => {
    // wait on the handle
    token.WaitHandle.WaitOne();
    // write out a message
    Console.WriteLine(">>>>> Wait handle released");
});


// wait for input before we start the task
Console.WriteLine("Press enter to start task");
Console.WriteLine("Press enter again to cancel task");
Console.ReadLine();

// start the tasks
task1.Start();
task2.Start();

// read a line from the console.
Console.ReadLine();

// cancel the task
Console.WriteLine("Cancelling task");
tokenSource.Cancel();

// wait for input before exiting
Console.WriteLine("Main method complete. Press enter to finish.");
Console.ReadLine();
        }
    }
}
```

Cancelling Several Tasks

You can use a single token when creating several Tasks and cancel them all with a single call to the CancellationTokenSource.Cancel() method. Listing 2-10 shows this in action.

Listing 2-10. Cancelling Multiple Tasks

```
using System;
using System.Threading;
using System.Threading.Tasks;

namespace Listing_10 {

    class Listing_10 {

        static void Main(string[] args) {

            // create the cancellation token source
            CancellationTokenSource tokenSource
                = new CancellationTokenSource();
            // create the cancellation token
            CancellationToken token = tokenSource.Token;

            // create the tasks
            Task task1 = new Task(() => {
                for (int i = 0; i < int.MaxValue; i++) {
                    token.ThrowIfCancellationRequested();
                    Console.WriteLine("Task 1 - Int value {0}", i);
                }
            }, token);

            Task task2 = new Task(() => {
                for (int i = 0; i < int.MaxValue; i++) {
                    token.ThrowIfCancellationRequested();
                    Console.WriteLine("Task 2 - Int value {0}", i);
                }
            }, token);

            // wait for input before we start the tasks
            Console.WriteLine("Press enter to start tasks");
            Console.WriteLine("Press enter again to cancel tasks");
            Console.ReadLine();

            // start the tasks
            task1.Start();
            task2.Start();

            // read a line from the console.
            Console.ReadLine();
```

```
            // cancel the task
            Console.WriteLine("Cancelling tasks");
            tokenSource.Cancel();

            // wait for input before exiting
            Console.WriteLine("Main method complete. Press enter to finish.");
            Console.ReadLine();
        }
    }
}
```

Creating a Composite Cancellation Token

You can create a token that is composed from several CancellationTokens that will be cancelled if any of the underlying tokens is cancelled. You do this by calling the System.Threading.
CancellationTokenSource.CreateLinkedTokenSource() method and passing in the CancellationTokens that you want to link. The result is a new CancellationToken that you can use normally. Listing 2-11 demonstrates creating and using a composite cancellation token.

Listing 2-11. Using a Composite Cancellation Token

```
using System;
using System.Threading;
using System.Threading.Tasks;

namespace Listing_11 {

    class Listing_11 {

        static void Main(string[] args) {

            // create the cancellation token sources
            CancellationTokenSource tokenSource1 = new CancellationTokenSource();
            CancellationTokenSource tokenSource2 = new CancellationTokenSource();
            CancellationTokenSource tokenSource3 = new CancellationTokenSource();

            // create a composite token source using multiple tokens
            CancellationTokenSource compositeSource =
                CancellationTokenSource.CreateLinkedTokenSource(
                    tokenSource1.Token, tokenSource2.Token, tokenSource3.Token);

            // create a cancellable task using the composite token
            Task task = new Task(() => {
                // wait until the token has been cancelled
                compositeSource.Token.WaitHandle.WaitOne();
                // throw a cancellation exception
                throw new OperationCanceledException(compositeSource.Token);
            }, compositeSource.Token);
```

```
        // start the task
        task.Start();

        // cancel one of the original tokens
        tokenSource2.Cancel();

        // wait for input before exiting
        Console.WriteLine("Main method complete. Press enter to finish.");
        Console.ReadLine();
      }
   }
}
```

Determining If a Task Was Cancelled

You can determine if a Task has been cancelled by checking the IsCancelled property, which will return true if the Task was cancelled. Listing 2-12 demonstrates the use of this property.

Listing 2-12. Using the Task.isCancelled Property

```
using System;
using System.Threading;
using System.Threading.Tasks;

namespace Listing_12 {

    class Listing_12 {

        static void Main(string[] args) {

            // create the cancellation token source
            CancellationTokenSource tokenSource1 = new CancellationTokenSource();
            // create the cancellation token
            CancellationToken token1 = tokenSource1.Token;

            // create the first task, which we will let run fully
            Task task1 = new Task(() => {
                for (int i = 0; i < 10; i++) {
                    token1.ThrowIfCancellationRequested();
                    Console.WriteLine("Task 1 - Int value {0}", i);
                }
            }, token1);

            // create the second cancellation token source
            CancellationTokenSource tokenSource2 = new CancellationTokenSource();
            // create the cancellation token
            CancellationToken token2 = tokenSource2.Token;
```

```
        // create the second task, which we will cancel
        Task task2 = new Task(() => {
            for (int i = 0; i < int.MaxValue; i++) {
                token2.ThrowIfCancellationRequested();
                Console.WriteLine("Task 2 - Int value {0}", i);
            }
        }, token2);

        // start all of the tasks
        task1.Start();
        task2.Start();

        // cancel the second token source
        tokenSource2.Cancel();

        // write out the cancellation detail of each task
        Console.WriteLine("Task 1 cancelled? {0}", task1.IsCanceled);
        Console.WriteLine("Task 2 cancelled? {0}", task2.IsCanceled);

        // wait for input before exiting
        Console.WriteLine("Main method complete. Press enter to finish.");
        Console.ReadLine();

    }
  }
}
```

The code in Listing 2-12 creates two Tasks, each of which is constructed using a CancellationToken from a different CancellationTokenSource. The CancellationTokenSource for the second Task is cancelled, but the first Task is allowed to complete normally. The values of the IsCanceled property are printed out for each of the tasks. Running the code produces results similar to the following:

```
Task 1 cancelled? False

Task 2 cancelled? True

Task 1 - Int value 0

...

Task 1 - Int value 9

Main method complete. Press enter to finish.
```

Waiting for Time to Pass

It can be useful to have a Task wait for a given period of time, for example, if you are periodically polling the status of something before continuing executing the Task. Making a Task wait like this is referred to as *sleeping*. You specify a period of time for the Task to sleep for, and it will wait until that period of time has elapsed, at which point the Task will wake up and continue execution.

Table 2-4. Putting Tasks to Sleep

Problem	Solution	Listing
Sleep using a wait handle.	Create a CancellationTokenSource, and use the CancellationToken wait handle by calling the CancallationToken.WaitHandle.WaitOne() instance method, specifying the number of milliseconds to sleep. The Task will sleep until the time specified has elapsed or the token has been cancelled.	2-13
Sleep using classic .NET threads.	Call the static Thread.Sleep() method, specifying the number of milliseconds to sleep for. This method does not monitor cancellation tokens.	2-14
Sleep using spin waiting.	Call the static Thread.SleepWait() method, specifying the number of CPU loops to wait for. Use this technique with caution.	2-15

Using a Cancellation Token Wait Handle

The best way to put Tasks to sleep is to use the wait handle of a CancellationToken, which you saw earlier in the "Cancelling Tasks" section. Create an instance of CancellationTokenSource, and read the Token property to obtain the CancellationToken instance. Use the WaitHandle property, and call the overloaded WaitOne() method. In the "Cancelling Tasks" section, you saw the version that takes no arguments, which causes the calling thread to wait until the CancellationTokenSource.Cancel() method is called. However, other overloads of this method allow you to specify a period to wait using either an Int32 or a TimeSpan. When you specify a time period, the WaitOne() method will put the task to sleep for the specific number of milliseconds or until the CancellationToken is cancelled, whichever happens first. Listing 2-13 demonstrates how this works.

Listing 2-13. Putting a Task to Sleep

```
using System;
using System.Threading;
using System.Threading.Tasks;

namespace Listing_13 {

    class Listing_13 {

        static void Main(string[] args) {

            // create the cancellation token source
            CancellationTokenSource tokenSource = new CancellationTokenSource();
            // create the cancellation token
            CancellationToken token = tokenSource.Token;
```

```
// create the first task, which we will let run fully
Task task1 = new Task(() => {
    for (int i = 0; i < Int32.MaxValue; i++) {
        // put the task to sleep for 10 seconds
        bool cancelled = token.WaitHandle.WaitOne(10000);
        // print out a message
        Console.WriteLine("Task 1 - Int value {0}. Cancelled? {1}",
            i, cancelled);
        // check to see if we have been cancelled
        if (cancelled) {
            throw new OperationCanceledException(token);
        }
    }
}, token);

// start task
task1.Start();

// wait for input before exiting
Console.WriteLine("Press enter to cancel token.");
Console.ReadLine();

// cancel the token
tokenSource.Cancel();

// wait for input before exiting
Console.WriteLine("Main method complete. Press enter to finish.");
Console.ReadLine();
    }
  }
}
```

Listing 2-13 creates a Task that prints out a message and then sleeps for 10 seconds using the WaitOne() method. If you run the code, the messages will be printed until you hit the return key, at which point the CancellationToken will be cancelled, causing the Task to wake up again. Remember, the WaitOne() method will wait until either the time specified has elapsed or the token has been cancelled, whichever happens first. The CancellationToken.WaitHandle.WaitOne() method returns true if the token has been cancelled and false if the time elapsed, causing the task has woken up because the time specified has elapsed.

I prefer this technique for putting tasks to sleep because of the immediate response to the token being cancelled. You'll see in a moment that this is an improvement over the classic threading model.

Using Classic Sleep

Because the TPL uses the classic .NET threading support behind the scenes, you can use the classic threading technique to put a Task to sleep. Call the static Thread.Sleep() method, and pass a time interval as an argument. Listing 2-14 reworks the previous example to use this technique.

Listing 2-14. Sleeping Using Classic Threads

```
using System;
using System.Threading;
using System.Threading.Tasks;

namespace Listing_14 {

    class Listing_14 {

        static void Main(string[] args) {

            // create the cancellation token source
            CancellationTokenSource tokenSource = new CancellationTokenSource();
            // create the cancellation token
            CancellationToken token = tokenSource.Token;

            // create the first task, which we will let run fully
            Task task1 = new Task(() => {
                for (int i = 0; i < Int32.MaxValue; i++) {
                    // put the task to sleep for 10 seconds
                    Thread.Sleep(10000);
                    // print out a message
                    Console.WriteLine("Task 1 - Int value {0}", i);
                    // check for task cancellation
                    token.ThrowIfCancellationRequested();
                }
            }, token);

            // start task
            task1.Start();

            // wait for input before exiting
            Console.WriteLine("Press enter to cancel token.");
            Console.ReadLine();

            // cancel the token
            tokenSource.Cancel();

            // wait for input before exiting
            Console.WriteLine("Main method complete. Press enter to finish.");
            Console.ReadLine();
        }
    }
}
```

The key difference with this technique is that cancelling the token doesn't immediately cancel the task, because the Thread.Sleep() method will block until the time specified has elapsed and only then check the cancellation status. In this simple example, this means that the task continues to exist, albeit asleep, for up to 10 seconds after the token has been cancelled.

Using Spin Waiting

The spin waiting technique is included in this chapter for completeness, but I recommend against using it. When you use the other two sleep techniques, the thread that is performing your task gives up its turn in the schedule when its sleeping, so any other threads can have a turn. The scheduler, which is responsible for managing the threads running at any given time, has to do some work to determine which thread should go next and make it happen. You can avoid the scheduler having to do this work by using a technique called spin waiting: the thread doesn't give up its turn; it just enters a very tight loop on the CPU. Listing 2-15 demonstrates how to perform spin waiting by using the `Thread.SpinWait()` method.

Listing 2-15. Sleeping by Spin Waiting

```
using System;
using System.Threading;
using System.Threading.Tasks;

namespace Listing_15 {

    class Listing_15 {

        static void Main(string[] args) {

            // create the cancellation token source
            CancellationTokenSource tokenSource = new CancellationTokenSource();
            // create the cancellation token
            CancellationToken token = tokenSource.Token;

            // create the first task, which we will let run fully
            Task task1 = new Task(() => {
                for (int i = 0; i < Int32.MaxValue; i++) {
                    // put the task to sleep for 10 seconds
                    Thread.SpinWait(10000);
                    // print out a message
                    Console.WriteLine("Task 1 - Int value {0}", i);
                    // check for task cancellation
                    token.ThrowIfCancellationRequested();
                }
            }, token);

            // start task
            task1.Start();

            // wait for input before exiting
            Console.WriteLine("Press enter to cancel token.");
            Console.ReadLine();

            // cancel the token
            tokenSource.Cancel();
```

```
            // wait for input before exiting
            Console.WriteLine("Main method complete. Press enter to finish.");
            Console.ReadLine();
        }
    }
}
```

The integer argument passed to the `Thread.SpinWait()` method is the number of times that the tight CPU loop should be performed, and the amount of time that this takes depends on the speed of your system. Spin waiting is most commonly used to acquire synchronization locks, which are described in the next chapter. The problem with spin waiting is that your task doesn't stop using the CPU; it just burns a specified number of CPU cycles. This approach distorts the behavior of the scheduling process, and you can get some quite odd behaviors from an application if you use spin locks wrongly. My advice is to avoid spin locking, because it can cause a lot more problems than it solves. There are very few applications that cannot rely on the more robust and predictable sleep techniques.

Waiting for Tasks

When I showed you how to get a result from a `Task`, you learned that calling the `Task.Result` waits until the task has completed. You can also wait for tasks to complete without reading a result by using other methods in the `Task` class. This is useful if you want to wait for a `Task` that doesn't return a result or if you need to do some basic coordination between tasks. You can wait for a single `Task` to complete, wait for a number of `Tasks` to complete or wait for the first of a number of `Tasks` to complete. Table 2-5 provides a quick summary of techniques for waiting for tasks.

Table 2-5. Waiting for Tasks

Problem	Solution	Listing
Wait for a single task.	Call the `Wait()` method on the `Task` instance, optionally providing a maximum duration to wait and a `CancellationToken` to monitor while waiting.	2-16
Wait for a set of tasks.	Call the static `Task.WaitForAll()` method, supplying a `Task` array as an argument and optionally specifying a maximum duration to wait and a `CancellationToken` to monitor while waiting.	2-17
Wait for the first of a set of tasks.	Call the static `Task.WaitAny()` method, supplying a `Task` array as an argument and optionally specifying a maximum duration to wait and a `CancellationToken` to monitor while waiting.	2-18

■ **Tip** Waiting for a task that has been cancelled will throw an exception; see the next section for details of handling exceptions in tasks.

Waiting for a Single Task

You can wait for a single `Task` to complete by calling the `Wait()` instance method. The calling method will not return until the `Task` instance has completed, been cancelled or thrown an exception. See the next section for details of how to handle exceptions and the previous section for details of cancelling tasks. You can wait conditionally on a task by using the overloaded versions of the `Wait()` method. Table 2-6 shows the overloaded versions.

Table 2-6. Overloaded Versions of Task.Wait() Instance Method

Method	Description
Wait()	Wait until the Task completes, is cancelled, or throws an exception.
Wait(CancellationToken)	Wait until the CancellationToken is cancelled or the Task completes, is cancelled, or throws an exception.
Wait(Int32)	Wait for the specified number of milliseconds to pass or for the Task to complete, be cancelled, or throw an exception (whichever happens first).
Wait(TimeSpan)	Wait until the specified TimeSpan has passed or for the Task to complete, be cancelled, or throw an exception (whichever happens first).
Wait(Int32, CancellationToken)	Wait for the specified number of milliseconds to pass, for the CancellationToken to be cancelled, or for the Task to complete, be cancelled, or throw an exception (whichever happens first).

Listing 2-16 illustrates how to use some of the overloaded versions of `Wait()`.

Listing 2-16. Waiting for a Single Task

```
using System;
using System.Threading;
using System.Threading.Tasks;

namespace Listing_16 {

    class Listing_16 {

        static void Main(string[] args) {

            // create the cancellation token source
            CancellationTokenSource tokenSource = new CancellationTokenSource();
            // create the cancellation token
            CancellationToken token = tokenSource.Token;

            // create and start the first task, which we will let run fully
            Task task = createTask(token);
            task.Start();
```

```
            // wait for the task
            Console.WriteLine("Waiting for task to complete.");
            task.Wait();
            Console.WriteLine("Task Completed.");

            // create and start another task
            task = createTask(token);
            task.Start();

            Console.WriteLine("Waiting 2 secs for task to complete.");
            bool completed = task.Wait(2000);
            Console.WriteLine("Wait ended - task completed: {0}", completed);

            // create and start another task
            task = createTask(token);
            task.Start();

            Console.WriteLine("Waiting 2 secs for task to complete.");
            completed = task.Wait(2000, token);
            Console.WriteLine("Wait ended - task completed: {0} task cancelled {1}",
                completed, task.IsCanceled);

            // wait for input before exiting
            Console.WriteLine("Main method complete. Press enter to finish.");
            Console.ReadLine();
        }

        static Task createTask(CancellationToken token) {
            return new Task(() => {
                for (int i = 0; i < 5; i++) {
                    // check for task cancellation
                    token.ThrowIfCancellationRequested();
                    // print out a message
                    Console.WriteLine("Task - Int value {0}", i);
                    // put the task to sleep for 1 second
                    token.WaitHandle.WaitOne(1000);
                }
            }, token);
        }
    }
}
```

The overloaded versions that specify a time period return a Boolean result, which will be **true** if the Task completed before the duration elapsed and **false** otherwise.

■ **Note** If an exception is thrown by a Task, it will be rethrown when the Wait() method is called. See the "Handling Exceptions in Tasks" section of this chapter for further details.

Waiting for Several Tasks

You can wait for a number of tasks to complete by using the static `Task.WaitAll()` method. This method will not return until all of the tasks passed as arguments have completed, been cancelled, or thrown an exception. The `WaitAll()` method is overloaded and follows the same pattern of signatures as the `Task.Wait()` instance method (see Table 2-5 for details). Listing 2-17 demonstrates how to wait for several tasks.

■ **Tip** When using this method, a `Task` is considered complete if it has finished its workload, been cancelled, or thrown an exception. If one or more of your tasks has thrown an exception, the `WaitAll()` method will throw an exception. See the "Handling Exceptions" section in this chapter for details.

Listing 2-17. Waiting for Several Tasks

```
using System;
using System.Threading;
using System.Threading.Tasks;

namespace Listing_17 {

    class Listing_17 {

        static void Main(string[] args) {

            // create the cancellation token source
            CancellationTokenSource tokenSource = new CancellationTokenSource();
            // create the cancellation token
            CancellationToken token = tokenSource.Token;

            // create the tasks
            Task task1 = new Task(() => {
                for (int i = 0; i < 5; i++) {
                    // check for task cancellation
                    token.ThrowIfCancellationRequested();
                    // print out a message
                    Console.WriteLine("Task 1 - Int value {0}", i);
                    // put the task to sleep for 1 second
                    token.WaitHandle.WaitOne(1000);
                }
                Console.WriteLine("Task 1 complete");
            }, token);

            Task task2 = new Task(() => {
                Console.WriteLine("Task 2 complete");
            }, token);
```

```
            // start the tasks
            task1.Start();
            task2.Start();

            // wait for the tasks
            Console.WriteLine("Waiting for tasks to complete.");
            Task.WaitAll(task1, task2);
            Console.WriteLine("Tasks Completed.");

            // wait for input before exiting
            Console.WriteLine("Main method complete. Press enter to finish.");
            Console.ReadLine();
        }
    }
}
```

In the listing, we create two tasks, one of which takes longer to complete than the other. Notice that we create cancellable tasks, because we want to use the CancellationToken wait handle to slow down the execution of the first task by putting it to sleep. We start both tasks and then call Task.WaitAll(), which blocks until both tasks are complete.

Waiting for One of Many Tasks

The Task.WaitAny() method waits for one of a set of tasks to complete, and this method has a number of overloads, all of which take a Task array. The method waits until any of the specified Tasks completes and returns the array index of the completed Task. If you use one of the overloads that accept additional arguments, a return value of -1 indicates that the time period expired or the CancellationToken was cancelled before any of the tasks completed. Listing 2-18 demonstrates the WaitAny() method.

■ **Tip** When using this method, a Task is considered complete if it has finished its workload, been cancelled, or thrown an exception. If one or more of your tasks has thrown an exception, the WaitAny() method will throw an exception. See the "Handling Exceptions" section in this chapter for details.

Listing 2-18. Using the WaitAny Method

```
using System;
using System.Threading;
using System.Threading.Tasks;

namespace Listing_18 {

    class Listing_18 {

        static void Main(string[] args) {
```

```
    // create the cancellation token source
    CancellationTokenSource tokenSource = new CancellationTokenSource();
    // create the cancellation token
    CancellationToken token = tokenSource.Token;

    // create the tasks
    Task task1 = new Task(() => {
        for (int i = 0; i < 5; i++) {
            // check for task cancellation
            token.ThrowIfCancellationRequested();
            // print out a message
            Console.WriteLine("Task 1 - Int value {0}", i);
            // put the task to sleep for 1 second
            token.WaitHandle.WaitOne(1000);
        }
        Console.WriteLine("Task 1 complete");
    }, token);

    Task task2 = new Task(() => {
        Console.WriteLine("Task 2 complete");
    }, token);

    // start the tasks
    task1.Start();
    task2.Start();

    // wait for the tasks
    Console.WriteLine("Waiting for tasks to complete.");
    int taskIndex = Task.WaitAny(task1, task2);
    Console.WriteLine("Task Completed. Index: {0}", taskIndex);

    // wait for input before exiting
    Console.WriteLine("Main method complete. Press enter to finish.");
    Console.ReadLine();
        }
    }
}
```

Handling Exceptions in Tasks

Another of the useful areas of standardization introduced by the TPL is in exception handling. It doesn't matter how well we design, write, and test our code, we still have to handle exceptions.

An exception that is thrown but dealt with is known as a *handled exception*. An exception that is thrown and not dealt with is an *unhandled exception*. Unhandled exceptions are something to avoid in general programming, but they are especially dangerous in when using the TPL, because by default, they will cause your program to exit unpredictably.

The TPL provides a consistent model for handling exceptions that occur while a task is executing them, and the following sections describe the different aspects of this model and show you how to leave all of your exceptions unhandled and override the default policy for dealing with unhandled exceptions.

Table 2-7 provides the quick guide for handling task exceptions.

Table 2-7. *Handling Task Exceptions*

Problem	Solution	Listing
Handle exceptions thrown by tasks.	Call a trigger member (Task.Wait(), Task.WaitAll(), Task,WaitAny(), Task.Result), and catch System.AggregateException. Get an enumerable collection of the exceptions thrown by calling AggregateException.InnerExceptions.	2-19
Use an exception handler.	Call the AggregateException.Handle() method, providing a delegate that takes a System.Exception and returns true if the exception has been handled and false if it should be escalated.	2-20
Read Task properties.	Call the IsCompleted, IsFaulted, IsCancelled and Exception properties of the Task class.	2-21
Set a custom escalation policy.	Register an event handler with System.Threading.Tasks.TaskScheduler.UnobservedTaskException.	2-22

Handling Basic Exceptions

Any exception that is thrown (and not caught) by a Task is squirreled away by the .NET Framework until you call a trigger member, such as Task.Wait(), Task.WaitAll(), Task.WaitAny(), or Task.Result, at which point the trigger member will throw an instance of System.AggregateException.

The AggregateException type is used to provider a wrapper around one or more exceptions, and this is useful because methods such as WaitAll() coordinate multiple Tasks and may need to present you with multiple exceptions. This feature is also useful for Task chaining, which is described in the next chapter. An AggregateException is always thrown by the trigger methods, even when there has been only one exception thrown.

An example is always the best illustration, so Listing 2-19 creates three Tasks, two of which throw exceptions. The main thread starts the tasks and then calls the static WaitAll() method, catches the AggregateException and prints out details of the exceptions thrown by the individual Tasks.

Listing 2-19. Basic Exception Handling

```
using System;
using System.Threading.Tasks;

namespace Listing_19 {

    class Listing_19 {

        static void Main(string[] args) {
```

```
        // create the tasks
        Task task1 = new Task(() => {
            ArgumentOutOfRangeException exception = new ArgumentOutOfRangeException();
            exception.Source = "task1";
            throw exception;
        });
        Task task2 = new Task(() => {
            throw new NullReferenceException();
        });
        Task task3 = new Task(() => {
            Console.WriteLine("Hello from Task 3");
        });

        // start the tasks
        task1.Start(); task2.Start(); task3.Start();

        // wait for all of the tasks to complete
        // and wrap the method in a try...catch block
        try {
            Task.WaitAll(task1, task2, task3);
        } catch (AggregateException ex) {
            // enumerate the exceptions that have been aggregated
            foreach (Exception inner in ex.InnerExceptions) {
                Console.WriteLine("Exception type {0} from {1}",
                    inner.GetType(), inner.Source);
            }
        }

        // wait for input before exiting
        Console.WriteLine("Main method complete. Press enter to finish.");
        Console.ReadLine();
    }
  }
}
```

To get the exceptions that have been aggregated, you call the InnerExceptions property of AggregateException, which returns a collections of exceptions that you can enumerate.

In the listing, tasks task1 and task2 throw exceptions, which are bundled up into an instance of AggregateException. This exception is thrown when we call the Task.WaitAll() trigger method. One shortcoming of this approach to handling exceptions is that there is no obvious way of correlating exceptions that have been thrown to the task that threw them. In the code listing, the Exception.Source property is used to indicate that task1 is the source of the ArgumentOutOfRangeException.

Using an Iterative Handler

Generally, you will need to differentiate between the exceptions that you were expecting and the ones that are unexpected and you need to propagate. The AggregateException class provides the Handle() method, which allows you to specify a function delegate that will be called for each exception. Your function or lambda expression should return true if the exception is one that you can handle and false otherwise.

The "Cancelling Tasks" section of this chapter explained that you should throw an instance of the OperationCanceledException to acknowledge a cancellation request. That type of exception is likely to be one you will have to process most frequently. Listing 2-20 shows you how to use the AggregateException.Handle() method to differentiate between an exception thrown for a cancellation and other kinds of exception.

Listing 2-20. Using an Iterative Exception Handler

```
using System;
using System.Threading;
using System.Threading.Tasks;

namespace Listing_20 {

    class Listing_20 {

        static void Main(string[] args) {

            // create the cancellation token source and the token
            CancellationTokenSource tokenSource = new CancellationTokenSource();
            CancellationToken token = tokenSource.Token;

            // create a task that waits on the cancellation token
            Task task1 = new Task(() => {
                // wait forever or until the token is cancelled
                token.WaitHandle.WaitOne(-1);
                // throw an exception to acknowledge the cancellation
                throw new OperationCanceledException(token);
            }, token);

            // create a task that throws an exception
            Task task2 = new Task(() => {
                throw new NullReferenceException();
            });

            // start the tasks
            task1.Start(); task2.Start();

            // cancel the token
            tokenSource.Cancel();

            // wait on the tasks and catch any exceptions
            try {
                Task.WaitAll(task1, task2);
            } catch (AggregateException ex) {
                // iterate through the inner exceptions using
                // the handle method
                ex.Handle((inner) => {
                    if (inner is OperationCanceledException) {
```

```
                // ...handle task cancellation...
                return true;
            } else {
                // this is an exception we don't know how
                // to handle, so return false
                return false;
            }
        });
    }

    // wait for input before exiting
    Console.WriteLine("Main method complete. Press enter to finish.");
    Console.ReadLine();
}
}
}
```

If you compile and run the code in Listing 2-20, you will see one of the exceptions—
NullReferenceException—being reported as unhandled. This is, of course, because the exception
handler only marks OperationCanceledExceptions as handled.

Reading the Task Properties

An alternative to catching the exceptions is to use the properties of the Task class, in particular, the
IsCompleted, IsFaulted, IsCancelled, and Exception properties. You still have to catch
AggregateException when you call any of the trigger methods, but you can use the properties to
determine if a task has completed, thrown an exception, or been cancelled, and if an exception was
thrown, you can get the details of the exception. Listing 2-21 shows you how to use the Task properties.

Listing 2-21. Exception Handling with Task Properties

```
using System;
using System.Threading;
using System.Threading.Tasks;

namespace Listing_21 {

    class Listing_21 {

        static void Main(string[] args) {

            CancellationTokenSource tokenSource = new CancellationTokenSource();

            // create a task that throws an exception
            Task task1 = new Task(() => {
                throw new NullReferenceException();
            });
```

```
Task task2 = new Task(() => {
    // wait until we are cancelled
    tokenSource.Token.WaitHandle.WaitOne(-1);
    throw new OperationCanceledException();
}, tokenSource.Token);

// start the tasks
task1.Start();
task2.Start();

// cancel the token
tokenSource.Cancel();

// wait for the tasks, ignoring the exceptions
try {
    Task.WaitAll(task1, task2);
} catch (AggregateException) {
    // ignore exceptions
}

// write out the details of the task exception
Console.WriteLine("Task 1 completed: {0}", task1.IsCompleted);
Console.WriteLine("Task 1 faulted: {0}", task1.IsFaulted);
Console.WriteLine("Task 1 cancelled: {0}", task1.IsCanceled);
Console.WriteLine(task1.Exception);

// write out the details of the task exception
Console.WriteLine("Task 2 completed: {0}", task2.IsCompleted);
Console.WriteLine("Task 2 faulted: {0}", task2.IsFaulted);
Console.WriteLine("Task 2 cancelled: {0}", task2.IsCanceled);
Console.WriteLine(task2.Exception);

// wait for input before exiting
Console.WriteLine("Main method complete. Press enter to finish.");
Console.ReadLine();
        }
    }
}
```

The code in the listing creates two tasks: one throws an exception, and the other waits for a CancellationToken to be cancelled. Once the tasks are started, we cancel the token and call Task.WaitAll() to allow the tasks to complete. We ignore any exceptions by catching and discarding AggregateException and then print the values of the Task properties to the console, getting the following results:

```
Task 1 completed: True

Task 1 faulted: True

Task 1 cancelled: False

System.AggregateException: One or more errors occurred. ---> System.NullReferenceException:

... details of exception...

Task 2 completed: True

Task 2 faulted: False

Task 2 cancelled: True


Main method complete. Press enter to finish.
```

The IsCompleted property will return true if the Task has completed and false otherwise. The IsFaulted property returns true if the Task has thrown an exception and false if it has not or if the Task has been cancelled. The IsCanceled property returns true if the Task has been cancelled.

Using a Custom Escalation Policy

If you don't catch AggregateException when you call a trigger method, the .NET Framework will escalate the exceptions. By default, this means that the unhandled exceptions will be thrown again when your Task is finalized and cause your program to be terminated. Because you don't know when the finalizer will be called, you won't be able to predict when this will happen.

But, if you are determined not to handle the exceptions using one of the techniques described in the previous sections, you can override the escalation policy and supply your own code to call when an exception is escalated. You do this by adding an event handler to the static System.Threading.Tasks.TaskScheduler.UnobservedTaskException member, as shown in the Listing 2-22. Don't worry about the other members of the TaskScheduler class; they are described in Chapter 4. Listing 2-22 shows how to implement an escalation policy that writes the exception type to the console.

Listing 2-22. Custom Escalation Policy

```
using System;
using System.Threading;
using System.Threading.Tasks;

namespace Listing_22 {

    class Listing_22 {

        static void Main(string[] args) {

            // create the new escalation policy
            TaskScheduler.UnobservedTaskException +=
                (object sender, UnobservedTaskExceptionEventArgs eventArgs) =>
                    {
                        // mark the exception as being handled
                        eventArgs.SetObserved();
                        // get the aggregate exception and process the contents
                        ((AggregateException)eventArgs.Exception).Handle(ex => {
                            // write the type of the exception to the console
                            Console.WriteLine("Exception type: {0}", ex.GetType());
                            return true;
                        });
                    };

            // create tasks that will throw an exception
            Task task1 = new Task(() => {
                throw new NullReferenceException();
            });
            Task task2 = new Task(() => {
                throw new ArgumentOutOfRangeException();
            });

            // start the tasks
            task1.Start(); task2.Start();

            // wait for the tasks to complete - but do so
            // without calling any of the trigger members
            // so that the exceptions remain unhandled
            while (!task1.IsCompleted || !task2.IsCompleted) {
                Thread.Sleep(500);
            }

            // wait for input before exiting
            Console.WriteLine("Press enter to finish and finalize tasks");
            Console.ReadLine();
        }
    }
}
```

The .NET Framework calls the event handler each time an unhandled exception is escalated. Notice that the `UnobservedTaskExceptionEventArgs.SetObserved()` method is called to tell the .NET Framework that the exception has been handled and should not be escalated any further. If you omit the call to `SetObserved()`, the exception will be escalated using the default policy. You can get the exception by calling the `UnobservedTaskExceptionEventArgs.Exception` property, which will return instances of `AggregateException`. See the previous sections for examples of how to process this type.

Getting the Status of a Task

One other area of standardization for parallel programming is the status information available from the `Task.Status` property, which returns a value from the `System.Threading.Tasks.TaskStatus` enumeration. The enumeration members are shown in Table 2-8.

Table 2-8. Members of the TaskStatus Enumeration

Member	Description
Created	The task has been initialized but not yet scheduled.
WaitingForActivation WaitingToRun	The task is waiting to be scheduled or has been scheduled and is awaiting execution.
Running	The task is running.
WaitingForChildrenToComplete	The task is waiting for a child task (covered in the next chapter) to complete.
RanToCompletion	The task completed without being cancelled and without an exception being thrown.
Canceled	The task was cancelled (see the " Cancelling Tasks" section in this chapter).
Faulted	The task threw an exception (see the "Handling Exceptions in Tasks" section in this chapter).
WaitingForChildrenToComplete	See Chapter 4 for details about this value.

Executing Tasks Lazily

If you want to perform some work in parallel only when the result is required for the first time, you can use lazy task execution, which combines lazy variable initialization and the `Task<>.Factory.StartNew()` method.

Lazy variables are not initialized until they are required, allowing you to avoid potentially expensive computations until they are needed or to avoid doing work for variables that may not be needed at all. You can combine lazy variables with tasks to create a task that is not executed until the lazy variable is read.

Listing 2-24 demonstrates lazy task execution using two examples: The first defines the task body as a function and then uses it to create a lazy variable. The second does the same thing in a single statement. I have included the first version because the code is a lot easier to understand when the two parts are created separately.

Listing 2-23. Lazy Task Execution

```
using System;
using System.Threading.Tasks;

namespace Listing_23 {

    class Listing_23 {

        static void Main(string[] args) {

            // define the function
            Func<string> taskBody = new Func<string>(() => {
                Console.WriteLine("Task body working...");
                return "Task Result";
            });

            // create the lazy variable
            Lazy<Task<string>> lazyData = new Lazy<Task<string>>(() =>
                Task<string>.Factory.StartNew(taskBody));

            Console.WriteLine("Calling lazy variable");
            Console.WriteLine("Result from task: {0}", lazyData.Value.Result);

            // do the same thing in a single statement
            Lazy<Task<string>> lazyData2 = new Lazy<Task<string>>(
                () => Task<string>.Factory.StartNew(() => {
                    Console.WriteLine("Task body working...");
                    return "Task Result";
                }));

            Console.WriteLine("Calling second lazy variable");
            Console.WriteLine("Result from task: {0}", lazyData2.Value.Result);

            // wait for input before exiting
            Console.WriteLine("Main method complete. Press enter to finish.");
            Console.ReadLine();
        }
    }
}
```

Understanding Common Problems and Their Causes

Take a look at the examples in this section for help in troubleshooting common Task programming problems.

Task Dependency Deadlock

If two or more Tasks depend on each other to complete, none can move forward without the others, so a *deadlock* (the condition where the Tasks involved cannot progress) occurs.

Solution

The only way to avoid this problem is to ensure that your Tasks do not depend on one another. This requires careful attention when writing your Task bodies and thorough testing. You can also use the debugging features of Visual Studio 2010 to help detect deadlocks (see Chapter 7 for details).

Example

In the following example, two Tasks depend upon one another, and each requires the result of the other to generate its own result. When the program is run, both Tasks are started by the main application thread and deadlock. Because the main thread waits for the Tasks to finish, the whole program seizes up and never completes.

```
using System;
using System.Threading.Tasks;

namespace Dependency_Deadlock {

    class Dependency_Deadlock {

        static void Main(string[] args) {

            // define an array to hold the Tasks
            Task<int>[] tasks = new Task<int>[2];

            // create and start the first task
            tasks[0] = Task.Factory.StartNew(() => {
                // get the result of the other task,
                // add 100 to it and return it as the result
                return tasks[1].Result + 100;
            });

            // create and start the second task
            tasks[1] = Task.Factory.StartNew(() => {
                // get the result of the other task,
                // add 100 to it and return it as the result
                return tasks[1].Result + 100;
            });
```

```
            // wait for the tasks to complete
            Task.WaitAll(tasks);

            // wait for input before exiting
            Console.WriteLine("Main method complete. Press enter to finish.");
            Console.ReadLine();
        }
    }
}
```

Local Variable Evaluation

Assume that you create a series of Tasks in a for loop and refer to the loop counter in your lambda expressions. All of the Tasks end up with the same value because of the way that the C# variable scoping rules are applied to lambda expressions.

Solution

The simplest way to fix this problem is to pass the loop counter in as a state object to the Task.

Example

In the following example, five Tasks print out a message that references the counter of the loop that created them, and they all print the same value. Another five Tasks do the same thing, but get their values as state objects, and these get the expected values.

```
using System;
using System.Threading.Tasks;

namespace Local_Variable_Evaluation {

    class Local_Variable_Evaluation {

        static void Main(string[] args) {

            // create and start the "bad" tasks
            for (int i = 0; i < 5; i++) {
                Task.Factory.StartNew(() => {
                    // write out a message that uses the loop counter
                    Console.WriteLine("Task {0} has counter value: {1}",
                        Task.CurrentId, i);
                });
            }

            // create and start the "good" tasks
            for (int i = 0; i < 5; i++) {
                Task.Factory.StartNew((stateObj) => {
                    // cast the state object to an int
                    int loopValue = (int)stateObj;
```

```
                    // write out a message that uses the loop counter
                    Console.WriteLine("Task {0} has counter value: {1}",
                        Task.CurrentId, loopValue);
                }, i);
            }

            // wait for input before exiting
            Console.WriteLine("Main method complete. Press enter to finish.");
            Console.ReadLine();
        }
    }
}
```

Excessive Spinning

Many programmers overestimate the performance impact of a `Task` waiting (either via `Thread.Sleep()` or by using a `CancellationToken` wait handle) and use spin waiting instead (through the `Thread.SpinWait()` method or by entering a code loop).

For anything other than exceptionally short waits, spin waiting and code loops will cripple the performance of your parallel program, because avoiding a wait also avoids freeing up a thread for execution.

Solution

Restrict your use of spin waiting and code loops to situations where you know that the condition that you are waiting for will take only a few CPU cycles. If you must avoid a full wait, use spin waiting in preference to code loops.

Example

In the following example, one `Task` enters a code loop to await the cancellation of another `Task`. Another `Task` does the same thing but uses spin waiting. On the quad-core machine that I used to write this book, this example burns roughly 30 percent of the available CPU, which is quite something for a program that does nothing at all. You may get different results if you have fewer cores.

```
using System;
using System.Threading;
using System.Threading.Tasks;

namespace Excessive_Spinning {

    class Excessive_Spinning {

        static void Main(string[] args) {

            // create a cancellation token source
            CancellationTokenSource tokenSource =
                new CancellationTokenSource();
```

```
// create the first task
Task t1 = Task.Factory.StartNew(() => {
    Console.WriteLine("Task 1 waiting for cancellation");
    tokenSource.Token.WaitHandle.WaitOne();
    Console.WriteLine("Task 1 cancelled");
    tokenSource.Token.ThrowIfCancellationRequested();
}, tokenSource.Token);

// create the second task, which will use a code loop
Task t2 = Task.Factory.StartNew(() => {
    // enter a loop until t1 is cancelled
    while (!t1.Status.HasFlag(TaskStatus.Canceled)) {
        // do nothing - this is a code loop
    }
    Console.WriteLine("Task 2 exited code loop");
});

// create the third loop which will use spin waiting
Task t3 = Task.Factory.StartNew(() => {
    // enter the spin wait loop
    while (t1.Status != TaskStatus.Canceled) {
        Thread.SpinWait(1000);
    }
    Console.WriteLine("Task 3 exited spin wait loop");
});

// prompt the user to hit enter to cancel
Console.WriteLine("Press enter to cancel token");
Console.ReadLine();
tokenSource.Cancel();

// wait for input before exiting
Console.WriteLine("Main method complete. Press enter to finish.");
Console.ReadLine();
    }
  }
}
```

Summary

This chapter introduced you to the basic building blocks that we will use to explore the Task Programming Library (TPL). You learned how to create and start Tasks, cancel Tasks as they are running, handle exceptions when things go wrong, and check the status of Tasks—all essential to writing parallel programs. In the next chapter, we'll look at one of the most common complexities that parallel programmers face, specifically sharing data between tasks.

CHAPTER 3

■ ■ ■

Sharing Data

Listing 3-1. Hello Task

```csharp
using System;
using System.Threading.Tasks;

namespace Listing_01 {

    class BankAccount {
        public int Balance {
            get;
            set;
        }
    }

    class Listing_01 {

        static void Main(string[] args) {

            // create the bank account instance
            BankAccount account = new BankAccount();

            // create an array of tasks
            Task[] tasks = new Task[10];

            for (int i = 0; i < 10; i++) {
                // create a new task
                tasks[i] = new Task(() => {
                    // enter a loop for 1000 balance updates
                    for (int j = 0; j < 1000; j++) {
                        // update the balance
                        account.Balance = account.Balance + 1;
                    }
                });
                // start the new task
                tasks[i].Start();
            }
```

```
        // wait for all of the tasks to complete
        Task.WaitAll(tasks);

        // write out the counter value
        Console.WriteLine("Expected value {0}, Counter value: {1}",
            10000, account.Balance);

        // wait for input before exiting
        Console.WriteLine("Press enter to finish");
        Console.ReadLine();
      }
    }
}
```

The Trouble with Data

Listing 3-1 creates ten Tasks, each of which increments the BankAccount.Balance property 1,000 times. We wait for all of the Tasks to complete and print out the value of Balance. If there are ten Tasks and each of them increments Balance 1,000 times, the final value of Balance should be 10,000 (10 × 1000). Running Listing 3-1 might produce the following results:

```
Expected value 10000, Balance: 8840

Press any key to continue . . .
```

You will certainly get a different result if you run the code. Repeatedly running the program produces a wide range of results. If we are fortunate, we might get the expected result once or twice. In this chapter, I explain why this happens and how to correct the problem.

Going to the Races

The odd behavior in Listing 3-1 is caused by a *data race*. Whenever we have two or more Tasks performing operations that update a shared piece data, there is the potential for a race. And if we don't manage the race properly, we get unexpected and undesirable results.

Incrementing the account balance in Listing 3-1 takes three steps:

1. Read the current balance from the BankAccount object.

2. Calculate the new value.

3. Update the BankAccount with the new balance.

Thinking of this as a three-step process is really a convenience. In fact, we don't know how the compiler, the runtime, and the operating system are going to perform or optimize our increment operation, but let's stick with three steps for the sake of simplicity.

We get a range of results with Listing 3-1 because there are slight variations in the timing of each Task. If you run the program several times, your machine will be in a different state each time: the CPU will be more or less busy; there will be different amounts of memory available, and so on. These differences influence the way in which the Tasks are created, scheduled, and run.

Figure 3-1 shows what can happen when two Tasks race. The Tasks are performing the steps of the balance update slightly out of phase with each other, because they have been started a short time apart. Task 1 reads the current balance and gets 0. A fraction of a second later, Task 2 reads the current balance of the counter and also gets 0—oops. Both Tasks calculate the new balance by incrementing the starting balance they received, so both produce a new balance of 1 —oops, again.

Task 1 stores its new value, and a fraction of a second later, Task 2 comes steaming along and does the same thing. We used two Tasks to perform two increments but got a result of 1. That's a data race—two Tasks competing to manipulate a piece of shared data without any coordination between them. You can imagine how bad things get in Listing 3-1 with ten Tasks performing 1,000 increments each.

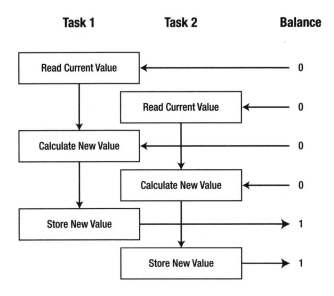

Figure 3-1. A simple data race

Creating Some Order

A data race is like a birthday party. The Tasks are the party guests, and when the cake is brought out, the guests can get a little wild. If all of the guests rush to get themselves some cake at the same time, order breaks down.

We created a mad scramble to read and write the shared data in Listing 3-1 and ended up with a data race. The cake in this example is the bank account balance. We have to manage a potential problem whenever multiple Tasks share and update the same data. There are four broad kinds of solution to shared data problems:

- Sequential execution: We stop parallelizing the work.

- *Immutability*: We stop Tasks being able to modify the data.

- *Isolation*: We stop sharing the data.

- *Synchronization*: We coordinate the actions of the Tasks so that they take turns instead of competing.

We discuss each of these solutions in the following sections and look at the various .NET features available to support them.

Executing Sequentially

Sequential execution solves the shared data problem by having only one active `Task`, in essence, going back to a single-threaded code model. Put another way, you don't need to share the cake if you are the only person at the party.

This is the least useful and interesting solution to the data race in a book on parallel programming, but don't be afraid of sequential execution if the problem you are trying to solve is not well suited to the parallel world.

Executing Immutably

Immutability solves the shared data problem by not allowing data to be changed. If data can't be changed, there is no scope for a data race. If sequential execution means that you get the cake to yourself, immutability means that you can look at the cake but can't eat.

C# supports immutability with the `readonly` and `const` keywords. Fields marked with the `const` modifier must be declared and assigned in a single statement, such as this:

```
public const int AccountNumber = 123456;
```

Once declared and assigned, the `const` value cannot be changed, and the field can only be accessed through the type name, not an instance of the type. The `readonly` keyword is accessible through type instances and can be modified in a constructor; this means that the value of a `readonly` field can depend on which constructor is used to instantiate an immutable type. Listing 3-2 shows demonstrates both keywords in use.

Listing 3-2. An Immutable Bank Account

```
using System;

namespace Listing_02 {

    class ImmutableBankAccount {
        public const int AccountNumber = 123456;
        public readonly int Balance;

        public ImmutableBankAccount(int InitialBalance) {
            Balance = InitialBalance;
        }

        public ImmutableBankAccount() {
            Balance = 0;
        }
    }
```

```
class Listing_02 {

    static void Main(string[] args) {

        // create a bank account with the default balance
        ImmutableBankAccount bankAccount1 = new ImmutableBankAccount();
        Console.WriteLine("Account Number: {0}, Account Balance: {1}",
            ImmutableBankAccount.AccountNumber, bankAccount1.Balance);

        // create a bank account with a starting balance
        ImmutableBankAccount bankAccount2 = new ImmutableBankAccount(200);
        Console.WriteLine("Account Number: {0}, Account Balance: {1}",
            ImmutableBankAccount.AccountNumber, bankAccount2.Balance);

        // wait for input before exiting
        Console.WriteLine("Press enter to finish");
        Console.ReadLine();
    }
}
}
```

Immutability is not a widely used solution in C#, because not being able to change data values is a huge limitation. In Listing 3-2, we ended up with a bank account whose balance can be read but not changed. Immutability is useful, however, for creating a clear separation between immutable reference data that can be safely shared between Tasks and mutable Task data that must be protected using a different technique.

■ **Tip** See the "Unexpected Immutability" example in the "Understanding Common Problems and Their Causes" section at the end of this chapter for an example of how misusing immutability can cause problems.

Executing in Isolation

Isolation solves the shared data problem by giving everyone their own piece of data. You don't need to share if everyone at the party gets their own cake.

We can provide a Task with isolated data by using the constructor overload that takes a state object, as described in Chapter 2. Listing 3-3 updates our simple bank account example to use isolation. Each Task is given the current balance as a state object when it is created. The data is isolated because each Task only modifies its own version of the balance. When all of the Tasks have completed, we read the results and combine them to accurately update the bank account.

Listing 3-3. Isolation by Convention

```csharp
using System;
using System.Threading.Tasks;

namespace Listing_03 {

    class BankAccount {
        public int Balance {
            get;
            set;
        }
    }

    class Listing_03 {

        static void Main(string[] args) {

            // create the bank account instance
            BankAccount account = new BankAccount();

            // create an array of tasks
            Task<int>[] tasks = new Task<int>[10];

            for (int i = 0; i < 10; i++) {
                // create a new task
                tasks[i] = new Task<int>((stateObject) => {

                    // get the state object
                    int isolatedBalance = (int)stateObject;

                    // enter a loop for 1000 balance updates
                    for (int j = 0; j < 1000; j++) {
                        // update the balance
                        isolatedBalance++;
                    }

                    // return the updated balance
                    return isolatedBalance;

                }, account.Balance);

                // start the new task
                tasks[i].Start();
            }

            // get the result from each task and add it to
            // the balance
            for (int i = 0; i < 10; i++) {
                account.Balance += tasks[i].Result;
            }
```

```
        // write out the counter value
        Console.WriteLine("Expected value {0}, Balance: {1}",
            10000, account.Balance);

        // wait for input before exiting
        Console.WriteLine("Press enter to finish");
        Console.ReadLine();
    }
  }
}
```

There is no data race in Listing 3-3, because the Tasks are only concerned with their own local version of the balance. This is an example of *isolation by convention*: the code is written so that the Tasks works in isolation but the isolation is not enforced by the .NET runtime; we have to take care to ensure that Tasks don't share data by mistake.

.NET provides the System.Threading.ThreadLocal class, which creates isolation that *is* enforced by the .NET Framework. ThreadLocal represents a special kind of data called thread local storage (TLS), where a single ThreadLocal results in each thread that accesses the data getting its own isolated instance.

TLS can be a little hard to understand, but try thinking of it like this—when we declare a ThreadLocal to hold, say, a string, we make the following call:

```
ThreadLocal<string> isolatedData = new ThreadLocal<string>();
```

Imagine that the .NET Framework creates Dictionary<Thread, string> behind the scenes and that whenever we call the ThreadLocal.Value property to get or set the isolated data value, the framework translates that into a query against the Dictionary so that we only read or write the value associated with the current thread and each thread has its own value.

TLS doesn't really use a Dictionary, but imagining that it does is a helpful way of understanding an unusual concept. The important thing to remember is each thread has its own isolated data value and can't read or write the value belonging to any other thread.

Now, notice that we are talking about threads and not Tasks, and remember from Chapter 1 that a single thread can be used to perform multiple Tasks. To ensure that you get the results you expect with Tasks, make sure that you set the ThreadLocal.Value property at the start of your Task body. Listing 3-4 shows ThreadLocal being used in our simple bank account program, with the isolated data value being set at the start of the Task body.

Listing 3-4. Using TLS

```
using System;
using System.Threading;
using System.Threading.Tasks;

namespace Listing_04 {

    class BankAccount {
        public int Balance {
            get;
            set;
        }
    }
```

```csharp
class Listing_04 {

    static void Main(string[] args) {

        // create the bank account instance
        BankAccount account = new BankAccount();

        // create an array of tasks
        Task<int>[] tasks = new Task<int>[10];

        // create the thread local storage
        ThreadLocal<int> tls = new ThreadLocal<int>();

        for (int i = 0; i < 10; i++) {
            // create a new task
            tasks[i] = new Task<int>((stateObject) => {

                // get the state object and use it
                // to set the TLS data
                tls.Value = (int)stateObject;

                // enter a loop for 1000 balance updates
                for (int j = 0; j < 1000; j++) {
                    // update the TLS balance
                    tls.Value++;
                }

                // return the updated balance
                return tls.Value;

            }, account.Balance);

            // start the new task
            tasks[i].Start();
        }

        // get the result from each task and add it to
        // the balance
        for (int i = 0; i < 10; i++) {
            account.Balance += tasks[i].Result;
        }

        // write out the counter value
        Console.WriteLine("Expected value {0}, Balance: {1}",
            10000, account.Balance);

        // wait for input before exiting
        Console.WriteLine("Press enter to finish");
        Console.ReadLine();
    }
}
}
```

Even though we have created only one instance of ThreadLocal<int>, each Task is able to initialize its own isolated instance of the data using the state object and perform updates without worrying about data races. ThreadLocal provides an overloaded constructor so you can supply a factory delegate that will initialize the isolated data value. This factory delegate is lazily initialized, meaning that it will not be called until the Task calls the ThreadLocal.Value property for the first time.

Be careful when using lazy initialization in TLS (or elsewhere in C#); it can trip you up. The factory delegate is not called until the first time that the variable is accessed, so any other data that you depend on will not be read until then. Remember also that TLS works on threads and not Tasks, so the value factory will only be called the first time a thread performs one of your Tasks. Take a look at Listing 3-5, which shows an ill-advised use of the value factory.

Listing 3-5. A TLS Value Factory That Produced Unexpected Results

```
using System;
using System.Threading;
using System.Threading.Tasks;

namespace Listing_05 {

    class BankAccount {
        public int Balance {
            get;
            set;
        }
    }

    class Listing_05 {

        static void Main(string[] args) {

            // create the bank account instance
            BankAccount account = new BankAccount();

            // create an array of tasks
            Task<int>[] tasks = new Task<int>[10];

            // create the thread local storage
            ThreadLocal<int> tls = new ThreadLocal<int>(() => {
                Console.WriteLine("Value factory called for value: {0}",
                    account.Balance);
                return account.Balance;
            });

            for (int i = 0; i < 10; i++) {
                // create a new task
                tasks[i] = new Task<int>(() => {
```

```
                        // enter a loop for 1000 balance updates
                        for (int j = 0; j < 1000; j++) {
                            // update the TLS balance
                            tls.Value++;
                        }

                        // return the updated balance
                        return tls.Value;

                });

                    // start the new task
                    tasks[i].Start();
            }

            // get the result from each task and add it to
            // the balance
            for (int i = 0; i < 10; i++) {
                account.Balance += tasks[i].Result;
            }

            // write out the counter value
            Console.WriteLine("Expected value {0}, Balance: {1}",
                10000, account.Balance);

            // wait for input before exiting
            Console.WriteLine("Press enter to finish");
            Console.ReadLine();
        }
    }
}
```

Running Listing 3-5 yields the following results:

```
Value factory called for value: 0

Value factory called for value: 0

Value factory called for value: 0

Value factory called for value: 0

Expected value 10000, Balance: 29000

Press enter to finish
```

We started ten Tasks, but the value factory was called to initialize the TLS only four times. Can you guess why? Yep, the code was run on a four-core machine, and four threads were used to execute the ten Tasks. As a consequence, the final balance from one Task was carried over to be the initial balance for another, and we ended up with an overall balance that was unexpected. TLS can be a useful technique if used carefully but can trip up the unwary.

Synchronizing Execution

If sequential execution means being the only person at the party, immutability is having a plastic cake, and isolation is giving everyone their own cake, then synchronization is having many guests and one cake and asking your great aunt Matilda to make everyone act politely. Matilda makes sure that everyone gets a piece of the cake by having the guests take turns and play nice.

Synchronization means making Tasks take turns, avoiding races by serializing access to shared data, usually only allowing one Task access to the shared data at any given time (although there are other options that we will cover in Chapter 4).

The two key elements to understanding synchronization are the critical region and the synchronization primitive. In party terms, critical regions are the cakes, or the things that we want to control access to in order to avoid problems. Synchronization primitives play the role of the great aunt, or the way in which we enforce order and politeness.

Defining Critical Regions

A *critical region* is one or more C# statements that we want to serialize access to so we can avoid a data race. For the bank account example in Listing 3-1, the critical region is the statement that increments the account balance, as shown in the following fragment:

```
for (int j = 0; j < 1000; j++) {
    // update the balance
    account.Balance = account.Balance + 1; // <-- critical region
}
```

More complex programs will have larger and more complex critical regions, of course. And classes can have more than one critical region. Imagine that we added new methods to our simple BankAccount type that read and update the balance. We must serialize access to the statements *within* each method but also *across* methods, so that a Task that calls one method doesn't start a data race with a Task calling the other method. Don't worry if the idea of critical regions doesn't immediately make sense; there are plenty of examples in this chapter and throughout the rest of this book that will help.

Defining Synchronization Primitives

A *synchronization primitive* is a special kind of data type that is used to coordinate Tasks' access to critical regions and, therefore, to shared data. A Task arrives at a point in its work where they need to access a critical region. The Task checks with the synchronization primitive to see if the critical section is already in use. If the critical section is free, then it proceeds to execute the code statements. If there is another Task already using the critical section, then the newly arrived Task is asked to wait. When the Task that is using the critical section has finished, it tells the synchronization primitive that it is done, so that another Task can be allowed to proceed.

When a primitive grants access to a critical section, the Task is said to *acquire* or *take* the *lock*. When a Task notifies the primitive that is leaving the critical section, it is said to *release* or *exit* the lock.

There are three kinds of synchronization primitives in the .NET Framework:

- Lightweight primitives

- Heavyweight (classic) primitives

- Wait handles

With .NET 4, Microsoft has introduced some new *lightweight* primitives, so called because they are more efficiently implemented than the equivalent classic threading classes. They can only provide synchronization within one application domain, but since this is usually what programmers require, you will find yourself using these primitives most frequently.

The *heavyweight* threading primitives have existed since the early versions of .NET and have been widely used with the classic .NET threading model. They don't perform as well as the lightweight primitives, but they can be used across application domains.

Wait handles use a feature of the Windows operating system and can be used to provide synchronization between processes. Wait handles are often used to coordinate `Tasks` (something we will cover at length in the next chapter), but they can be used to avoid data races as well. They can also be used to provide synchronization across different processes.

■ **Note** This note is for you particularly detail-oriented readers. You know from Chapter 1 that tasks are executed by threads. The .NET synchronization primitives actually operate at the thread level, but since the threads are executing `Tasks`, we will discuss synchronization as though it operated at the task level. There is no effective difference and keeping everything at the task level makes for clearer examples.

Getting to grips with synchronization is one of the most challenging aspects of parallel programming, and it trips up everyone at some point. When you encounter problems (and you almost certainly will), stop and think about what you are trying to achieve and ask yourself a couple of questions. Have I selected the right synchronization primitive? And am I using it correctly. Nine times out of ten, the problem can be found in the answers to those two questions.

Using Synchronization Wisely

Before we cover the different synchronization primitives, let me set out some advice that you should consider if you want to write effective parallel programs:

- Don't synchronize too much.

- Don't synchronize too little.

- Pick the lightest tool to do the job.

- Don't write you own synchronization primitives.

Don't Synchronize Too Much

Most programmers go through a transition period when they come to parallel programming in which they write the program structure as though they planned for sequential execution and apply parallel features later. Data races arise, which are then fixed using synchronization applied like a Band-Aid.

Because the program was designed for sequential use, the programmer finds it hard to synchronize with any granularity and ends up synchronizing everything.

As I said earlier, synchronization has a cost and can reduce performance. Synchronizing with a heavy hand means that your code will end up running restricting parallelism but still incur the synchronization overheads.

Don't Synchronize Too Little

The natural reaction to having produced a program with too much synchronization is to over-compensate and use too little. Now, we end up with a program that performs well because the number of synchronization points is drastically reduced but doesn't protect all of the shared data and so suffers from data races.

Pick the Lightest Tool

The .NET Framework includes synchronization primitives from the classic .NET threading era and some new primitives introduced as part of the TPL. The new primitives are more efficient, but some of them lack useful features available in the heavyweight older primitives.

It may sound obvious, but you should pick the most efficient primitive that meets your program requirements. As programmers, we tend to end up with a shortlist of types and primitives that we use again and again because we understand them and have confidence in them. While that is fine for general programming, it can easily produce problems in parallel programming by either introducing a performance penalty or by not delivering the required level of synchronization.

Don't Write Your Own Synchronization Primitives

At some point, every parallel programmer struggles to use a particular synchronization primitive in a particular way and thinks, "hmmm, maybe I should write my own." You will have those thoughts, too. Don't do it; don't give in and write your own. I guarantee you that you will end up making things much, much worse.

Synchronization primitives are very difficult to write correctly. Most of the primitives in the .NET Framework rely on features of the operating system and, in some cases, of the machine hardware. My advice to you is to change the code whenever you can't get one of the .NET primitives to fit in with your code model. That solution will be simpler and quicker, and you have a far greater chance of producing working code than if you try to write your own primitive.

Using Basic Synchronization Primitives

The following sections describe the basic .NET synchronization primitives. Each of these classes can be used to ensure that only one **Task** is able to enter a critical region. The next chapter will describe some advanced synchronization primitives that will allow you to work with different numbers of **Task**s.

Table 3-1. *Synchronization Primtives*

Problem	Solution	Listing
Serialize access to a critical region.	Use the `lock` keyword or `System.Threading.Montor` class, or use the `System.Threading.SpinLock` class.	3-6, 3-7, and 3-10
Increment or decrement a numeric value.	Use the static members of the `System.Threading.Interlocked` class.	3-8 and 3-9
Create cross process synchronization.	Use the `System.Threading.Mutex` class to create a named `mutex`.	3-11
Perform synchronization using multiple locks.	Use `WaitAll()` method of a primitive that extends `System.Threading.WaitHandle`.	3-12
Synchronize all of the methods in a class.	Use declarative synchronization.	3-14
Create locks that permit multiple readers.	Use a reader-writer lock.	3-15 and 3-16

Locking and Monitoring

The simplest way to use synchronization in C# is with the **lock** keyword, which is a two-stage process. First, you must create a lock object that is visible to all of your **Task**s. Second, you must wrap the critical section in a **lock** block using the lock, as follows:

```
lock (lockObj) {
    ...critical section code...
}
```

Listing 3-6 shows the application of the **lock** keyword to the critical region of the bank account example from Listing 3-1.

Listing 3-6. *Applying the lock Keyword*

```
using System;
using System.Threading.Tasks;

namespace Listing_06 {

    class BankAccount {
        public int Balance {
            get;
            set;
        }
    }
```

```
class Listing_06 {

    static void Main(string[] args) {

        // create the bank account instance
        BankAccount account = new BankAccount();

        // create an array of tasks
        Task[] tasks = new Task[10];

        // create the lock object
        object lockObj = new object();

        for (int i = 0; i < 10; i++) {
            // create a new task
            tasks[i] = new Task(() => {
                // enter a loop for 1000 balance updates
                for (int j = 0; j < 1000; j++) {
                    lock (lockObj) {
                        // update the balance
                        account.Balance = account.Balance + 1;
                    }
                }
            });
            // start the new task
            tasks[i].Start();
        }

        // wait for all of the tasks to complete
        Task.WaitAll(tasks);

        // write out the counter value
        Console.WriteLine("Expected value {0}, Balance: {1}",
            10000, account.Balance);

        // wait for input before exiting
        Console.WriteLine("Press enter to finish");
        Console.ReadLine();
    }
}
}
```

The lock keyword is a C# shortcut for using the System.Threading.Monitor class, which is a heavyweight primitive.

```
lock (lockObj) {
    ...critical region code...
}
```

The preceding fragment is equivalent to the following:

```
bool lockAcquired;
try {
    Monitor.Enter(lockObj, ref lockAcquired);
    ...critical region code...
} finally {
    if (lockAcquired) Monitor.Exit(lockObj);
}
```

The members of the `Monitor` class are static, which is why you must provide a `lock` object—this tells the `Monitor` class which critical region a `Task` is trying to enter.

■ **Tip** It is important to ensure that all of your `Task`s use the same `lock` object when entering a given critical region. See the discussion of the Isolated Lock References antipattern in this chapter for more details.

The `lock` keyword automatically takes care of acquiring and releasing the lock for the critical region by calling `Monitor.Enter()` and `Monitor.Exit()` for you. If you decide to use the `Monitor` class directly (and there are some reasons for this that we'll come to in a moment), you should ensure that you call `Monitor.Exit()` within a `finally` block, just as in the preceding fragment. If you do not, you run the risk of encountering the orphaned locks problem described at the end of this chapter.

`Monitor.Enter()` takes a lock object and a pass-by-reference `bool` as arguments. The `bool` is set to `true` when the lock is acquired and should be checked before releasing the lock with `Monitor.Exit()`. There are some conditions under which you risk trying to release a lock that you have not acquired.

When one `Task` has acquired the lock, no other `Task` can enter the critical region. Calls to `Monitor.Enter()` will block until the first `Task` releases the lock by calling `Monitor.Exit()`. If there are `Task`s waiting when the lock is released, `Monitor` selects one of them and allows it to acquire the lock. `Task`s may acquire the lock in any sequence; the order in which `Task`s arrive at the critical region doesn't guarantee anything about the order in which they will acquire the lock.

You can try to acquire the lock by calling one of the overloads of the `Monitor.TryEnter()` method, which will let your `Task` try and acquire the lock without waiting indefinitely for it to become available. The overloads are listed in Table 3-2.

Table 3-2. Overloads of the System.Threading.Monitor.TryEnter Method

Overload	Description
`Monitor.TryEnter` `(Object, Boolean)`	Attempt to acquire a lock using a given lock object. The **Boolean** argument is set to **true** if the lock was acquired and **false** otherwise.
`Monitor.TryEnter` `(Object, Int32, Boolean)`	Attempt to acquire a lock using the lock object, waiting a maximum of **Int32** milliseconds. The **Boolean** argument is set to **true** if the lock was acquired and **false** otherwise.
`Monitor.TryEnter` `(Object,TimeSpan,Boolean)`	Attempt to acquire a lock using the **lock** object, waiting for the **TimeSpan** to see if the lock becomes available. The **Boolean** argument is set to **true** if the lock was acquired and **false** otherwise.

The same lock object, as I have said, must always be used for a given critical region. If you wish to protect two related critical regions (perhaps because they update the same shared data), the same object should be used to enter either region.

Listing 3-7 extends our simple bank account example to serialize access to critical regions. There are two groups of **Tasks**, one of which wants to increment the balance while the other wants to decrement it. By using the same lock object, we ensure that there is at most one **Task** working in the pair of critical regions.

Listing 3-7. Using a Single Lock Object to Serialize Access to Two Critical Regions

```
using System;
using System.Threading.Tasks;

namespace Listing_07 {

    class BankAccount {
        public int Balance {
            get;
            set;
        }
    }

    class Listing_07 {

        static void Main(string[] args) {

            // create the bank account instance
            BankAccount account = new BankAccount();

            // create an array of tasks
            Task[] incrementTasks = new Task[5];
            Task[] decrementTasks = new Task[5];
```

```
// create the lock object
object lockObj = new object();

for (int i = 0; i < 5; i++) {
    // create a new task
    incrementTasks[i] = new Task(() => {
        // enter a loop for 1000 balance updates
        for (int j = 0; j < 1000; j++) {
            lock (lockObj) {
                // increment the balance
                account.Balance++;
            }
        }
    });
    // start the new task
    incrementTasks[i].Start();
}

for (int i = 0; i < 5; i++) {
    // create a new task
    decrementTasks[i] = new Task(() => {
        // enter a loop for 1000 balance updates
        for (int j = 0; j < 1000; j++) {
            lock (lockObj) {
                // decrement the balance
                account.Balance = account.Balance -2;
            }
        }
    });
    // start the new task
    decrementTasks[i].Start();
}

// wait for all of the tasks to complete
Task.WaitAll(incrementTasks);
Task.WaitAll(decrementTasks);

// write out the counter value
Console.WriteLine("Expected value: -5000");
Console.WriteLine("Balance: {0}", account.Balance);

// wait for input before exiting
Console.WriteLine("Press enter to finish");
Console.ReadLine();
        }
    }
}
```

Using Interlocked Operations

The `System.Threading.Interlocked` class provides a set of static methods that use special features of the operating system and hardware to provide high-performance synchronized operations. All of the methods in `Interlocked` are static and synchronized. Table 3-3 provides a summary of the key members.

Table 3-3. Selected Members of the System.Threading.Interlocked Class

Member	Description

`Exchange(ref Double, Double)`
`Exchange(ref Int32, Int32)`
`Exchange(ref Int64, Int64)`
`Exchange(ref Single, Single)`
`Exchange(ref Object, Object)`
`Exchange<T>(ref T, T)`
	Set a value.

`Add(ref Int32, Int32)` `Add(ref Int64, Int64)`	Add two 32-bit or 64-bit integers
`Increment(ref Int32)` `Increment(ref Int64)`	Increment a 32-bit or 64-bit integer.
`Decrement(ref Int32)` `Decrement(ref Int64)`	Decrement a 32-bit or a 64-bit integer.

`CompareExchange(ref Double, Double, Double)`
`CompareExchange(ref Int32, Int32, Int32)`
`CompareExchange(ref Int64, Int64, Int64)`
`CompareExchange(ref Single, Single, Single)`
`CompareExchange(ref Object, Object, Object)`
`CompareExchange<T>(ref T, T, T)`
	Compare two values, and if they are equal, replace one of them.

The `Interlocked.Exchange()` method sets the value of a variable. The following statements are functionally equivalent, but manage synchronization using different techniques:

```
int myval = 99;

lock (lockObj) {
    // change value
    myval = 100;
}

// change value - synchronized
Interlocked.Exchange(ref myval, 101);
```

The `Add()`, `Increment()`, and `Decrement()` methods are convenient shortcuts when using integers and work the way that you would expect. Listing 3-8 shows how we can use `Interlocked.Increment()` to fix the data race from Listing 3-1. Notice that we have had to change the `BankAccount` class to expose the balance as an integer, because Interlocked methods require arguments modified by the ref keyword and values from properties cannot be used with ref.

Listing 3-8. Using Interlocked.Increment()

```csharp
using System;
using System.Threading;
using System.Threading.Tasks;

namespace Listing_08 {

    class BankAccount {
        public int Balance = 0;
    }

    class Listing_08 {

        static void Main(string[] args) {

            // create the bank account instance
            BankAccount account = new BankAccount();

            // create an array of tasks
            Task[] tasks = new Task[10];

            for (int i = 0; i < 10; i++) {
                // create a new task
                tasks[i] = new Task(() => {
                    // enter a loop for 1000 balance updates
                    for (int j = 0; j < 1000; j++) {
                        // update the balance
                        Interlocked.Increment(ref account.Balance);
                    }
                });
                // start the new task
                tasks[i].Start();
            }

            // wait for all of the tasks to complete
            Task.WaitAll(tasks);

            // write out the counter value
            Console.WriteLine("Expected value {0}, Balance: {1}",
                10000, account.Balance);

            // wait for input before exiting
            Console.WriteLine("Press enter to finish");
            Console.ReadLine();
        }
    }
}
```

The CompareExchange() method checks to see if a variable has a given value and, if it does, changes the value of variable. This is not as obtuse as it sounds, because this method allows you to tell if another Task has updated a shared variable and act accordingly. Using CompareExchange allows you to mix isolated data and then merge the isolated values with the shared data.

Listing 3-9 updates the previous example so that individual Tasks make a note of the starting balance and work with isolated balances to perform their updates. When they have calculated their local balances, they use CompareExchange() to update the shared value. If the shared data has not changed, the account balance is updated; otherwise, a message is printed out. In a real program, instead of simply noting that the shared data has changed, you could repeat the Task calculation or try a different method to update the shared data. For example, in the listing, we could have tried to add the local balance to the shared value.

Listing 3-9. Convergent Isolation with Interlocked.CompareExchange()

```
using System;
using System.Threading;
using System.Threading.Tasks;

namespace Listing_09 {

    class BankAccount {
        public int Balance = 0;
    }

    class Listing_09 {

        static void Main(string[] args) {

            // create the bank account instance
            BankAccount account = new BankAccount();

            // create an array of tasks
            Task[] tasks = new Task[10];

            for (int i = 0; i < 10; i++) {
                // create a new task
                tasks[i] = new Task(() => {

                    // get a local copy of the shared data
                    int startBalance = account.Balance;
                    // create a local working copy of the shared data
                    int localBalance = startBalance;

                    // enter a loop for 1000 balance updates
                    for (int j = 0; j < 1000; j++) {
                        // update the local balance
                        localBalance++;
                    }
```

```
                    // check to see if the shared data has changed since we started
                    // and if not, then update with our local value
                    int sharedData = Interlocked.CompareExchange(
                        ref account.Balance, localBalance, startBalance);

                    if (sharedData == startBalance) {
                        Console.WriteLine("Shared data updated OK");
                    } else {
                        Console.WriteLine("Shared data changed");
                    }
                });
                // start the new task
                tasks[i].Start();
            }

            // wait for all of the tasks to complete
            Task.WaitAll(tasks);

            // write out the counter value
            Console.WriteLine("Expected value {0}, Balance: {1}",
                10000, account.Balance);

            // wait for input before exiting
            Console.WriteLine("Press enter to finish");
            Console.ReadLine();
        }
    }
}
```

Using Spin Locking

We encountered spinning in the last chapter. Typically, when waiting to acquire a regular synchronization primitive, your Task is taken out of the schedule waits until it has acquired the primitive and can run again. Spinning takes a different approach; the Task enters a tight execution loop, periodically trying to acquire the primitive.

Spinning avoids the overhead of rescheduling the Task because it never stops running, but it doesn't allow another Task to take its place. Spinning is useful if you expect the wait to acquire the primitive to be very short.

The System.Threading.Spinlock class is a lightweight, spin-based synchronization primitive. It has a similar structure to other primitives in that it relies on Enter(), TryEnter(), and Exit() methods to acquire and release the lock. Listing 3-10 shows the bank account example implemented using SpinLock.

Listing 3-10. *Using the SpinLock Primitive*

```
using System;
using System.Threading;
using System.Threading.Tasks;
```

```
namespace Listing_10 {

    class BankAccount {
        public int Balance {
            get;
            set;
        }
    }

    class Listing_10 {

        static void Main(string[] args) {

            // create the bank account instance
            BankAccount account = new BankAccount();

            // create the spinlock
            SpinLock spinlock = new SpinLock();

            // create an array of tasks
            Task[] tasks = new Task[10];

            for (int i = 0; i < 10; i++) {
                // create a new task
                tasks[i] = new Task(() => {
                    // enter a loop for 1000 balance updates
                    for (int j = 0; j < 1000; j++) {
                        bool lockAcquired = false;
                        try {
                            spinlock.Enter(ref lockAcquired);
                            // update the balance
                            account.Balance = account.Balance + 1;
                        } finally {
                            if (lockAcquired) spinlock.Exit();
                        }
                    }
                });
                // start the new task
                tasks[i].Start();
            }

            // wait for all of the tasks to complete
            Task.WaitAll(tasks);

            // write out the counter value
            Console.WriteLine("Expected value {0}, Balance: {1}",
                10000, account.Balance);
```

```
            // wait for input before exiting
            Console.WriteLine("Press enter to finish");
            Console.ReadLine();
        }
    }
}
```

The constructor for SpinLock has an overload that enables or disables owner tracking, which simply means that the primitive keeps a record of which Task has acquired the lock. SpinLock doesn't support recursive locking, so if you have already acquired the lock, you must not try to acquire it again. If you have enabled owner tracking, attempting recursive locking will cause a System.Threading.LockRecursionException to be thrown. If you have disabled owner tracking and try to lock recursively, a deadlock will occur. SpinLock has three properties that can help you avoid inadvertent recursive lock attempts, described in Table 3-4.

Table 3-4. System.Threading.SpinLock Properties

Property	Description
IsHeld	Return true if the lock is held by any thread.
IsHeldByCurrentThread	Return true if the lock is held by the thread executing the current Task.
IsThreadOwnerTrackingEnabled	Return true if owner tracking was enabled when the primitive instance was created.

Using Wait Handles and the Mutex Class

Wait handles are wrappers around a Windows feature called *synchronization handles*. Several .NET synchronization primitives that are based on wait handles, and they all derive from the System.Threading.WaitHandle class. Each class has slightly different characteristics, and we'll walk through each of them in the next chapter when we explore coordinating Tasks.

The wait handle class that has most relevance to avoiding data races and is System.Threading.Mutex. Listing 3-11 shows the basic use of the Mutex class to solve the bank account data race problem. You acquire the lock on Mutex by calling the WaitOne() method and release the lock by calling ReleaseMutex().

Listing 3-11. Basic Use of the Mutex Class

```
using System;
using System.Threading;
using System.Threading.Tasks;

namespace Listing_11 {
```

```csharp
class BankAccount {
    public int Balance {
        get;
        set;
    }
}

class Listing_11 {

    static void Main(string[] args) {

        // create the bank account instance
        BankAccount account = new BankAccount();

        // create the mutex
        Mutex mutex = new Mutex();

        // create an array of tasks
        Task[] tasks = new Task[10];

        for (int i = 0; i < 10; i++) {
            // create a new task
            tasks[i] = new Task(() => {
                // enter a loop for 1000 balance updates
                for (int j = 0; j < 1000; j++) {
                    // acquire the mutex
                    bool lockAcquired = mutex.WaitOne();
                    try {
                        // update the balance
                        account.Balance = account.Balance + 1;
                    } finally {
                        // release the mutext
                        if (lockAcquired) mutex.ReleaseMutex();
                    }
                }
            });
            // start the new task
            tasks[i].Start();
        }

        // wait for all of the tasks to complete
        Task.WaitAll(tasks);

        // write out the counter value
        Console.WriteLine("Expected value {0}, Balance: {1}",
            10000, account.Balance);
```

```
                    // wait for input before exiting
                    Console.WriteLine("Press enter to finish");
                    Console.ReadLine();
                }
            }
        }
```

Acquiring Multiple Locks

All classes that extend from WaitHandle inherit three methods that can be used to acquire the lock. You have seen the WaitOne() instance method in Listing 3-11. In addition, the static WaitAll() and WaitAny() methods allow you to acquire multiple locks with one call. Listing 3-12 demonstrates the WaitAll() method, which causes the Task to block until all of the locks can be acquired.

The listing creates two BankAccounts and two Mutexes. Two Tasks are created that modify the balance of one of the two accounts, and each acquires the lock from the Mutex for the account it is working with. The third Task changes the balance of both accounts and, therefore, needs to acquire the lock from both Mutexes to avoid starting a data race with one of the other Tasks.

Listing 3-12. Acquiring Multiple Locks with Mutex.WaitAll()

```
using System;
using System.Threading;
using System.Threading.Tasks;

namespace Listing_12 {

    class BankAccount {
        public int Balance {
            get;
            set;
        }
    }

    class Listing_12 {

        static void Main(string[] args) {

            // create the bank account instances
            BankAccount account1 = new BankAccount();
            BankAccount account2 = new BankAccount();

            // create the mutexes
            Mutex mutex1 = new Mutex();
            Mutex mutex2 = new Mutex();

            // create a new task to update the first account
            Task task1 = new Task(() => {
                // enter a loop for 1000 balance updates
                for (int j = 0; j < 1000; j++) {
```

```
            // acquire the lock for the account
            bool lockAcquired = mutex1.WaitOne();;
            try {
                // update the balance
                account1.Balance++;
            } finally {
                if (lockAcquired) mutex1.ReleaseMutex();
            }
        }
    });

    // create a new task to update the first account
    Task task2 = new Task(() => {
        // enter a loop for 1000 balance updates
        for (int j = 0; j < 1000; j++) {
            // acquire the lock for the account
            bool lockAcquired = mutex2.WaitOne();
            try {
                // update the balance
                account2.Balance += 2;
            } finally {
                if (lockAcquired) mutex2.ReleaseMutex();
            }
        }
    });

    // create a new task to update the first account
    Task task3 = new Task(() => {
        // enter a loop for 1000 balance updates
        for (int j = 0; j < 1000; j++) {
            // acquire the locks for both accounts
            bool lockAcquired = Mutex.WaitAll(new WaitHandle[] { mutex1, mutex2});
            try {
                // simulate a transfer between accounts
                account1.Balance++;
                account2.Balance--;
            } finally {
                if (lockAcquired) {
                    mutex1.ReleaseMutex();
                    mutex2.ReleaseMutex();
                }
            }
        }
    });

    // start the tasks
    task1.Start();
    task2.Start();
    task3.Start();
```

```
            // wait for the tasks to complete
            Task.WaitAll(task1, task2, task3);

            // write out the counter value
            Console.WriteLine("Account1 balance {0}, Account2 balance: {1}",
                account1.Balance, account2.Balance);

            // wait for input before exiting
            Console.WriteLine("Press enter to finish");
            Console.ReadLine();
        }
    }
}
```

The `WaitAll()` method is inherited from the `WaitHandle` class and takes an array of `WaitHandle`s as the set of locks to acquire. Notice that although you can acquire multiple locks in a single step, you must release them individually using the `Mutex.ReleaseMutex()` method. The `WaitAny()` method returns when any of the locks have been acquired, and it returns an `int` that tells you the position of the acquired lock in the `WaitHandle` array passed in as a parameter.

The `WaitOne()`, `WaitAll()`, and `WaitAny()` methods are all overridden so that you can attempt to acquire a lock or set of locks for a given period of time; see the .NET Framework documentation for details.

Configuring Interprocess Synchronization

Wait handles can be shared between processes. The `Mutex`es in the previous two listings were *local*, meaning that they were only usable in one process; a local `Mutex` is created when you use the default constructor.

You can also create a *named system* `Mutex`, which is the kind that can be shared between processes. You do this by using the overloaded constructors that take a name argument. When using a named `Mutex`, it is important to see if the `Mutex` you are looking for has already been created, because it is possible to create several `Mutex`es with the same name that exist independently of one another.

You can test to see if a `Mutex` exists by using the static `Mutex.OpenExisting()` method, which takes a `string` argument as the name of the `Mutex` you wish to create. If a `Mutex` with the name you have provided exists, it is returned by the `OpenExisting()` method. A `System.Threading.WaitHandleCannotBeOpenedException` is thrown if a `Mutex` has not already been created with that name. Listing 3-13 shows how to use the `OpenExisting()` method and the overloaded constructor to test for, create, and use a shared `Mutex`. To test this listing, you must run two or more instances of the compiled program. Control of the `Mutex` will pass from process to process each time you press the `Enter` key. If you compile and run the code in this listing, the program will loop forever, so you can safely close the console window when you have had enough.

Listing 3-13. Interprocess Mutex Use

```csharp
using System;
using System.Threading;
using System.Threading.Tasks;

namespace Listing_13 {

    class Listing_13 {

        static void Main(string[] args) {

            // declare the name we will use for the mutex
            string mutexName = "myApressMutex";

            // declare the mutext
            Mutex namedMutext;

            try {
                // test to see if the named mutex already exists
                namedMutext = Mutex.OpenExisting(mutexName);
            } catch (WaitHandleCannotBeOpenedException) {
                // the mutext does not exist - we must create it
                namedMutext = new Mutex(false, mutexName);
            }

            // create the task
            Task task = new Task(() => {
                while (true) {
                    // acquire the mutex
                    Console.WriteLine("Waiting to acquire Mutex");
                    namedMutext.WaitOne();
                    Console.WriteLine("Acquired Mutex - press enter to release");
                    Console.ReadLine();
                    namedMutext.ReleaseMutex();
                    Console.WriteLine("Released Mutex");
                }
            });

            // start the task
            task.Start();

            // wait for the task to complete
            task.Wait();
        }
    }
}
```

■ **Tip** You must be careful to pick a distinctive name for your Mutex to avoid conflicting with other programs running on the same machine. You will get some very odd behavior if you share a Mutex with someone else's application.

Using Declarative Synchronization

So far, I have showed you how to *selectively* apply synchronization to critical regions. An alternative is to *declaratively* synchronize all of the fields and methods in a class by applying the Synchronization attribute. Your class must extend System.ContextBoundObject and import the System.Runtime.Remoting.Contexts namespace in order to be able to use the Synchronization attribute.

To demonstrate declarative synchronization with our bank account example, let's change the BankAccount class so that the balance can be read with the GetBalance() method and incremented with the IncrementBalance() method, as shown in Listing 3-14. Now, all of the code statements are contained in a single class and can be synchronized by applying the Synchronization attribute and having the BankAccount class extend ContextBoundObject.

Listing 3-14. Using Declarative Synchronization

```
using System;
using System.Runtime.Remoting.Contexts;
using System.Threading.Tasks;

namespace Listing_14 {

    [Synchronization]
    class BankAccount : ContextBoundObject {
        private int balance = 0;

        public void IncrementBalance() {
            balance++;
        }

        public int GetBalance() {
            return balance;
        }
    }

    class Listing_14 {

        static void Main(string[] args) {

            // create the bank account instance
            BankAccount account = new BankAccount();

            // create an array of tasks
            Task[] tasks = new Task[10];
```

```
for (int i = 0; i < 10; i++) {
    // create a new task
    tasks[i] = new Task(() => {
        // enter a loop for 1000 balance updates
        for (int j = 0; j < 1000; j++) {
            // update the balance
            account.IncrementBalance();
        }
    });
    // start the new task
    tasks[i].Start();
}

// wait for all of the tasks to complete
Task.WaitAll(tasks);

// write out the counter value
Console.WriteLine("Expected value {0}, Balance: {1}",
    10000, account.GetBalance());

// wait for input before exiting
Console.WriteLine("Press enter to finish");
Console.ReadLine();
        }
    }
}
```

The problem with using the Synchronization attribute is that every field and method of your class, even if they don't modify shared data, becomes synchronized using a single lock, and this can cause a performance problem. Declarative synchronization is a heavy-handed approach to avoiding data races and should be used with caution.

Using Reader-Writer Locks

The synchronization primitives discussed so far consider all Tasks as equally likely to cause a data race. That idea is reasonable, but in many situations, it is not true. Often, there will be many Tasks that only need to read shared data and only a few that need to modify it. Lots of Tasks can read a data value concurrently without causing a data race—only changing data causes problems.

A reader-writer lock is a common performance optimization and contains two locks—one for reading data and one for writing data—and allows multiple reader Tasks to acquire the read lock simultaneously. When a writer comes along and requests the write lock, it is made to wait for any active readers to release the read lock before being allowed to proceed, at which point the reader acquires both the read and write locks and has exclusive access to the critical region. This means that any requests by readers or writers to acquire either lock are made to wait until the active writer has finished with the critical region and releases the locks.

Using the ReaderWriterLockSlim Class

The System.Threading.ReaderWriterLockSlim class provides a convenient implementation of reader-writer locking that takes care of managing the locks. This class is a lightweight alternative for the heavyweight `System.Threading.ReaderWriter`, which Microsoft no longer recommends using. The lightweight version is simpler to use, offers better performance, and avoids some potential deadlocks.

You acquire and release the `ReaderWriterLockSlim` read lock by calling the `EnterReadLock()` and `ExitReadLock()` methods. Similarly, you acquire and release the write lock by calling `EnterWriteLock` and `ExitWriteLock()`. The `ReaderWriterLockSlim` class only provides the synchronization primitives; it does not enforce the separation between read and write operations in your code. You must be careful to avoid modifying shared data in a `Task` that has only acquired the read lock. Listing 3-15 demonstrates the use of the `ReaderWriterLockSlim` class.

Listing 3-15. *Using the ReaderWriterLockSlim Class*

```
using System;
using System.Threading;
using System.Threading.Tasks;

namespace Listing_15 {

    class Listing_15 {

        static void Main(string[] args) {

            // create the reader-writer lock
            ReaderWriterLockSlim rwlock = new ReaderWriterLockSlim();

            // create a cancellation token source
            CancellationTokenSource tokenSource = new CancellationTokenSource();

            // create an array of tasks
            Task[] tasks = new Task[5];

            for (int i = 0; i < 5; i++) {
                // create a new task
                tasks[i] = new Task(() => {
                    while (true) {
                        // acqure the read lock
                        rwlock.EnterReadLock();
                        // we now have the lock
                        Console.WriteLine("Read lock acquired - count: {0}",
                            rwlock.CurrentReadCount);
                        // wait - this simulates a read operation
                        tokenSource.Token.WaitHandle.WaitOne(1000);
                        // release the read lock
                        rwlock.ExitReadLock();
                        Console.WriteLine("Read lock released - count {0}",
                            rwlock.CurrentReadCount);
                        // check for cancellation
                        tokenSource.Token.ThrowIfCancellationRequested();
                    }
                }, tokenSource.Token);
```

```
            // start the new task
            tasks[i].Start();
        }

        // prompt the user
        Console.WriteLine("Press enter to acquire write lock");
        // wait for the user to press enter
        Console.ReadLine();

        // acquire the write lock
        Console.WriteLine("Requesting write lock");
        rwlock.EnterWriteLock();

        Console.WriteLine("Write lock acquired");
        Console.WriteLine("Press enter to release write lock");
        // wait for the user to press enter
        Console.ReadLine();
        // release the write lock
        rwlock.ExitWriteLock();

        // wait for 2 seconds and then cancel the tasks
        tokenSource.Token.WaitHandle.WaitOne(2000);
        tokenSource.Cancel();

        try {
            // wait for the tasks to complete
            Task.WaitAll(tasks);
        } catch (AggregateException) {
            // do nothing
        }

        // wait for input before exiting
        Console.WriteLine("Press enter to finish");
        Console.ReadLine();
    }
  }
}
```

The example creates five Tasks that acquire the read lock, wait for one second, and then release the read lock, repeating this sequence until they are cancelled. As the read lock is acquired and released, a message is printed to the console, and this message shows the number of holders of the read lock, which is available by reading the CurrentReadCount property.

When you press the Enter key, the main application thread acquires the write lock, which is held for two seconds and then released. You can see from the following results that once the write lock has been requested, the number of Tasks holding the read lock starts to drop. This is because calls to EnterReadLock() will now wait until the writer lock has been released to ensure writer exclusivity.

```
...

Read lock released - count 4

Read lock acquired - count: 5


Requesting write lock

Read lock released - count 4

Read lock released - count 3

Read lock released - count 2

Read lock released - count 1

Read lock released - count 0

Write lock acquired

Press enter to release write lock


Read lock acquired - count: 1

Read lock acquired - count: 3

Read lock acquired - count: 2

Read lock acquired - count: 4

Read lock acquired - count: 5

Read lock released - count 4

...
```

If you press Enter again, the main application thread releases the write lock, which allows the Tasks to continue their acquire/release sequence once more.

Using Recursion and Upgradable Read Locks

Listing 3-15 separates the code that reads the shared data from the code that modifies it. Often, you will want to read data and make a change only if some condition is met. You could acquire the write lock to do this, but that requires exclusive access. Because you don't know in advance if you actually need to make changes, that would be a potential performance problem.

But you are thinking, "Aha! I can acquire the (nonexclusive) read lock, perform the test, and then acquire the (exclusive) write lock if I need to make modifications." In that case, you would produce some code similar to the following fragment:

```
ReaderWriterLockSlim rwlock = new ReaderWriterLockSlim();

rwlock.EnterReadLock();
if (needToWrite) {
    // acquire write lock
    rwlock.EnterWriteLock();
    // ...perform write operations ...
    // release the write lock
    rwlock.ExitWriteLock();
}
// release the read lock
rwlock.ExitReadLock();
```

Unfortunately, when you came to run this code, you would get the following exception:

```
Unhandled Exception: System.Threading.LockRecursionException: Write lock

  may not be acquired with read lock held. This pattern is prone to deadlocks.

Please ensure that read locks are released before taking a write lock.

If an upgrade is necessary, use an upgrade lock in place of the read lock.

  at System.Threading.ReaderWriterLockSlim.TryEnterWriteLockCore(Int32

 millisecondsTimeout)

...
```

Acquiring the lock on a primitive when you already have a lock is called *lock recursion*. The ReaderWriterLockSlim class doesn't support lock recursion by default, because lock recursion has the potential to create deadlocks. Instead, you should use an *upgradable read lock*, which allows you to read the shared data, perform your test, and safely acquire exclusive write access if you need it. You acquire and release an upgradable read lock by calling the EnterUpgradeableReadLock() and ExitUpgradeableReadLock() methods and then acquire and release the write lock (if needed) by calling the EnterWriteLock() and ExitWriteLock() as before.

■ **Note** Although it is not recommended, you can enable lock recursion in `ReaderWriterLockSlim` by using an overloaded constructor. See the .NET Framework documentation for details, but don't be surprised when your application deadlocks.

Once the upgradable lock is acquired, requests for the write lock and further requests for the upgradable read lock will block until `ExitUpgradeableReadLock()` is called, but multiple holders of the read lock are allowed. Upgrading the lock by calling `EnterWriteLock()` waits for all of the current holders of the read lock to call `ExitReadLock()` before the write lock is granted. Listing 3-16 demonstrates the use of the upgradable read lock by having five `Task`s that read shared data and two that use the upgradable read lock to make changes.

Listing 3-16. Avoiding Lock Recursion by Using an Upgradable Read Lock

```
using System;
using System.Threading;
using System.Threading.Tasks;

namespace Listing_16 {

    class Listing_16 {

        static void Main(string[] args) {

            // create the reader-writer lock
            ReaderWriterLockSlim rwlock = new ReaderWriterLockSlim();

            // create a cancellation token source
            CancellationTokenSource tokenSource = new CancellationTokenSource();

            // create some shared data
            int sharedData = 0;

            // create an array of tasks
            Task[] readerTasks = new Task[5];

            for (int i = 0; i < readerTasks.Length; i++) {
                // create a new task
                readerTasks[i] = new Task(() => {
                    while (true) {
                        // acqure the read lock
                        rwlock.EnterReadLock();
                        // we now have the lock
                        Console.WriteLine("Read lock acquired - count: {0}",
                            rwlock.CurrentReadCount);

                        // read the shared data
                        Console.WriteLine("Shared data value {0}", sharedData);
```

```
            // wait - slow things down to make the example clear
            tokenSource.Token.WaitHandle.WaitOne(1000);

            // release the read lock
            rwlock.ExitReadLock();
            Console.WriteLine("Read lock released - count {0}",
                rwlock.CurrentReadCount);

            // check for cancellation
            tokenSource.Token.ThrowIfCancellationRequested();
        }
    }, tokenSource.Token);
    // start the new task
    readerTasks[i].Start();
}

Task[] writerTasks = new Task[2];
for (int i = 0; i < writerTasks.Length; i++) {
    writerTasks[i] = new Task(() => {
        while (true) {
            // acquire the upgradeable lock
            rwlock.EnterUpgradeableReadLock();

            // simulate a branch that will require a write
            if (true) {
                // acquire the write lock
                rwlock.EnterWriteLock();
                // print out a message with the details of the lock
                Console.WriteLine("Write Lock acquired - waiting readers {0},
                    writers {1}, upgraders {2}",
                    rwlock.WaitingReadCount, rwlock.WaitingWriteCount,
                    rwlock.WaitingUpgradeCount);

                // modify the shared data
                sharedData++;

                // wait - slow down the example to make things clear
                tokenSource.Token.WaitHandle.WaitOne(1000);
                // release the write lock
                rwlock.ExitWriteLock();
            }

            // release the upgradable lock
            rwlock.ExitUpgradeableReadLock();

            // check for cancellation
            tokenSource.Token.ThrowIfCancellationRequested();
        }
```

```
            }, tokenSource.Token);
            // start the new task
            writerTasks[i].Start();
        }

        // prompt the user
        Console.WriteLine("Press enter to cancel tasks");
        // wait for the user to press enter
        Console.ReadLine();

        // cancel the tasks
        tokenSource.Cancel();

        try {
            // wait for the tasks to complete
            Task.WaitAll(readerTasks);
        } catch (AggregateException agex) {
            agex.Handle(ex => true);
        }

        // wait for input before exiting
        Console.WriteLine("Press enter to finish");
        Console.ReadLine();
    }
}
}
```

Only one holder of the upgradable lock is allowed at a time, which means you should partition your requests for locks carefully to have as few requests as possible for upgradable and write locks. You may be tempted to separate your read and write requests so that you release the read lock and then try to acquire the write lock only if you need to make a change, as shown in the following fragment:

```
ReaderWriterLockSlim rwlock = new ReaderWriterLockSlim();

bool writeFlag = false;

rwlock.EnterReadLock();
if (needToWrite) {
    writeFlag = true;
}

// release the read lock
rwlock.ExitReadLock();

if (writeFlag) {

    // acquire write lock
    rwlock.EnterWriteLock();
```

```
    // ...perform write operations ...

    // release the write lock
    rwlock.ExitWriteLock();
}
```

This creates a data race, because between the point at which you release the read lock and acquire the write lock, another Task could have modified the shared data and changed the condition that you were looking for. The only way this approach works is if there is only one Task that can change the shared data. If that is the case, there is no performance impact in using an upgradable lock, because there will be no other upgrade requests to contend with.

Working with Concurrent Collections

One of the most common ways of sharing data is through collection classes. Often, you will want to use Tasks to parallel process the contents of a collection or use a collection to gather the results produced by Tasks. Sharing a collection between Tasks creates the same kinds of data races as sharing other types.

Listing 3-17 demonstrates a collection data race. A System.Collections.Generic.Queue<int> with 1,000 items is processed by ten Tasks. While there are still items in the collection, the Tasks remove the first item and increment a counter, and the counter is synchronized using interlocked operations.

Listing 3-17. A data Race Sharing a Collection

```
using System;
using System.Collections.Generic;
using System.Threading;
using System.Threading.Tasks;

namespace Listing_17 {

    class Listing_17 {

        static void Main(string[] args) {

            // create a shared collection
            Queue<int> sharedQueue = new Queue<int>();
            // populate the collection with items to process
            for (int i = 0; i < 1000; i++) {
                sharedQueue.Enqueue(i);
            }

            // define a counter for the number of processed items
            int itemCount = 0;

            // create tasks to process the list
            Task[] tasks = new Task[10];
            for (int i = 0; i < tasks.Length; i++) {
                // create the new task
                tasks[i] = new Task(() => {
```

```
                    while (sharedQueue.Count > 0) {
                        // take an item from the queue
                        int item = sharedQueue.Dequeue();
                        // increment the count of items processed
                        Interlocked.Increment(ref itemCount);
                    }

                });
                // start the new task
                tasks[i].Start();
            }

            // wait for the tasks to complete
            Task.WaitAll(tasks);

            // report on the number of items processed
            Console.WriteLine("Items processed: {0}", itemCount);

            // wait for input before exiting
            Console.WriteLine("Press enter to finish");
            Console.ReadLine();
        }
    }
}
```

The example gives rise to two kinds of data race. The first is where the counter value exceeds 1,000, which happens because the steps in the `Queue.Dequeue()` method are not synchronized so `Tasks` are reading the same value several times from the head of the queue. The second is a `System.InvalidOperationException`, thrown when calls to `Queue.Dequeue()` are made when the queue is empty; this happens because the check to see if there are items left in the queue (`sharedQueue.Count > 0`) and the request to take an item from the queue (`sharedQueue.Dequeue()`) are not protected in a critical region.

There are three kinds of collection in the .NET Framework, and each requires a different approach to sharing them safely.

Using .NET 4 Concurrent Collection Classes

.NET 4 includes a set of collection classes in the `System.Collections.Concurrent` namespace. These classes are type safe and synchronized using the lightweight synchronization primitives described earlier in the chapter. You should use the new concurrent collection classes whenever you need to share a collection during parallel programming, because the combination of type safety and lightweight synchronization makes them safe to share and fast to use. Table 3-5 summarizes the four concurrent collection classes, each of which is detailed in the following sections.

■ **Note** There is a fifth concurrent collection class, `BlockingCollection`. We will discuss this class in the next chapter.

Table 3-5. Concurrent Collection Classes

Problem	Solution	Listing
Safely collect data on a first-in, first-out basis.	Use the `System.Threading.Tasks.ConcurrentQueue` class.	3-18
Safely collect data on a first-in, last-out basis.	Use the `System.Threading.Tasks.ConcurrentStack` class.	3-19
Safely collect data without a specific ordering.	Use the `System.Threading.Tasks.ConcurrentBag` class.	3-20
Safely collect key-value pairs.	Use the `System.Threading.Tasks.ConcurrentDictionary` class.	3-21

■ **Tip** Each of the concurrent collection classes implement a set of useful extension methods that range from `Count()`, to return the number of items in the collection, through to methods to calculate averages or search for items. See the .NET Framework documentation for details.

ConcurrentQueue

The `ConcurrentQueue` class implements a first in, first out (FIFO) queue, which means that when you take items from the queue, you get them in the same order in which they were added. To place an item into a `ConcurrentQueue`, you call the `Enqueue()` method. To take the first item in the queue, you call `TryDequeue()` and to get the first item in the queue without taking it, you call `TryPeek()`.

`TryDequeue()` and `TryPeek()` take a parameter of the collection type, modified by the `out` keyword and return a `bool` result. If the result is `true`, the parameter will contain the data item. If it is `false`, no data item could be obtained. Listing 3-18 shows how to use the `ConcurrentQueue` class to resolve the data race demonstrated in Listing 3-17.

Listing 3-18. Using the ConcurrentQueue Class

```
using System;
using System.Collections.Concurrent;
using System.Threading;
using System.Threading.Tasks;

namespace Listing_18 {

    class Listing_18 {

        static void Main(string[] args) {
```

```
        // create a shared collection
        ConcurrentQueue<int> sharedQueue = new ConcurrentQueue<int>();

        // populate the collection with items to process
        for (int i = 0; i < 1000; i++) {
            sharedQueue.Enqueue(i);
        }

        // define a counter for the number of processed items
        int itemCount = 0;

        // create tasks to process the list
        Task[] tasks = new Task[10];
        for (int i = 0; i < tasks.Length; i++) {
            // create the new task
            tasks[i] = new Task(() => {

                while (sharedQueue.Count > 0) {
                    // define a variable for the dequeue requests
                    int queueElement;
                    // take an item from the queue
                    bool gotElement = sharedQueue.TryDequeue(out queueElement);
                    // increment the count of items processed
                    if (gotElement) {
                        Interlocked.Increment(ref itemCount);
                    }
                }

            });
            // start the new task
            tasks[i].Start();
        }

        // wait for the tasks to complete
        Task.WaitAll(tasks);

        // report on the number of items processed
        Console.WriteLine("Items processed: {0}", itemCount);

        // wait for input before exiting
        Console.WriteLine("Press enter to finish");
        Console.ReadLine();
    }
  }
}
```

The TryDequeue() and TryPeek() methods force you to code for possible failure, that is, for the eventuality that no data item is available. Listing 3-18 checks to see if there are items in the queue by reading the Count property. However, we can't assume that there will still be items by the time our call to TryDequeue() is executed, so we have to check the bool result from TryDequeue() to see if we received data to process. Table 3-6 describes the key members of the ConcurrentQueue class.

Table 3-6. Key Members of System.Collections.Concurrent.ConcurrentQueue

Member	Description
Enqueue(T)	Add an item of type T to the queue.
TryPeek(out T)	Try to return an element from the head of the queue without removing it. Return **true** if a data item was returned. The element is set to the **out** parameter.
TryDequeue(out T)	Try to remove and return an element from the head of the queue. Return **true** if a data item was returned. The element is set to the **out** parameter.

ConcurrentStack

The `System.Collections.Concurrent.ConcurrentStack` class implements a last in, first out (LIFO) queue—taking an item from the queue returns the most recently added item. Items are added to the stack using the `Push()` and `PushRange()` methods and inspected and retrieved using the `TryPeek()`, `TryPop()`, and `TryPopRange()` methods. Listing 3-19 demonstrates the use of the `ConcurrentStack` collection.

Listing 3-19. Using the ConcurrentStack Class

```
using System;
using System.Collections.Concurrent;
using System.Threading;
using System.Threading.Tasks;

namespace Listing_19 {

    class Listing_19 {

        static void Main(string[] args) {

            // create a shared collection
            ConcurrentStack<int> sharedStack = new ConcurrentStack<int>();

            // populate the collection with items to process
            for (int i = 0; i < 1000; i++) {
                sharedStack.Push(i);
            }

            // define a counter for the number of processed items
            int itemCount = 0;

            // create tasks to process the list
            Task[] tasks = new Task[10];
            for (int i = 0; i < tasks.Length; i++) {
                // create the new task
                tasks[i] = new Task(() => {
```

91

```
                    while (sharedStack.Count > 0) {
                        // define a variable for the dequeue requests
                        int queueElement;
                        // take an item from the queue
                        bool gotElement = sharedStack.TryPop(out queueElement);
                        // increment the count of items processed
                        if (gotElement) {
                            Interlocked.Increment(ref itemCount);
                        }
                    }

                });
                // start the new task
                tasks[i].Start();
            }

            // wait for the tasks to complete
            Task.WaitAll(tasks);

            // report on the number of items processed
            Console.WriteLine("Items processed: {0}", itemCount);

            // wait for input before exiting
            Console.WriteLine("Press enter to finish");
            Console.ReadLine();
        }
    }
}
```

Table 3-7 describes the key members of the ConcurrentStack class.

Table 3-7. Key members of System.Collections.Concurrent.ConcurrentStack

Member	Description
Push(T)	Insert an element at the head of the stack.
PushRange(T[]) PushRange(T[], int, int)	Insert multiple elements at the head of the stack.
TryPeek(out T)	Try to return an element from the head of the stack without removing it. Return **true** if a data item was returned.
TryPop(out T)	Try to remove and return an element from the head of the stack. Return **true** if a data item was returned.
TryPopRange(out T[]) TryPopRange(out T[], int, int)	Try to remove and return multiple elements from the head of the stack. Return the number of data items returned.

ConcurrentBag

The ConcurrentBag class implements an unordered collection, such that the order in which items are added does not guarantee the order in which they will be returned. Items are added with the Add() method, returned and removed from the collection with the TryTake() method, and returned without being removed with the TryPeek() method. Listing 3-20 demonstrates use of the ConcurrentBag collection.

Listing 3-20. Using the ConcurrentBag Class

```csharp
using System;
using System.Collections.Concurrent;
using System.Threading;
using System.Threading.Tasks;

namespace Listing_20 {

    class Listing_20 {

        static void Main(string[] args) {

            // create a shared collection
            ConcurrentBag<int> sharedBag = new ConcurrentBag<int>();

            // populate the collection with items to process
            for (int i = 0; i < 1000; i++) {
                sharedBag.Add(i);
            }

            // define a counter for the number of processed items
            int itemCount = 0;

            // create tasks to process the list
            Task[] tasks = new Task[10];
            for (int i = 0; i < tasks.Length; i++) {
                // create the new task
                tasks[i] = new Task(() => {

                    while (sharedBag.Count > 0) {
                        // define a variable for the dequeue requests
                        int queueElement;
                        // take an item from the queue
                        bool gotElement = sharedBag.TryTake(out queueElement);
                        // increment the count of items processed
                        if (gotElement) {
                            Interlocked.Increment(ref itemCount);
                        }
                    }
                }
```

```
            });
            // start the new task
            tasks[i].Start();
        }

        // wait for the tasks to complete
        Task.WaitAll(tasks);

        // report on the number of items processed
        Console.WriteLine("Items processed: {0}", itemCount);

        // wait for input before exiting
        Console.WriteLine("Press enter to finish");
        Console.ReadLine();
    }
  }
}
```

Table 3-8 describes the key members of the ConcurrentBag class.

Table 3-8. Key members of System.Collections.Concurrent.ConcurrentBag

Member	Description
Add(T)	Add an element to the collection.
TryPeek(out T)	Try to return an element from the collection without removing it. Return **true** if a data item was returned.
TryTake(out T)	Try to remove and return an element from the collection. Return **true** if a data item was returned.

ConcurrentDictionary

The ConcurrentDictionary class implements a collection of key-value pairs. Like the other collection classes in the System.Collections.Concurrent namespace, ConcurrentDictionary provides methods whose names are prefixed with **Try** and returns **bool** results if they operate successfully. Table 3-9 describes the key members of the ConcurrentDictionary class.

Table3-9. Key members of System.Collections.Concurrent.ConcurrentDictionary

Member	Description
TryAdd(TKey, TVal)	Try to add a new key-value pair to the collection. Return **true** if the pair was added successfully.
TryGetValue(TKey, out TVal)	Try to get the value associated with the specified key. Return **true** if the value was obtained and placed in the **out** parameter.
TryRemove(TKey, out TVal)	Try to remove a key-value pair from the collection. The value will be placed in the **out** parameter. Return **true** if the key-value pair was removed successfully.
TryUpdate(TKey, TVal, TVal)	Try to update the value associated with a key. The first value parameter will be used to update the key-value pair if the current value in the collection is equal to the second value parameter. Return **true** if the value was updated.
ContainsKey(TKey)	Return **true** if the collection contains a key-value pair with the specified key.

Bear in mind that the state of the collection may change between calls to individual methods. For example, if you call the ContainsKey() method and then call TryGetValue() using the key you have checked for, there is no guarantee that it will still be present, so your method calls may be interleaved with those from another parallel Task.

Listing 3-21 shows the ConcurrentDictionary class being used to implement a variant of the data isolation pattern to allow multiple Tasks to keep track of their own account balances.

Listing 3-21. Using the ConcurrentDictionary Class

```
using System;
using System.Collections.Concurrent;
using System.Threading.Tasks;

namespace Listing_21 {

    class BankAccount {
        public int Balance {
            get;
            set;
        }
    }

    class Listing_21 {

        static void Main(string[] args) {
```

```
// create the bank account instance
BankAccount account = new BankAccount();

// create a shared dictionary
ConcurrentDictionary<object, int> sharedDict
    = new ConcurrentDictionary<object, int>();

// create tasks to process the list
Task<int>[] tasks = new Task<int>[10];
for (int i = 0; i < tasks.Length; i++) {

    // put the initial value into the dictionary
    sharedDict.TryAdd(i, account.Balance);

    // create the new task
    tasks[i] = new Task<int>((keyObj) => {

        // define variables for use in the loop
        int currentValue;
        bool gotValue;

        // enter a loop for 1000 balance updates
        for (int j = 0; j < 1000; j++) {
            // get the current value from the dictionary
            gotValue = sharedDict.TryGetValue(keyObj, out currentValue);
            // increment the value and update the dictionary entry
            sharedDict.TryUpdate(keyObj, currentValue + 1, currentValue);
        }

        // define the final result
        int result;
        // get our result from the dictionary
        gotValue = sharedDict.TryGetValue(keyObj, out result);
        // return the result value if we got one
        if (gotValue) {
            return result;
        } else {
            // there was no result available - we have encountered a problem
            throw new Exception(
                String.Format("No data item available for key {0}", keyObj));
        }
    }, i);

    // start the new task
    tasks[i].Start();
}

// update the balance of the account using the task results
for (int i = 0; i < tasks.Length; i++) {
    account.Balance += tasks[i].Result;
}
```

```
        // write out the counter value
        Console.WriteLine("Expected value {0}, Balance: {1}",
            10000, account.Balance);

        // wait for input before exiting
        Console.WriteLine("Press enter to finish");
        Console.ReadLine();

        }
    }
}
```

Using First-Generation Collections

The first-generation collection classes are those that were included in .NET since version 1.0. These classes include two features to help with synchronization, but neither is ideal, and you should use the new concurrent collections wherever possible.

The first synchronization helper is the static `Synchronized` method, which creates a wrapper around your collection instance. The wrapper synchronizes all of the methods of the collection, rather like the declarative synchronization demonstrated earlier in the chapter. Listing 3-22 shows the use of the `Synchronized` method for a `System.Collections.Queue`.

Listing 3-22. Synchronizing a First-Generation Collection Class

```
using System;
using System.Collections;
using System.Threading.Tasks;

namespace Listing_22 {

    class Listing_22 {

        static void Main(string[] args) {

            // create a collection
            Queue sharedQueue = Queue.Synchronized(new Queue());

            // create tasks to process the list
            Task[] tasks = new Task[10];
            for (int i = 0; i < tasks.Length; i++) {
                // create the new task
                tasks[i] = new Task(() => {

                    for (int j = 0; j < 100; j++) {
                        sharedQueue.Enqueue(j);
                    }
```

```
            });
            // start the new task
            tasks[i].Start();
        }

        // wait for the tasks to complete
        Task.WaitAll(tasks);

        // report on the number of items enqueued
        Console.WriteLine("Items enqueued: {0}", sharedQueue.Count);

        // wait for input before exiting
        Console.WriteLine("Press enter to finish");
        Console.ReadLine();
    }
  }
}
```

The **Synchronized** method works in Listing 3-22 because we are using it to stop multiple enqueue operations colliding. But while each method is synchronized, there is no support for maintaining consistency *across* method calls. If you need to perform multiple operations on the collection, such as checking that there are items in the queue and then removing one of them, the **Synchronized** method won't help.

The second synchronization helper is the **SyncRoot** instance member, which returns an object that you can use to perform locking with the **lock** keyword. Listing 3-23 demonstrates the use of **SyncRoot**.

Listing 3-23. Manually Synchronizing a First-Generation Collection Class

```
using System;
using System.Collections;
using System.Threading;
using System.Threading.Tasks;

namespace Listing_23 {

    class Listing_23 {

        static void Main(string[] args) {

            // create a collection
            Queue sharedQueue = new Queue();

            // populate the collection with items to process
            for (int i = 0; i < 1000; i++) {
                sharedQueue.Enqueue(i);
            }

            // define a counter for the number of processed items
            int itemCount = 0;
```

```
        // create tasks to process the list
        Task[] tasks = new Task[10];
        for (int i = 0; i < tasks.Length; i++) {
            // create the new task
            tasks[i] = new Task(() => {

                while (sharedQueue.Count > 0) {
                    // get the lock using the collections sync root
                    lock (sharedQueue.SyncRoot) {
                        // check that there are still items
                        if (sharedQueue.Count > 0) {
                            // take an item from the queue
                            int queueElement = (int)sharedQueue.Dequeue();
                            // increment the count of items processed
                            Interlocked.Increment(ref itemCount);
                        }
                    }
                }

            });
            // start the new task
            tasks[i].Start();
        }

        // wait for the tasks to complete
        Task.WaitAll(tasks);

        // report on the number of items processed
        Console.WriteLine("Items processed: {0}", itemCount);

        // wait for input before exiting
        Console.WriteLine("Press enter to finish");
        Console.ReadLine();
    }
  }
}
```

In Listing 3-23, we make two calls to the Count property: one to keep the Task body running and one to check that there are still items in the queue once we have acquired sole access to the critical region. We need the second call because, unlike the concurrent classes, the first-generation collections are not designed to cope with interleaved parallel requests. When sharing first-generation collections between Tasks, you have to either write additional checks inside of the critical region or catch the exceptions that will be thrown when the state is out of kilter, for example, trying to dequeue from an empty queue.

The other issue with the first-generation collections is that they are not type safe. We have to cast the result from the Dequeue() method to an int and deal with the exceptions that arise if a type other than an int is added to the collection.

Using Generic Collections

Generic collections are those from the System.Collections.Generic namespace. These collections are type safe but provide no support for synchronization. You must use one of the synchronization primitives described earlier in this chapter when sharing these classes. Wherever possible, use the concurrent collections instead.

Common Problems and Their Causes

Sharing data safely between Tasks is one of the most error-prone aspects of parallel programming. You will almost certainly make mistakes as you come to terms with the nuances of parallel programming and strive to strike a balance between performance and safety. This section describes and demonstrates four of the most common problems in the hope that you will be able to more quickly determine the cause of a problem when it arises.

Unexpected Mutability

Types that are assumed to be immutable are built from mutable types whose states are changed by another Task. Unexpected and inconsistent program results from the point at which the state change occurs.

Solution

There is no programmatic solution to the Unexpected Mutability antipattern. The only way to avoid this problem is to check the field modifiers for all types that you are relying on as being immutable to make sure that they can't be changed.

Example

C# does not enforce immutability of complex types; it is possible to declare a field to be readonly and still modify the members of the type instance assigned to it. For example, the following listing shows the type MyImmutableType, which declares a readonly field of the type MyReferenceData. The PI field of MyReferenceData is not readonly and is changed by the main thread of the program, causing incorrect calculations.

```
using System;
using System.Threading;
using System.Threading.Tasks;

namespace Mistaken_Immutability {

    class MyReferenceData {
        public double PI = 3.14;
    }

    class MyImmutableType {
        public readonly MyReferenceData refData = new MyReferenceData();
        public readonly int circleSize = 1;
    }

    class MistakenImmutability {

        static void Main(string[] args) {
```

```
            // create a new instance of the immutable type
            MyImmutableType immutable = new MyImmutableType();

            // create a cancellation token source
            CancellationTokenSource tokenSource = new CancellationTokenSource();

            // create a task that will calculate the circumference
            // of a 1 unit circle and check the result
            Task task1 = new Task(() => {
                while (true) {
                    // perform the calculation
                    double circ = 2 * immutable.refData.PI * immutable.circleSize;
                    Console.WriteLine("Circumference: {0}", circ);
                    // check for the mutation
                    if (circ == 4) {
                        // the mutation has occurred - break
                        // out of the loop
                        Console.WriteLine("Mutation detected");
                        break;
                    }
                    // sleep for a moment
                    tokenSource.Token.WaitHandle.WaitOne(250);
                }
            }, tokenSource.Token);

            // start the task
            task1.Start();

            // wait to let the task start work
            Thread.Sleep(1000);

            // perform the mutation
            immutable.refData.PI = 2;

            // join the task
            task1.Wait();

            // wait for input before exiting
            Console.WriteLine("Press enter to finish");
            Console.ReadLine();
        }
    }
}
```

Multiple Locks

In a multiple lock scenario, multiple critical sections modify the same shared data, and each has its own lock or synchronization primitive. Access to each critical region is synchronized, but there is no overall coordination which means that a data race can still occur.

Solution

Ensure that every Task that enters the critical region uses the same reference to acquire the synchronization lock.

Example

The following example shows two locks being used to synchronize access to critical regions that access the same shared data, in this case, the balance of our bank account example. Ten Tasks are created in two groups of five: members of the first group uses one lock to synchronize their balance updates, and the second group uses the other lock.

```
using System;
using System.Threading.Tasks;

namespace Multiple_Locks {

    class BankAccount {
        public int Balance {
            get;
            set;
        }
    }

    class Multiple_Locks {

        static void Main(string[] args) {

            // create the bank account instance
            BankAccount account = new BankAccount();

            // create two lock objects
            object lock1 = new object();
            object lock2 = new object();

            // create an array of tasks
            Task[] tasks = new Task[10];

            // create five tasks that use the first lock object
            for (int i = 0; i < 5; i++) {
                // create a new task
                tasks[i] = new Task(() => {
                    // enter a loop for 1000 balance updates
                    for (int j = 0; j < 1000; j++) {
                        lock (lock1) {
                            // update the balance
                            account.Balance++;
                        }
                    }
                });
            }
```

```
            // create five tasks that use the second lock object
            for (int i = 5; i < 10; i++) {
                // create a new task
                tasks[i] = new Task(() => {
                    // enter a loop for 1000 balance updates
                    for (int j = 0; j < 1000; j++) {
                        lock (lock2) {
                            // update the balance
                            account.Balance++;
                        }
                    }
                });
            }

            // start the tasks
            foreach (Task task in tasks) {
                task.Start();
            }

            // wait for all of the tasks to complete
            Task.WaitAll(tasks);

            // write out the counter value
            Console.WriteLine("Expected value {0}, Balance: {1}",
                10000, account.Balance);

            // wait for input before exiting
            Console.WriteLine("Press enter to finish");
            Console.ReadLine();

        }
    }
}
```

Lock Acquisition Order

You may run into a lock acquisition order issue if you acquire multiple locks in a nested code block but do so in a different order in two or more critical regions. The following fragment demonstrates a nested block:

```
lock (lockObj1) {
    lock (lockObj2) {
        ...critical region...
    }
}
```

If you repeat this nested acquisition to protect another critical region but don't acquire the locks in the same order (i.e., acquire lockObj2 and then lockObj1), you create a potential deadlock where neither of the two Tasks (or any other Task that will wish to acquire either lock) can continue.

Solution

If you are using wait-handle–based primitives, the best solution is to use the `WaitAll()` method demonstrated in the "Acquiring Multiple Locks" section of this chapter. This method will acquire the lock on multiple wait handles in a single step, which avoids the deadlock.

If you are using another kind of primitive, the only solution is to ensure that you always acquire the locks in the same order. A simple trick is to name the primitive instances sequentially (`lock1`, `lock2`, etc.) and always acquire the lowest ordered name first. Ensuring that you don't duplicate primitive instance names in your code is a lot easier than debugging a deadlock.

Example

The following example creates two objects used with the lock keyword. Two `Task`s are created, and they acquire one of the locks, wait for 500 ms, and then acquire the second lock. The lock acquisition order is different for each `Task` and deadlock occurs.

```
using System;
using System.Threading;
using System.Threading.Tasks;

namespace Lock_Acquisition_Order {

    class Lock_Acquisition_Order {

        static void Main(string[] args) {

            // create two lock objects
            object lock1 = new object();
            object lock2 = new object();

            // create a task that acquires lock 1
            // and then lock 2
            Task task1 = new Task(() => {
                lock (lock1) {
                    Console.WriteLine("Task 1 acquired lock 1");
                    Thread.Sleep(500);
                    lock (lock2) {
                        Console.WriteLine("Task 1 acquired lock 2");
                    }
                }
            });

            // create a task that acquires lock 2
            // and then lock 1
            Task task2 = new Task(() => {
                lock (lock2) {
                    Console.WriteLine("Task 2 acquired lock 2");
                    Thread.Sleep(500);
```

```
                    lock (lock1) {
                        Console.WriteLine("Task 2 acquired lock 1");
                    }
                }
            });

            // start the tasks
            task1.Start();
            task2.Start();

            // wait for input before exiting
            Console.WriteLine("Press enter to finish");
            Console.ReadLine();
        }
    }
}
```

Orphaned Locks

The .NET synchronization primitives require you to explicitly acquire and release the lock. An orphaned lock is one that has been acquired but, because of an exception or poor programming, will never be released.

Because the lock is never released, any Tasks that try to acquire the lock will wait indefinitely.

Solution

Ensure that you do not return from a method before releasing a lock and handle exceptions by releasing your lock in the finally block of a try. . .catch. . .finally sequence. Alternatively, use the lock keyword (although this may offer poor performance compared with one of the lightweight synchronization primitives).

Example

The following example uses a Mutex to demonstrate an orphaned lock. The first Task created repeatedly acquires and releases the Mutex. The second Task acquires the Mutex and then throws an exception, so the Mutex is never released. The first Task deadlocks waiting to acquire the Mutex and cannot move forward. The Mutex remains orphaned even when the second Task has finished and its exception has been processed.

```
using System;
using System.Threading;
using System.Threading.Tasks;

namespace Orphaned_Locks {

    class Orphaned_Locks {

        static void Main(string[] args) {
```

```csharp
// create the sync primitive
Mutex mutex = new Mutex();

// create a cancellation token source
CancellationTokenSource tokenSource = new CancellationTokenSource();

// create a task that acquires and releases the mutex
Task task1 = new Task(() => {
    while (true) {
        mutex.WaitOne();
        Console.WriteLine("Task 1 acquired mutex");
        // wait for 500ms
        tokenSource.Token.WaitHandle.WaitOne(500);
        // exit the mutex
        mutex.ReleaseMutex();
        Console.WriteLine("Task 1 released mutex");
    }
}, tokenSource.Token);

// create a task that acquires and then abandons the mutex
Task task2 = new Task(() => {
    // wait for 2 seconds to let the other task run
    tokenSource.Token.WaitHandle.WaitOne(2000);
    // acquire the mutex
    mutex.WaitOne();
    Console.WriteLine("Task 2 acquired mutex");
    // abandon the mutex
    throw new Exception("Abandoning Mutex");
}, tokenSource.Token);

// start the tasks
task1.Start();
task2.Start();

// put the main thread to sleep
tokenSource.Token.WaitHandle.WaitOne(3000);

// wait for task 2
try {
    task2.Wait();
} catch (AggregateException ex) {
    ex.Handle((inner) => {
        Console.WriteLine(inner);
        return true;
    });
}
```

```
        // wait for input before exiting
        Console.WriteLine("Press enter to finish");
        Console.ReadLine();

    }
  }
}
```

Summary

In this chapter, we tackled the difficult topic of sharing data between tasks. Of the problems that you are likely to encounter as you write parallel programs, problems of this type are the most commonly occurring. Taking the time to make sure you understand how your data is shared between your tasks can save many hours of debugging. In the next chapter, we'll look at how you can coordinate several tasks to build more complex parallel programs.

CHAPTER 4

Coordinating Tasks

Listing 4-1. Task Continuation

```csharp
using System;
using System.Threading.Tasks;

namespace Listing_01 {

    class BankAccount {
        public int Balance {
            get;
            set;
        }
    }

    class Listing_01 {

        static void Main(string[] args) {

            Task<BankAccount> task = new Task<BankAccount>(() => {
                // create a new bank account
                BankAccount account = new BankAccount();
                // enter a loop
                for (int i = 0; i < 1000; i++) {
                    // increment the account total
                    account.Balance++;
                }
                // return the bank account
                return account;
            });

            task.ContinueWith((Task<BankAccount> antecedent) => {
                Console.WriteLine("Final Balance: {0}", antecedent.Result.Balance);
            });

            // start the task
            task.Start();
```

```
            // wait for input before exiting
            Console.WriteLine("Press enter to finish");
            Console.ReadLine();


        }
    }
}
```

Doing More with Tasks

One of the most useful features of the TPL is the flexible way you can coordinate what groups of Tasks do to build complex parallel programs. In this chapter, we'll look at the main approaches to coordination.

The first two are *task continuations* and *child tasks*. Continuations let you create chains of Tasks that are executed one after the other. Child tasks are run in the body of another Task and let you break down work into smaller pieces in order to increase concurrency. Listing 4-1 demonstrates a simple task continuation.

We'll also build on the previous chapter to apply what you learned about synchronization; there are some advanced synchronization primitives that can be used to manage how Tasks interact with one another. This chapter describes these primitives and shows you how to use them.

A core building block in many parallel programs is the Parallel Producer/Consumer pattern, which has one group of Tasks creating items which are then processed by a second group of Tasks. You'll use this pattern time and time again. The .NET Framework includes a class that makes implementing this pattern very simple, and this chapter shows you how to create and customize this important programming model—if you only read one part of this chapter closely, make it this one.

This chapter finishes up by showing you how to implement a custom task scheduler. The task scheduler is responsible for taking the Tasks that you create and having them executed by the classic threads that underpin the TPL. This is the only part of the book where you see the classic threads, and you'll need to have some knowledge of how they work to follow along. But this is very much an optional (and advanced) topic. You can use the default TPL task scheduler without having any needing any experience with threads and, in fact, that's exactly what I recommend you do.

Using Task Continuations

Task continuations allow you to chains of Tasks, which are performed in order, so when one Task in the chain finishes, the next one begins.

In a simple continuation, each Task in the chain is followed by one other Task, which can be useful but not deeply so. The true power of continuations arises with multitask and selective continuations. *Multitask continuations* schedule several Tasks when one finishes, or schedule one Task when several finish. They create the potential for fine-grained parallelism, where steps that were performed sequentially inside a larger Task body can now be performed in parallel. *Selective continuations* allow you to schedule Tasks based on the status of the previous Task in the chain, allowing you to create complex, yet natural, sets of Tasks to represent complex application states.

The following sections show you how to create and manage different types of continuations, building on what we learned in the previous chapter, as summarized in Table 4-1.

Table 4-1. Task Continuations

Problem	Solution	Listing
Create a simple continuation.	Use the `Task.ContinueWith()` method for each `Task` continuation.	4-1 and 4-2
Create selective continuations.	Use the `Task.ContinueWith()` method, and specify a value from the `TaskContinuationOptions` enumeration.	4-4
Create many-to-one and any-to-one continuations.	Use the `TaskFactory.ContinueWhenAll()` and `Task.Factory.ContinueWhenAny()` methods.	4-5 and 4-6
Canceling continuations.	Use a `CancellationToken` when using the `ContinueWith()` method and, optionally, the `NotOnCanceled` value from the `TaskContinuationOptions` enumeration.	4-7
Handle exceptions in task continuations.	Use selective continuations with the `OnlyOnFaulted` and `NotOnFaulted` values from the `TaskContinuationOptions` enumeration or propagate exceptions by handling and re-throwing them in continuations.	4-8 and 4-9

Creating Simple Continuations

Listing 4-1, at the start of this chapter, demonstrates a simple task continuation. Creating a simple continuation is a two step process:

1. Create a new `Task` instance.

2. Call the `ContinueWith()` method on the new `Task`, supplying a `System.Action<Task>` delegate as the method parameter.

■ **Note** In Listing 4-1 and throughout this chapter, we will be using lambda expressions to create anonymous `Action` delegates. See Chapter 2 for more information about lambda expressions.

Performing these steps creates two `Tasks`. The first `Task` is called the *antecedent*. The second `Task`, returned by the `ContinueWith()` method, is called the *continuation*.

Once both `Tasks` have been created, calling the antecedent `Start()` method schedules the `Task` as usual and, when it has been completed, automatically schedules the continuation `Task`. Note that I used the word "schedules" here; other `Tasks` may be executed between the antecedent `Task` completing and the continuation `Task` being performed.

In Listing 4-1, the antecedent increments the balance of a `BankAccount`, and the continuation prints out the final balance. But look closely, and you will see something interesting: the antecedent is defined to be a `Task<BankAccount>`, so the `Task` body returns the `BankAccount` instance when the `Task` completes.

The Task.ContinueWith() method takes a System.Action<Task> argument and uses this to pass the antecedent Task to the continuation, meaning that all of the methods and properties of the antecedent Task are available to you in your continuation code. Listing 4-1 uses this feature to get the BankAccount instance from the antecedent's Result property.

Using Task.ContinueWith<T>() allows you to create continuation Tasks that return a result, just like you did with stand-alone Tasks in the previous chapter. The result type of a continuation can differ from that of the antecedent. Listing 4-2 demonstrates a continuation that obtains a BankAccount instance from the antecedent Task and returns double the value of the Balance property as its own result. Notice that, in order to get the result from the continuation, we declare a Task<int> to hold the result from the Task.ContinueWith<int>() method so that we can read the Result property.

Listing 4-2. Returning Results with Continuation Tasks

```
using System;
using System.Threading.Tasks;

namespace Listing_02 {

    class BankAccount {
        public int Balance {
            get;
            set;
        }
    }

    class Listing_02 {

        static void Main(string[] args) {

            Task<BankAccount> task = new Task<BankAccount>(() => {
                // create a new bank account
                BankAccount account = new BankAccount();
                // enter a loop
                for (int i = 0; i < 1000; i++) {
                    // increment the account total
                    account.Balance++;
                }
                // return the bank account
                return account;
            });

            Task<int> continuationTask
                = task.ContinueWith<int>((Task<BankAccount> antecedent) => {
                    Console.WriteLine("Interim Balance: {0}", antecedent.Result.Balance);
                    return antecedent.Result.Balance * 2;
                });

            // start the task
            task.Start();
```

```
        Console.WriteLine("Final balance: {0}", continuationTask.Result);

        // wait for input before exiting
        Console.WriteLine("Press enter to finish");
        Console.ReadLine();

    }
  }
}
```

■ **Note** The `Task` returned from the `Task.ContinueWith()` method cannot be started using the `Task.Start()` method. It will be scheduled to run as a continuation when an antecedent has completed.

There are five overloaded versions of the `ContinueWith()` method. The most complete version takes four arguments: `ContinueWith(Action(Task), CancellationToken, TaskContinuationOptions, TaskScheduler)`.

The `Action(Task)` is the task body and is required for all of the method versions. The `CancellationToken` is optional; see the "Canceling Continuations" section later in this chapter for details. The `TaskContinationsOptions` enumeration is described in Table 4-2 and allows you to create selective continuations. The `TaskScheduler` is described later in the "Using a Custom Task Scheduler" section of this chapter. When using the simpler overloads, default values are used for the `ContinuationOptions` and `TaskScheduler` while the `CancellationToken` is omitted.

Creating One-to-Many Continuations

An antecedent `Task` can have multiple continuations; that is to say that more than one `Task` can be automatically scheduled when the antecedent `Task` has completed. You call `ContinueWith()` for each continuation you need to create. And you can create chains of continuations by giving each of your continuations its own continuation. To do so, you just call the `ContinueWith()` method on the `Tasks` returned by your previous calls `ContinueWith()`.

Listing 4-3 demonstrates multiple and chained continuations through a variation of our bank account example. The antecedent task creates a `BankAccount`, increments the balance, and returns it as the result. Two second-generation continuations are created: one doubles the balance from the antecedent, and the other halves the balance. Each of the second-generation `Tasks` has a third-generation continuation that prints out its antecedent result, in this case, the final balance. One set of continuations is built up in stages while the others are created in a single statement.

Listing 4-3. Using Multiple Generations of Continuation

```
using System;
using System.Threading.Tasks;

namespace Listing_03 {
```

```
class BankAccount {
    public int Balance {
        get;
        set;
    }
}

class Listing_03 {

    static void Main(string[] args) {

        Task<BankAccount> rootTask = new Task<BankAccount>(() => {
            // create a new bank account
            BankAccount account = new BankAccount();
            // enter a loop
            for (int i = 0; i < 1000; i++) {
                // increment the account total
                account.Balance++;
            }
            // return the bank account
            return account;
        });

        // create the second-generation task, which will double the antecdent balance
        Task<int> continuationTask1
            = rootTask.ContinueWith<int>((Task<BankAccount> antecedent) => {
                Console.WriteLine("Interim Balance 1: {0}", antecedent.Result.Balance);
                return antecedent.Result.Balance * 2;
            });

        // create a third-generation task, which will print out the result
        Task continuationTask2
            = continuationTask1.ContinueWith((Task<int> antecedent) => {
                Console.WriteLine("Final Balance 1: {0}", antecedent.Result);
            });

        // create a second and third-generation task in one step
        rootTask.ContinueWith<int>((Task<BankAccount> antecedent) => {
            Console.WriteLine("Interim Balance 2: {0}", antecedent.Result.Balance);
            return antecedent.Result.Balance / 2;
        }).ContinueWith((Task<int> antecedent) => {
            Console.WriteLine("Final Balance 2: {0}", antecedent.Result);
        });

        // start the task
        rootTask.Start();
```

```
            // wait for input before exiting
            Console.WriteLine("Press enter to finish");
            Console.ReadLine();

        }
    }
}
```

Creating Selective Continuations

By default, continuation `Tasks` are automatically scheduled when the antecedent `Task` completes. We can be selective about scheduling continuations by using the values of the `System.Threading.Tasks.TaskContinuationOptions` enumeration when calling the `Task.ContinueWith()` method. Table 4-2 details the enumeration values.

Table 4-2. Key Values of the `System.Threading.Tasks.TaskContinuationOptions` Enumeration

Enumeration Value	Description
None	This is equivalent to not specifying a value; that is, the continuation will be scheduled to run when the antecedent completes.
OnlyOnRanToCompletion	The continuation will be scheduled if the antecedent completed successfully; that is, the antecedent is not cancelled and does not throw an unhandled exception.
NotOnRanToCompletion	The continuation will be scheduled if the antecedent is cancelled or throws an unhandled exception.
OnlyOnFaulted	The continuation will be scheduled if the antecedent throws an unhandled exception.
NotOnFaulted	The continuation will be scheduled if the antecedent does not throw an unhandled exception.
OnlyOnCancelled	The continuation will be scheduled if the antecedent is cancelled.
NotOnCancelled	The continuation will be scheduled if the antecedent is not cancelled.

Listing 4-4 demonstrates using the `OnlyOnFaulted` and `NotOnFaulted` values. The antecedent `Task` contains a code statement that throws a `System.Exception`. If the statement is commented out, the second continuation `Task` is scheduled on completion of the antecedent. If the line is left active, and the `Exception` is thrown, and the first continuation `Task` is scheduled.

Listing 4-4. Continuations Based on Exceptions

```
using System;
using System.Threading.Tasks;

namespace Listing_04 {

    class Listing_04 {

        static void Main(string[] args) {

            // create the first generation task
            Task firstGen = new Task(() => {
                Console.WriteLine("Message from first generation task");
                // comment out this line to stop the fault
                throw new Exception();
            });

            // create the second-generation task - only to run on exception
            Task secondGen1 = firstGen.ContinueWith(antecedent => {
                // write out a message with the antecedent exception
                Console.WriteLine("Antecedent task faulted with type: {0}",
                    antecedent.Exception.GetType());
            }, TaskContinuationOptions.OnlyOnFaulted);

            // create the second-generation task - only to run on no exception
            Task secondGen2 = firstGen.ContinueWith(antecedent => {
                Console.WriteLine("Antecedent task NOT faulted");
            }, TaskContinuationOptions.NotOnFaulted);

            // start the first generation task
            firstGen.Start();

            // wait for input before exiting
            Console.WriteLine("Press enter to finish");
            Console.ReadLine();

        }
    }
}
```

■ **Tip** The continuation that runs OnlyOnFaulted reads the Exception property of the antecedent. If this was not the case, the exception would have remained unhandled. See the "Handling Exceptions" section for more information about exceptions in continuation chains.

Creating Many-to-One and Any-To-One Continuations

The continuations we have seen so far have been one-to-one or one-to-many; that is, one antecedent has one or more continuations. You can also perform many-to-one continuations using the `ContinueWhenAll()` and `ContinueWhenAny()` methods of the `System.Threading.Tasks.TaskFactory` class. You obtain an instance of `TaskFactory` through the static `Task.Factory` property.

The `ContinueWhenAll()` and `ContinueWhenAny()` methods both take an array of `Tasks` argument. — `ContinueWhenAll()` schedules a continuation to be performed when all of the `Tasks` in the array have completed, whereas `ContineWhenAny()` schedules a continuation to be performed when any single `Task` in the array has completed. Listing 4-5 demonstrates a simple multitask continuation applied to the Isolation example from the previous chapter.

Listing 4-5. A Multitask Continuation

```
using System;
using System.Threading.Tasks;

namespace Listing_05 {

    class BankAccount {
        public int Balance {
            get;
            set;
        }
    }

    class Listing_05 {

        static void Main(string[] args) {

            // create the bank account instance
            BankAccount account = new BankAccount();

            // create an array of tasks
            Task<int>[] tasks = new Task<int>[10];

            for (int i = 0; i < 10; i++) {
                // create a new task
                tasks[i] = new Task<int>((stateObject) => {

                    // get the state object
                    int isolatedBalance = (int)stateObject;

                    // enter a loop for 1000 balance updates
                    for (int j = 0; j < 1000; j++) {
                        // update the balance
                        isolatedBalance++;
                    }
```

```
                // return the updated balance
                return isolatedBalance;

        }, account.Balance);
    }

    // set up a multitask continuation
    Task continuation = Task.Factory.ContinueWhenAll<int>(tasks, antecedents => {
        // run through and sum the individual balances
        foreach (Task<int> t in antecedents) {
            account.Balance += t.Result;
        }
    });

    // start the atecedent tasks
    foreach (Task t in tasks) {
        t.Start();
    }

    // wait for the contination task to complete
    continuation.Wait();

    // write out the counter value
    Console.WriteLine("Expected value {0}, Balance: {1}", 10000, account.Balance);

    // wait for input before exiting
    Console.WriteLine("Press enter to finish");
    Console.ReadLine();
        }
    }
}
```

In the listing, there are ten antecedent Tasks, each of which updates its own isolated bank account balance. The TaskFactory.ContinueWhenAll() method is used to create a multitask continuation that is scheduled when all of the antecedents have completed. In Listing 4-5, the continuation Task reads the Result property of each antecedent Task and adds it to the account balance.

The syntax of the ContinueWhenAll() method is slightly awkward if you are using lambda expressions because the array of antecedent Tasks appears twice, once as the first argument to the method and again as the input to the lambda expression.

The other oddity of the ContinueWhenAll() syntax is the way in which you specify the results of the antecedent Tasks and the result that you want for the continuation Task. The format is as follows:

```
Task<TAType>[] antecedents;
Task<TCType> continuation;

continuation = Task<TCType>.Factory.ContinueWhenAll<TAType>(antecedents,
    antecedentsParam => {

        ... task body...

});
```

Table 4-3 shows the main permutations of Task results and the generic versions of Task and ContinueWhenAll() or ContinueWhenAny() that you must use to get them.

Table 4-3. Antecedent and Continuation Type Calls

Antecedent Result	Continuation Result	Generic Form
None	None	`Task.Factory.ContineWhenAll()` `Task.Factory.ContineWhenAny()`
None	TCType	`Task<TCType>.Factory.ContineWhenAll()` `Task<TCType>.Factory.ContineWhenAny()`
TAType	None	`Task.Factory.ContinueWhenAll<TAType>()` `Task.Factory.ContinueWhenAny<TAType>()`
TAType	TCType	`Task<TCType>.Factory.ContinueWhenAll<TAType>()` `Task<TCType>.Factory.ContinueWhenAny<TAType>()`

The ContinueWhenAny() method works in a very similar way to ContinueWhenAll(), except that the continuation Task will be scheduled to run as soon as any of the antecedent Tasks has completed. The delegate argument for the ContinueWhenAny() method is the antecedent Task that completed first. Listing 4-6 demonstrates this kind of continuation. A set of ten antecedent Tasks uses a random number generator to wait for a period of time, and the first Task to wake up finishes and becomes the antecedent to the continuation Task.

Listing 4-6. Using TaskFactory.ContinueWhenAny()

```
using System;
using System.Threading;
using System.Threading.Tasks;

namespace Listing_06 {

    class Listing_06 {

        static void Main(string[] args) {

            // create an array of tasks
            Task<int>[] tasks = new Task<int>[10];

            // create a cancellation token source
            CancellationTokenSource tokenSource = new CancellationTokenSource();

            // create the random number generator
            Random rnd = new Random();

            for (int i = 0; i < 10; i++) {
```

```
        // create a new task
        tasks[i] = new Task<int>(() => {
            // define the variable for the sleep interval
            int sleepInterval;
            // acquire exclusive access to the random
            // number generator and get a random value
            lock (rnd) {
                sleepInterval = rnd.Next(500, 2000);
            }
            // put the task thread to sleep for the interval
            tokenSource.Token.WaitHandle.WaitOne(sleepInterval);
            // check to see the current task has been cancelled
            tokenSource.Token.ThrowIfCancellationRequested();
            // return the sleep interval as the result
            return sleepInterval;
        }, tokenSource.Token);
    }

    // set up a when-any multitask continuation
    Task continuation = Task.Factory.ContinueWhenAny<int>(tasks,
        (Task<int> antecedent) => {
            // write out a message using the antecedent result
            Console.WriteLine("The first task slept for {0} milliseconds",
                antecedent.Result);
        });

    // start the atecedent tasks
    foreach (Task t in tasks) {
        t.Start();
    }

    // wait for the contination task to complete
    continuation.Wait();

    // cancel the remaining tasks
    tokenSource.Cancel();

    // wait for input before exiting
    Console.WriteLine("Press enter to finish");
    Console.ReadLine();
        }
    }
}
```

Canceling Continuations

The techniques to handle cancellations for single Tasks, which we covered in the previous chapter, can be applied to continuations. The Task.ContinueWith(), TaskFactory.ContinueWhenAll(), and TaskFactory.ContinueWhenAny() methods all have overloaded versions that accept a CancellationToken, which you can obtain by creating an instance of CancellationTokenSource.

Listing 4-7 demonstrates canceling continuations. An antecedent Task is created and waits using a
CancellationToken wait handle. When the user presses the enter key, the CancellationTokenSource, and
therefore the antecedent Task, are cancelled.

Listing 4-7. Cancelling Continuations

```csharp
using System;
using System.Threading;
using System.Threading.Tasks;

namespace Listing_07 {

    class Listing_07 {

        static void Main(string[] args) {

            // create a cancellation token source
            CancellationTokenSource tokenSource
                = new CancellationTokenSource();

            // create the antecedent task
            Task task = new Task(() => {
                // write out a message
                Console.WriteLine("Antecedent running");
                // wait indefinately on the token wait handle
                tokenSource.Token.WaitHandle.WaitOne();
                // handle the cancellation exception
                tokenSource.Token.ThrowIfCancellationRequested();
            }, tokenSource.Token);

            // create a selective continuation
            Task neverScheduled = task.ContinueWith(antecedent => {
                // write out a message
                Console.WriteLine("This task will never be scheduled");
            }, tokenSource.Token);

            // create a bad selective contination
            Task badSelective = task.ContinueWith(antecedent => {
                // write out a message
                Console.WriteLine("This task will never be scheduled");
            }, tokenSource.Token, TaskContinuationOptions.OnlyOnCanceled,
            TaskScheduler.Current);

            // create a good selective contiuation
            Task continuation = task.ContinueWith(antecedent => {
                // write out a message
                Console.WriteLine("Continuation running");
            }, TaskContinuationOptions.OnlyOnCanceled);

            // start the task
            task.Start();
```

```
                // prompt the user so they can cancel the token
                Console.WriteLine("Press enter to cancel token");
                Console.ReadLine();
                // cancel the token source
                tokenSource.Cancel();

                // wait for the good continuation to complete
                continuation.Wait();

                // wait for input before exiting
                Console.WriteLine("Press enter to finish");
                Console.ReadLine();
            }
        }
    }
```

Each of the three continuation Tasks behaves in a different way. The neverScheduled Task has been created with the same CancellationToken as the antecedent and so is never scheduled to be run.

The second Task, called badSelective, is created using the OnlyOnCanceled value from the TaskContinuationOptions enumeration. Unfortunately, it is created using the same CancellationToken as the antecedent, so the options and the token can never be in a state where the Task will be scheduled. Tasks that rely on the OnlyOnCanceled value should not share a CancellationToken with their antecedent. The final Task, named continuation, shows a selective continuation that will run properly when the antecedent is cancelled.

Waiting for Continuations

Waiting for continuation Tasks works in just the same way as for single Tasks; you can use the Task instances created by the ContinueWith(), ContineWhenAll(), and ContinueWhenAny() methods with the Task.Wait() and Task.WaitAll() methods.

Waiting on a Task does not mean waiting on its continuations. Each Task is scheduled separately, and a call to Task.Wait() on an antecedent will return when the antecedent itself has completed. If you want to wait for a continuation chain to complete, you should wait on the last continuation in the sequence.

Handling Exceptions

There are no special features for propagating exceptions through a continuation chain. Any exceptions thrown by any Task in a continuation chain must be processed, or they will be treated as unhandled exceptions when the finalizer for the Task is performed. See the previous chapter for details of processing Task exceptions. Listing 4-8 illustrates the problem with exceptions in chains.

Listing 4-8. Unhandled Exceptions in Continuation Chains

```
using System;
using System.Threading.Tasks;

namespace Listing_08 {

    class Listing_08 {
```

```
static void Main(string[] args) {

    // create a first generation task
    Task gen1 = new Task(() => {
        // write out a message
        Console.WriteLine("First generation task");
    });

    // create a second-generation task
    Task gen2 = gen1.ContinueWith(antecedent => {
        // write out a message
        Console.WriteLine("Second generation task - throws exception");
        throw new Exception();
    });

    // create a third-generation task
    Task gen3 = gen2.ContinueWith(antecedent => {
        // write out a message
        Console.WriteLine("Third generation task");
    });

    // start the first gen task
    gen1.Start();

    // wait for the last task in the chain to complete
    gen3.Wait();

    // wait for input before exiting
    Console.WriteLine("Press enter to finish");
    Console.ReadLine();
    }
  }
}
```

The second-generation Task throws an exception, but the third-generation Task still runs. The main thread waits for the last Task in the chain to complete and prompts the user to press the Enter key. The program then exits, causing the finalizer to be called, at which point the exception from the second-generation continuation is propagated, producing the following output:

```
First generation task

Second generation task - throws exception

Third generation task

Press enter to finish


Unhandled Exception: System.AggregateException: A Task's exception(s) were not

observed either by Waiting on the Task or accessing its Exception property. As a result,

the unobserved exception was rethrown by the finalizer thread. --->

System.Exception: Exception of type 'System.Exception' was thrown.

    at Listing_08.Listing_08.<Main>b__1(Task antecedent)

    at System.Threading.Tasks.Task.<>c__DisplayClassb.<ContinueWith>b__a(Object obj)

    at System.Threading.Tasks.Task.InnerInvoke()

    at System.Threading.Tasks.Task.Execute()

    --- End of inner exception stack trace ---

    at System.Threading.Tasks.TaskExceptionHolder.Finalize()
```

The best way to handle this kind of problem is to have each continuation **Task** check the status of the antecedent and handle the exception. You can rethrow the same exception to propagate it throughout the continuation chain. Doing so will cause all of the tasks in a chain to be scheduled and executed, but it does reduce the chance of an unhandled exception. Listing 4-9 demonstrates this check-and-propagate approach.

Listing 4-9. Propagating Exceptions Along a Continuation Chain

```csharp
using System;
using System.Threading.Tasks;

namespace Listing_09 {

    class Listing_09 {

        static void Main(string[] args) {
```

```
    // create a first generation task
    Task gen1 = new Task(() => {
        // write out a message
        Console.WriteLine("First generation task");
    });

    // create a second-generation task
    Task gen2 = gen1.ContinueWith(antecedent => {
        // write out a message
        Console.WriteLine("Second generation task - throws exception");
        throw new Exception();
    });

    // create a third-generation task
    Task gen3 = gen2.ContinueWith(antecedent => {
        // check to see if the antecedent threw an exception
        if (antecedent.Status == TaskStatus.Faulted) {
            // get and rethrow the antecedent exception
            throw antecedent.Exception.InnerException;
        }
        // write out a message
        Console.WriteLine("Third generation task");
    });

    // start the first gen task
    gen1.Start();

    try {
        // wait for the last task in the chain to complete
        gen3.Wait();
    } catch (AggregateException ex) {
        ex.Handle(inner => {
            Console.WriteLine("Handled exception of type: {0}", inner.GetType());
            return true;
        });
    }

    // wait for input before exiting
    Console.WriteLine("Press enter to finish");
    Console.ReadLine();
        }
    }
}
```

By having the continuation process the exceptions thrown by the antecedent, we can catch exceptions thrown by the last Task in the chain and be sure to avoid unhandled exceptions. Note that the Exception property of an antecedent returns an instance of AggregateException. The InnerException property is read in the continuation Task to avoid nested instances of AggregateException, unpacking the nesting in the exception handler would also work. See the previous chapter for details of how to process instances of AggregateException.

The same issue exists when performing multitask continuations. If any of the antecedent Tasks have thrown an exception that you don't process, that exception becomes unhandled and will cause problems later. Processing antecedent exceptions with the ContinueWhenAll() method is simply a matter of checking each antecedent, such as with the following fragment:

```
Task[] tasks;

Task.Factory.ContinueWhenAll(tasks, antecedents => {
    foreach (Task t in antecedents) {
        if (t.Status == TaskStatus.Faulted) {
            // ...process or propagate...
        }
    }
    //...task contination code...
});
```

Handling exceptions when using the ContinueWhenAny() method is more difficult. The continuation has one antecedent, but one of the other Tasks from the previous generation may throw an exception and this might well happen after the continuation has been executed. The best way to avoid unhandled exceptions in this situation is to combine a selective ContinueWhenAny() continuation with a ContinueWhenAll() that exists purely to process exceptions, as in the following fragment:

```
Task[] tasks;

Task.Factory.ContinueWhenAny(tasks, antecedent => {
    // ...task continuaton code...
}, TaskContinuationOptions.NotOnFaulted);

Task.Factory.ContinueWhenAll(tasks, antecedents => {
    foreach (Task t in antecedents) {
        if (t.Status == TaskStatus.Faulted) {
            // ...process exceptions...
        }
    }
});
```

Creating Child Tasks

A *child* Task, sometimes known as a *nested* Task, is one that is created inside the Task body of another. The Task in which the child is created is known as the *parent*. There are two kinds of child Task—*detached* and *attached*. A detached Task, as demonstrated in Listing 4-10, has no special relationship with its parent; the child will be scheduled and can be performed concurrently with the parent but has no impact on the parent itself.

Table 4-4. Child Tasks

Problem	Solution	Listing
Create a detached child Task.	Create a new Task within the body of an existing one.	4-10
Create an attached child Task.	Create a new Task within the body of an existing one, specifying the AttachedToParent value from the TaskCreationOptions enumeration	4-11
Create a continuation of an attached child.	Call the ContinueWith() method of the attached child, specifying the AttachedToParent value from the TaskContinuationOptions enumeration	4-11

Listing 4-10. A Simple Child Task

```csharp
using System;
using System.Threading;
using System.Threading.Tasks;

namespace Listing_10 {

    class Listing_10 {

        static void Main(string[] args) {

            // create the parent task
            Task parentTask = new Task(() => {

                // create the first child task
                Task childTask = new Task(() => {
                    // write out a message and wait
                    Console.WriteLine("Child task running");
                    Thread.Sleep(1000);
                    Console.WriteLine("Child task finished");
                    throw new Exception();
                });

                Console.WriteLine("Starting child task...");
                childTask.Start();
            });

            // start the parent task
            parentTask.Start();

            // wait for the parent task
            Console.WriteLine("Waiting for parent task");
            parentTask.Wait();
            Console.WriteLine("Parent task finished");
```

```
            // wait for input before exiting
            Console.WriteLine("Press enter to finish");
            Console.ReadLine();
        }
    }
}
```

Attached child tasks are much more interesting and do have a special relationship with their parents. There are three parts to the relationship:

- The parent Task waits for attached child Tasks to complete before it completes.

- The parent Task throws any exceptions thrown by attached child Tasks.

- The status of the parent Task depends on the status of attached child Tasks.

You create an attached child by specifying the AttachedToParent value from the System.Threading. Tasks.TaskCreationOptions enumeration as a constructor argument. This establishes the relationship with the parent Task. Listing 4-11 demonstrates an attached child Task.

Listing 4-11. An Attached Child Task

```
using System;
using System.Threading;
using System.Threading.Tasks;

namespace Listing_11 {

    class Listing_11 {

        static void Main(string[] args) {

            // create the parent task
            Task parentTask = new Task(() => {

                // create the first child task
                Task childTask = new Task(() => {
                    // write out a message and wait
                    Console.WriteLine("Child 1 running");
                    Thread.Sleep(1000);
                    Console.WriteLine("Child 1 finished");
                    throw new Exception();
                }, TaskCreationOptions.AttachedToParent);

                // create an attached continuation
                childTask.ContinueWith(antecedent => {
                    // write out a message and wait
                    Console.WriteLine("Continuation running");
                    Thread.Sleep(1000);
                    Console.WriteLine("Continuation finished");
                },
```

```
        TaskContinuationOptions.AttachedToParent
        | TaskContinuationOptions.OnlyOnFaulted);

        Console.WriteLine("Starting child task...");
        childTask.Start();
    });

    // start the parent task
    parentTask.Start();

    try {
        // wait for the parent task
        Console.WriteLine("Waiting for parent task");
        parentTask.Wait();
        Console.WriteLine("Parent task finished");
    } catch (AggregateException ex) {
        Console.WriteLine("Exception: {0}", ex.InnerException.GetType());
    }

    // wait for input before exiting
    Console.WriteLine("Press enter to finish");
    Console.ReadLine();
    }
  }
}
```

The `Wait()` call on the parent `Task` will not return until the parent and all of its attached children have finished. You will see that the child `Task` throws an exception, which is packaged up by the parent `Task` and thrown again, allowing us to catch it when calling a trigger method on the parent. The exception will be a nested `AggregateException`; in other words, the original exception will have been packaged into an `AggregateException` by the child, and that will be packaged again into another `AggregateException` by the parent. The third part of the relationship relates to `Task` status. When a parent `Task` has finished executing and is waiting for its attached children to finish, its status will be `TaskStatus.WaitingForChildrenToComplete`.

You can extend the scope of the attached child relationship to `Task` continuations by using the `TaskContinuationOptions.AttachedToParent` value as an argument when calling the `ContinueWith()` method on an attached child `Task`. Listing 4-11 demonstrates how this done and shows how you can combine values from the `TaskContinuationOptions` enumeration to create continuations that are both selective and attached.

Using Synchronization to Coordinate Tasks

In this section, we revisit the topic of synchronization primitives, this time using them to coordinate activity between and amongst groups of `Tasks`.

We want one group of `Tasks` (called the *supervisors*) to exert some direction over another group of `Tasks` (called the *workers*). A synchronization primitive is used to mediate between the two groups and allows them to communicate. The communication between the supervisors and the workers is limited to two messages—go and wait.

The synchronization primitive keeps track of a *condition*. Worker `Tasks` check with the primitive to see if the condition has been satisfied. If it has, they are told to go and will continue their work. If the condition has not been satisfied, they are made to wait until it is.

The details of the condition vary from one type of primitive to another, but what they all share in common is that they are satisfied by when the supervisors *signal* the primitive

In effect, the workers are waiting for signals from the supervisors channeled through the synchronization primitive. Worker `Tasks` wait for the signals by calling the primitive's `Wait()` method (or `WaitOne()` for classic primitives). the `Wait()` method blocks (does not return) until the expected signals have been received and the primitive condition has been satisfied. When a primitive tells a worker `Task` that has been waiting that it may now proceed because the condition has been satisfied, the primitive is said to *wake*, *notify*, or *release* the waiting `Task`.

You could write your own code to allow supervisors to signal workers, but I recommend that you don't. First, writing synchronization primitives correctly is very hard , and the odds are that you will make mistakes unless you are very experienced in parallel programming. Second, the primitives included in the .NET class library cover the vast majority of situations that parallel programmers encounter and are implemented using a broadly consistent interface. If the type of condition you need your primitive to manage should change, it is a relatively simple thing to switch from one standard primitive to another. Table 4-5 summarizes the main uses for the most commonly used primitives.

Table 4-5. Coordinating Tasks

Problem	Solution	Listing
Implement a cooperative multi-phase algorithm.	Use the `System.Threading.Barrier` class.	4-12, 4-13, and 4-14
Coordinate `Tasks` so that multiple supervisors signal the primitive before the workers are released	Use the `System.Threading.CountDownEvent` class.	4-15
Coordinate `Tasks` so that one signal releases all workers.	Use the `System.Threading.ManualResetEventSlim` class.	4-16
Coordinate `Tasks` so that one signal releases one worker.	Use the `System.Threading.AutoResetEvent` class.	4-17
Coordinate `Tasks` so that one signal releases a specified number of workers.	Use the `System.Threading.SemaphoreSlim` class.	4-18

For some primitives, both classic and lightweight versions are available. The lightweight versions have names that end with "slim," such as `ManualResetEventSlim`. The lightweight versions have better performance characteristics for most uses when compared with the classic versions, because a call to `Wait()` on a lightweight primitive is initially handled by spinning, which is ideally suited to short waiting periods. See Chapter 2 for a description of spinning. The lightweight versions also support waiting using a `CancellationToken`, which is something that I find endlessly useful. I use the lightweight implementations for preference and recommend that you do the same.

Barrier

When using the System.Threading.Barrier primitive, the supervisors and the workers are the same Tasks, making Barrier useful for coordinating Tasks performing a *multiphase parallel algorithm.* Multiphase algorithms are broken down into several stages (called *phases*), where all of the Tasks participating in the work must reach the end of one phase before the next one can begin. This behavior is useful if the results produced in one phase are required as inputs for the next.

When a Task calls the SignalAndWait() method, the primitive is signaled (as though the Task were a supervisor), and the condition is checked (as though the Task were a worker). The condition for the Barrier class is satisfied when all of the Tasks participating in the algorithm have called the SignalAndWait() method. If a Task calls the method before the required number of calls has been made, it is made to wait. The number of calls is specified in the class constructor and can be altered using the AddParticipant() and RemoveParticipant() methods.

The Tasks performing the algorithm call the SignalAndWait() method when they reach the end of a phase. Not only does the Barrier release any waiting Tasks when the current phase ends, but it *resets* automatically, meaning that subsequent calls to SignalAndWait() will make Tasks wait until the counter reaches 0 again and another phase is complete.

When creating a new instance of Barrier, you can specify a System.Action that will be performed at the end of each phase and before the Tasks are notified that they should start the next one. you can see an example of this in the listing below. Table 4-6 summarizes key members of the Barrier class.

Table 4-6. Selected Members of the System.Threading.Barrier Class

Member	Description
AddParticipant() AddParticipants(int)	Increment the number of calls that must be made to SignalAndWait() before a phase completes.
RemoveParticpant() RemoveParticpants(int)	Decrement the number of calls that must be made to SignalAndWait() before a phase completes.
SignalAndWait()	Signal the primitive that the current Task has completed the current phase, and wait indefinitely for the other Tasks to do the same.
SignalAndWait(CancellationToken) SignalAndWait(Int32) SignalAndWait(TimeSpan) SignalAndWait(Int32, CancellationToken) SignalAndWait(TimeSpan, CancellationToken)	Function like SignalAndWait(), but give up waiting for the other Tasks if they have not all signaled the primitive before the specified time has passed or the specified cancellation token is cancelled.
CurrentPhaseNumber	Report the current phase number, incremented each time the SignalAndWait() method has been called the number of times specified in the constructor.

Continued

Member	Description
ParticipantCount	Return the number of calls to the SignalAndWait() method that will mark the end of a phase and release any waiting Tasks.
ParticipantsRemaining	Return the number of participants that have yet to signal the end of the current phase.

Listing 4-12 demonstrates how to create and use the Barrier class. When the Barrier instance is created, two constructor arguments are supplied: the number of Tasks that must call SignalAndWait() before the primitive condition is met and a System.Action(Barrier) that will be called each time the condition is met (the listing uses a lambda expression to define System.Action).

In the example, we create an array of BankAccounts and a set of Tasks that perform a simple multiphase algorithm against using the accounts. In the first phase, the Tasks enter a loop to add random amounts to the account they are working with and then signal the Barrier to indicate they have reached the end of the current phase.

The Barrier then executes the constructor Action, which sums the individual balances into the totalBalance variable. The second phase of the algorithm begins, where each Task reduces the balance of its account by 10 percent of the difference between the current balance and the total balance, a procedure that would not have been possible prior to all Tasks completing the first phase. At the end of the phase, the Tasks signal the Barrier again, which marks the end of the second phase and triggers the constructor action again.

Listing 4-12. Using the Barrier Class

```
using System;
using System.Threading;
using System.Threading.Tasks;

namespace Listing_12 {

    class BankAccount {
        public int Balance {
            get;
            set;
        }
    }

    class Listing_12 {

        static void Main(string[] args) {
```

```
// create the array of bank accounts
BankAccount[] accounts = new BankAccount[5];
for (int i = 0; i < accounts.Length; i++) {
    accounts[i] = new BankAccount();
}

// create the total balance counter
int totalBalance = 0;

// create the barrier
Barrier barrier = new Barrier(5, (myBarrier) => {
    // zero the balance
    totalBalance = 0;
    // sum the account totals
    foreach (BankAccount account in accounts) {
        totalBalance += account.Balance;
    }
    // write out the balance
    Console.WriteLine("Total balance: {0}", totalBalance);
});

// define the tasks array
Task[] tasks = new Task[5];

// loop to create the tasks
for (int i = 0; i < tasks.Length; i++) {
    tasks[i] = new Task((stateObj) => {

        // create a typed reference to the account
        BankAccount account = (BankAccount)stateObj;

        // start of phase
        Random rnd = new Random();
        for (int j = 0; j < 1000; j++) {
            account.Balance += rnd.Next(1, 100);
        }
        // end of phase

        // tell the user that this task has has completed the phase
        Console.WriteLine("Task {0}, phase {1} ended",
            Task.CurrentId, barrier.CurrentPhaseNumber);

        // signal the barrier
        barrier.SignalAndWait();

        // start of phase
        // alter the balance of this Task's account using the total balance
        // deduct 10% of the difference from the total balance
        account.Balance -= (totalBalance - account.Balance) / 10;
        // end of phase
```

```
                    // tell the user that this task has has completed the phase
                    Console.WriteLine("Task {0}, phase {1} ended",
                        Task.CurrentId, barrier.CurrentPhaseNumber);

                    // signal the barrier
                    barrier.SignalAndWait();
                },
                accounts[i]);
            }

            // start the task
            foreach (Task t in tasks) {
                t.Start();
            }

            // wait for all of the tasks to complete
            Task.WaitAll(tasks);

            // wait for input before exiting
            Console.WriteLine("Press enter to finish");
            Console.ReadLine();
        }
    }
}
```

Signaling the Barrier at the end of the final phase is not essential; in Listing 4-12, I wanted to calculate the final total balance. Listing 4-12 shows you how to make use of the Barrier class, but omits one major hazard. There is a deadlock if a Task doesn't signal the Barrier, because it throws an exception. The current phase will never end, and the waiting Tasks will never be released.

There are two ways to deal with exceptions in this situation. The first is to abandon the Task that has thrown the exception but carry on with the other Tasks. You can do this by creating a selective continuation with the OnlyOnFaulted value and calling the RemoveParticipant() method, which decreases the number of calls to SignalAndWait() that Barrier requires to mark the end of a phase. This approach works as long as you can continue without the result that the abandoned Task would have otherwise provided. Listing 4-13 demonstrates this technique.

Listing 4-13. Dealing with Exceptions by Reducing Participation

```
using System;
using System.Threading;
using System.Threading.Tasks;

namespace Listing_13 {

    class Listing_13 {

        static void Main(string[] args) {

            // create a barrier
            Barrier barrier = new Barrier(2);
```

```
            // create a task that will complete
            Task.Factory.StartNew(() => {
                Console.WriteLine("Good task starting phase 0");
                barrier.SignalAndWait();
                Console.WriteLine("Good task starting phase 1");
                barrier.SignalAndWait();
                Console.WriteLine("Good task completed");
            });

            // create a task that will throw an exception
            // with a selective continuation that will reduce the
            // particpant count in the barrier
            Task.Factory.StartNew(() => {
                Console.WriteLine("Bad task 1 throwing exception");
                throw new Exception();

            }).ContinueWith(antecedent => {
                // reduce the particpant count
                Console.WriteLine("Reducing the barrier participant count");
                barrier.RemoveParticipant();
            }, TaskContinuationOptions.OnlyOnFaulted);

            // wait for input before exiting
            Console.WriteLine("Press enter to finish");
            Console.ReadLine();
        }
    }
}
```

The second technique is to use a `CancellationToken` when creating the `Tasks` and use a version of the `Barrier.SignalAndWait()` method that takes a `CancellationToken` as an argument. A selective continuation `Task` cancels the token, which causes calls to `SignalAndWait()` to throw an `OperationCancelledException`, stopping all of the `Tasks` from continuing. This technique works if you don't want any of the `Tasks` to continue if any of them throw an exception. Listing 4-14 demonstrates this technique. Remember that the exception that was thrown in the first place is unhandled and will have to be dealt with using one of the techniques described in Chapter 2.

Listing 4-14. Dealing with Exceptions Using Cancellation

```
using System;
using System.Threading;
using System.Threading.Tasks;

namespace Listing_14 {

    class Listing_14 {

        static void Main(string[] args) {

            // create a barrier
            Barrier barrier = new Barrier(2);
```

```
        // create a cancellation token source
        CancellationTokenSource tokenSource
            = new CancellationTokenSource();

        // create a task that will complete
        Task.Factory.StartNew(() => {
            Console.WriteLine("Good task starting phase 0");
            barrier.SignalAndWait(tokenSource.Token);
            Console.WriteLine("Good task starting phase 1");
            barrier.SignalAndWait(tokenSource.Token);
        }, tokenSource.Token);

        // create a task that will throw an exception
        // with a selective continuation that will reduce the
        // particpant count in the barrier
        Task.Factory.StartNew(() => {
            Console.WriteLine("Bad task 1 throwing exception");
            throw new Exception();

        }, tokenSource.Token).ContinueWith(antecedent => {
            // reduce the particpant count
            Console.WriteLine("Cancelling the token");
            tokenSource.Cancel();
        }, TaskContinuationOptions.OnlyOnFaulted);

        // wait for input before exiting
        Console.WriteLine("Press enter to finish");
        Console.ReadLine();
    }
  }
}
```

CountDownEvent

The `System.Threading.CountDownEvent` is similar to `Barrier` in that it requires a number of calls to a method to satisfy the primitive condition. But unlike `Barrier`, `CountDownEvent` separates signaling from waiting.

Calls to the `CountDownEvent.Wait()` method block until the `Signal()` method has been called the number of times specified in the constructor; each call to `Signal()` decrements a counter. Once the counter reaches zero, any waiting `Tasks` are released. At this point, the event represented by the `CountDownEventClass` is said to be *signaled* or *set*.

Once the event is set, calls to the `Wait()` method will not cause the `Task` to wait. `CountDownEvent` must be manually reset, by calling the `Reset()` method. Once the event has been reset, we start over again. Calls to `Wait()` will block until the `Signal()` method has been called the required number of times. This is in contrast to the `Barrier` class, which resets automatically.

You can call the `AddCount()` or `TryAddCount()` methods to increment the counter but only if the event is not set. If you call `AddCount()` after the event has set without first calling `Reset()`,an exception will be thrown. Table 4-7 details the key members of the `CountDownEvent` class.

Table 4-7. Selected Members of the System.Threading.CountDownEvent Class

Member	Description
AddCount() AddCount(int)	Increment the condition counter.
Reset() Reset(int)	Reset the event using the original counter value or the value specified.
Signal() Signal(int)	Decrement the condition counter by one or by the amount specified.
TryAddCount() TryAddCount(int)	Try to increment the condition counter, and return true if the counter is incremented.
Wait()	Wait indefinitely for the event to be set.
Wait(CancellationToken) Wait(int) Wait(TimeSpan) Wait(int, CancellationToken) Wait(TimeSpan, CancellationToken)	Wait for the event to be set, for a period of time to pass, or for a cancellation token to be cancelled.
CurrentCount	Return the number of times that Signal() must be called before the event is set.
InitialCount	Return the initial value of the condition counter.
IsSet	Return true if the event is set; false otherwise.

Listing 4-15 demonstrates using CountDownEvent. A set of five supervisor Tasks is created, each of which sleeps for a random amount of time and then calls Signal(). The sixth Task, a worker, calls the CountDownEvent.Wait() method, which blocks until each of the Tasks have signaled the CountDownEvent, setting the event.

Listing 4-15. Using the CountDownEvent Primitive

```
using System;
using System.Threading;
using System.Threading.Tasks;

namespace Listing_15 {

    class Listing_15 {

        static void Main(string[] args) {
```

```
// create a CountDownEvent with a condition
// counter of 5
CountdownEvent cdevent = new CountdownEvent(5);

// create a Random that we will use to generate
// sleep intervals
Random rnd = new Random();

// create 5 tasks, each of which will wait for
// a random period and then signal the event
Task[] tasks = new Task[6];
for (int i = 0; i < tasks.Length; i++) {
    // create the new task
    tasks[i] = new Task(() => {
        // put the task to sleep for a random period
        // up to one second
        Thread.Sleep(rnd.Next(500, 1000));
        // signal the event
        Console.WriteLine("Task {0} signalling event", Task.CurrentId);
        cdevent.Signal();
    });
};

// create the final task, which will rendezous with the other 5
// using the count down event
tasks[5] = new Task(() => {
    // wait on the event
    Console.WriteLine("Rendezvous task waiting");
    cdevent.Wait();
    Console.WriteLine("Event has been set");

});

// start the tasks
foreach (Task t in tasks) {
    t.Start();
}

Task.WaitAll(tasks);

// wait for input before exiting
Console.WriteLine("Press enter to finish");
Console.ReadLine();
        }
    }
}
```

The example shows how one group (the five supervisors) directs the behavior of another group (the single worker). The worker is made to wait until the supervisors have all reached a given state and have signaled the primitive. It is important to note that although we created five supervisors, we could have achieved the same effect by having one supervisor call **Signal()** five times. Synchronization primitives care about which methods are called, not how they are called.

ManualResetEventSlim

The **System.Threading.ManualResetEventSlim** class provides a simpler approach than **CountDownEvent**. A single call to **Set()** signals the event, and any waiting **Task**s are released. New calls to **Wait()** don't block until the **Reset()** method is called. Table 4-8 summarizes the key members of this primitive.

Table 4-8. Key Members of the System.Threading.ManualResetEvent Class

Member	Description
Set()	Set the event, releasing any waiting **Task**s. While the event is set, calls to **Wait()** do not block until the **Reset()** method is called.
Reset()	Reset the event.
Wait() Wait(CancellationToken) Wait(int) Wait(TimeSpan) Wait(int, CancellationToken) Wait(TimeSpan, CancellationToken)	Calls to this method block until the event is set, the specified time period has passed, or the specified token is cancelled.
IsSet	Return **true** if the event is set and **false** otherwise.
SpinCount	Get and set the number of spins that a call to **Wait()** will result in before a normal wait occurs. See Chapter 2 for more information about spinning.

■ **Note** The ManualResetEventSlim class is the lightweight equivalent to System.Threading.ManualResetEvent.

Listing 4-16 demonstrates the use of the **ManualResetEventSlim** class. Two **Task**s are created: one worker that repeatedly waits on the event and one supervisor that sets and unsets the event. While the event is set, calls to the **Wait()** method do not block, and the worker **Task** proceeds without waiting. When the event is reset, calls to **Wait()** block until the supervisor sets the event once again.

■ **Tip** The default constructor creates an instance of ManualResetEventSlim with the event initially unset, but you can explicitly specify the initial state of the event by using the overloaded version of the constructor.

Listing 4-16. Using the ManualResetEventSlim Class

```csharp
using System;
using System.Threading;
using System.Threading.Tasks;

namespace Listing_16 {

    class Listing_16 {

        static void Main(string[] args) {

            // create the primtive
            ManualResetEventSlim manualResetEvent
                = new ManualResetEventSlim();

            // create the cancellation token source
            CancellationTokenSource tokenSource
                = new CancellationTokenSource();

            // create and start the task that will wait on the event
            Task waitingTask =  Task.Factory.StartNew(() => {
                while (true) {
                    // wait on the primitive
                    manualResetEvent.Wait(tokenSource.Token);
                    // print out a message
                    Console.WriteLine("Waiting task active");
                }
            }, tokenSource.Token);

            // create and start the signalling task
            Task signallingTask = Task.Factory.StartNew(() => {
                // create a random generator for sleep periods
                Random rnd = new Random();
                // loop while the task has not been cancelled
                while (!tokenSource.Token.IsCancellationRequested) {
                    // go to sleep for a random period
                    tokenSource.Token.WaitHandle.WaitOne(rnd.Next(500, 2000));
                    // set the event
                    manualResetEvent.Set();
                    Console.WriteLine("Event set");
                    // go to sleep again
                    tokenSource.Token.WaitHandle.WaitOne(rnd.Next(500, 2000));
```

```
        // reset the event
        manualResetEvent.Reset();
        Console.WriteLine("Event reset");
    }
    // if we reach this point, we know the task has been cancelled
    tokenSource.Token.ThrowIfCancellationRequested();
}, tokenSource.Token);

// ask the user to press return before we cancel
// the token and bring the tasks to an end
Console.WriteLine("Press enter to cancel tasks");
Console.ReadLine();

// cancel the token source and wait for the tasks
tokenSource.Cancel();
try {
    Task.WaitAll(waitingTask, signallingTask);
} catch (AggregateException) {
    // discard exceptions
}

// wait for input before exiting
Console.WriteLine("Press enter to finish");
Console.ReadLine();
        }
    }
}
```

AutoResetEvent

AutoResetEvent is similar to ManualResetEventSlim, but the event is reset automatically after each call to the Set() method, and only one waiting worker Task is released each time the event is set. There is no lightweight alternative to AutoResetEvent, and being a classic primitive, it has no method that allows waiting using a CancellationToken. Table 4-9 describes the key members of the AutoResetEvent class.

Table 4-9. Key Members of the System.Threading.AutoResetEvent Class

Member	Description
Set()	Set the event, releasing one waiting Task.
WaitOne() WaitOne(int) WaitOne(TimeSpan)	Wait until the event is signaled or the specified time period has passed.

Listing 4-17 demonstrates the use of the **AutoResetEvent** class. The constructor requires you to specify whether the event is initially set. We create three worker **Task**s, each of which calls the **WaitOne()** method of the **AutoResetEvent**. A fourth **Task**, the supervisor, sets the event every 500 milliseconds. Each time the event is set, one waiting worker **Task** is released. If you run the program, you will see long sequences where a given worker **Task** is never released, or seems to be the one constantly being released—the **AutoResetEvent** class makes no guarantees about which waiting **Task** will be released when the event is set, and you should be careful not to make assumptions about the order in which workers are released when using this class.

Listing 4-17. Using the AutoResetEvent Class

```
using System;
using System.Threading;
using System.Threading.Tasks;

namespace Listing_17 {

    class Listing_17 {

        static void Main(string[] args) {

            // create the primtive
            AutoResetEvent arEvent = new AutoResetEvent(false);

            // create the cancellation token source
            CancellationTokenSource tokenSource
                = new CancellationTokenSource();

            // create and start the task that will wait on the event
            for (int i = 0; i < 3; i++) {
                Task.Factory.StartNew(() => {
                    while (!tokenSource.Token.IsCancellationRequested) {
                        // wait on the primtive
                        arEvent.WaitOne();
                        // print out a message when we are released
                        Console.WriteLine("Task {0} released", Task.CurrentId);

                    }
                    // if we reach this point, we know the task has been cancelled
                    tokenSource.Token.ThrowIfCancellationRequested();
                }, tokenSource.Token);
            }
```

```
        // create and start the signalling task
        Task signallingTask = Task.Factory.StartNew(() => {
            // loop while the task has not been cancelled
            while (!tokenSource.Token.IsCancellationRequested) {
                // go to sleep for a random period
                tokenSource.Token.WaitHandle.WaitOne(500);
                // set the event
                arEvent.Set();
                Console.WriteLine("Event set");
            }
            // if we reach this point, we know the task has been cancelled
            tokenSource.Token.ThrowIfCancellationRequested();
        }, tokenSource.Token);

        // ask the user to press return before we cancel
        // the token and bring the tasks to an end
        Console.WriteLine("Press enter to cancel tasks");
        Console.ReadLine();

        // cancel the token source and wait for the tasks
        tokenSource.Cancel();

        // wait for input before exiting
        Console.WriteLine("Press enter to finish");
        Console.ReadLine();
    }
  }
}
```

SemaphoreSlim

The `System.Threading.SemaphoreSlim` class allows you to specify how many waiting worker `Tasks` are released when the event is set, which is useful when you want to restrict the degree of concurrency among a group of `Tasks`. The supervisor releases workers by calling the `Release()` method. The default version releases one `Task`, and you can specify how many `Tasks` are released by providing an `integer` argument. The constructor requires that you specify how many calls to the `Wait()` method can be made before the event is reset for the first time. Specifying `0` resets the event immediately, and any other value sets the event initially and then allows the specified number of calls to the `Wait()` method to be made without blocking before the event is reset.

■ **Note** The `SemaphoreSlim` class is the lightweight equivalent to `System.Threading.Semaphore`

Table 4-10 describes the key members of `SemaphoreSlim`.

Table 4-10. Key Members of the System.Threading.SemaphoreSlim Class

Member	Description
`Release()` `Release(int)`	Release one or a specified number of **Tasks**.

`Wait()`
`Wait(CancellationToken)`
`Wait(int)`
`Wait(TimeSpan)`
`Wait(int, CancellationToken)`
`Wait(TimeSpan, CancellationToken)`
	Calls to this method block until the event is set, the specified time period has passed, or the specified token is cancelled.

`CurrentCount`	Return the number of **Tasks** that will be released or the number of times that `Wait()` can be called without blocking if there are no waiting **Tasks**.

Listing 4-18 demonstrates the use of this class. Ten worker **Tasks** are created and call the `SemaphoreSlim.Wait()` method. A supervisor **Task** periodically releases two threads by signaling the primitive by calling `SemaphoreSlim.Release(2)`.

Listing 4-18. Using the SemaphoreSlim Class

```
using System;
using System.Threading;
using System.Threading.Tasks;

namespace Listing_18 {

    class Listing_18 {

        static void Main(string[] args) {

            // create the primtive
            SemaphoreSlim semaphore = new SemaphoreSlim(2);

            // create the cancellation token source
            CancellationTokenSource tokenSource
                = new CancellationTokenSource();
```

```
            // create and start the task that will wait on the event
            for (int i = 0; i < 10; i++) {
                Task.Factory.StartNew(() => {
                    while (true) {
                        semaphore.Wait(tokenSource.Token);
                        // print out a message when we are released
                        Console.WriteLine("Task {0} released", Task.CurrentId);
                    }
                }, tokenSource.Token);
            }

            // create and start the signalling task
            Task signallingTask = Task.Factory.StartNew(() => {
                // loop while the task has not been cancelled
                while (!tokenSource.Token.IsCancellationRequested) {
                    // go to sleep for a random period
                    tokenSource.Token.WaitHandle.WaitOne(500);
                    // signal the semaphore
                    semaphore.Release(2);
                    Console.WriteLine("Semaphore released");
                }
                // if we reach this point, we know the task has been cancelled
                tokenSource.Token.ThrowIfCancellationRequested();
            }, tokenSource.Token);

            // ask the user to press return before we cancel
            // the token and bring the tasks to an end
            Console.WriteLine("Press enter to cancel tasks");
            Console.ReadLine();

            // cancel the token source and wait for the tasks
            tokenSource.Cancel();

            // wait for input before exiting
            Console.WriteLine("Press enter to finish");
            Console.ReadLine();
        }
    }
}
```

There are no guarantees about which of the waiting Tasks will be released when the Release() method is called. If you compile and run the listing, you will see something similar to the following output, which illustrates that the order in which Tasks call the Wait() method has no relationship to the order in which they are released:

...

Semaphore released

Task 4 released

Task 3 released

Semaphore released

Task 6 released

Task 9 released

Semaphore released

Task 10 released

Task 7 released

Semaphore released

Task 2 released

Task 4 released

...

If there are no Tasks waiting when you call Release(),the event remains set until the Wait() method has been called. If you specified a number to release by providing an integer argument, the event remains set until the Wait() method has been called the number of times you specified.

Using the Parallel Producer/Consumer Pattern

One of the most common coordination techniques is called the *Producer/Consumer pattern*. One group of Tasks (the *producers*) creates data items that are processed by another group of Tasks (the *consumers*).

The flow of work from the producers to the consumers is mediated by a collection, typically a queue: producers place work items in the collection so that the consumers can remove and process them. At any given moment, the content of the collection represents the outstanding work items (i.e., those which have been produced, but have yet to be consumed) is the content. A synchronization primitive is used so that the producers can signal the consumers when work items are available to be processed.

The collection and primitive combination is valuable because it allows us to decouple the production from the consumption of items. We can vary the ratio of producer and consumer Tasks based on the relative time taken to produce or consume an item. We can use the number of outstanding items to regulate production if consumption gets backed up. We can use the collection to smooth out the effects of peaks and troughs on one side of the equation or the other.

     `System.Collections.Concurrent.BlockingCollection` combines the collection and the synchronization primitive into one class, which makes it ideal for implementing the producer/consumer pattern.

Creating the Pattern

We need three things to create the basic producer/consumer implementation: producer and consumer `Tasks` and an instance of `BlockingCollection` to handle the coordination. Listing 4-19 illustrates how to create and use all three.

Listing 4-19. Creating a Producer/Consumer Implementation

```
using System;
using System.Collections.Concurrent;
using System.Threading.Tasks;

namespace Listing_19 {

    class BankAccount {
        public int Balance {
            get;
            set;
        }
    }

    class Deposit {
        public int Amount {
            get;
            set;
        }
    }

    class Listing_19 {

        static void Main(string[] args) {


            // create the blocking collection
            BlockingCollection<Deposit> blockingCollection
                = new BlockingCollection<Deposit>();

            // create and start the producers, which will generate
            // deposits and place them into the collection
            Task[] producers = new Task[3];
            for (int i = 0; i < 3; i++) {
                producers[i] = Task.Factory.StartNew(() => {
                    // create a series of deposits
                    for (int j = 0; j < 20; j++) {
                        // create the transfer
                        Deposit deposit = new Deposit { Amount = 100 };
```

```
                                    // place the transfer in the collection
                                    blockingCollection.Add(deposit);
                                }
                        });
                };

                // create a many to one continuation that will signal
                // the end of production to the consumer
                Task.Factory.ContinueWhenAll(producers, antecedents => {
                    // signal that production has ended
                    Console.WriteLine("Signalling production end");
                    blockingCollection.CompleteAdding();
                });

                // create a bank account
                BankAccount account = new BankAccount();

                // create the consumer, which will update
                // the balance based on the deposits
                Task consumer = Task.Factory.StartNew(() => {
                    while (!blockingCollection.IsCompleted) {
                        Deposit deposit;
                        // try to take the next item
                        if (blockingCollection.TryTake(out deposit)) {
                            // update the balance with the transfer amount
                            account.Balance += deposit.Amount;
                        }
                    }
                    // print out the final balance
                    Console.WriteLine("Final Balance: {0}", account.Balance);
                });

                // wait for the consumer to finish
                consumer.Wait();

                // wait for input before exiting
                Console.WriteLine("Press enter to finish");
                Console.ReadLine();
            }
        }
    }
```

Creating a BlockingCollection instance

The first step in the listing is creating the BlockingCollection, which I have done using the default constructor. The class is strongly typed, so I have had to declare the type that will be in the collection, in this case Deposit.

```
// create the blocking collection
BlockingCollection<Deposit> blockingCollection = new BlockingCollection<Deposit>();
```

The default constructor creates *unbounded* collections, which means that there is no limit to the number of outstanding work items in the collection. The producers can put items in the collection at a much faster rate than the consumers are taking them out again, but the collection will continue to accept new items and let the backlog grow.

You create a *bounded* collection by using a constructor version that takes an `int` argument, as in the following statement:

```
BlockingCollection<Deposit> blockingCollection = new BlockingCollection<Deposit>(5);
```

This creates an instance of `BlockingCollection` that allows up to five items to be in the collection at any given time. If a producer tries to add an item when there are more than five items, the `Add()` method will block until a consumer has removed an item using the `Take()` mTake() method.

Selecting the Collection Type

`BlockingCollection` acts as a wrapper around one of the concurrent collection classes described in the previous chapter. The default constructor causes `BlockingCollection` to use the `ConcurrentQueue` class, but you can use `ConcurrentBag`, `ConcurrentStack`, or any class that implements the `System.Collections.Concurrent.IProducerConsumerCollection` interface.

Changing the underlying collection type that `BlockingCollection` uses will change the order in which the consumers receive items. Using a queue implementation, for example, means that the consumers take the items in the order that the producers added them, while a stack ensures that the most recently added item is consumed first. The following fragment creates a stack-based `BlockingCollection` bounded to five items.

```
ConcurrentStack<Deposit> stack = new ConcurrentStack<Deposit>();
BlockingCollection<Deposit> blockingCollection = new BlockingCollection<Deposit>(stack, 5);
```

Creating the Producers

The next step is to create the producers. In this example, we create three `Tasks` to produce instances of `Deposit` and add them to the collection:

```
// create and start the producers, which will generate
// deposits and place them into the collection
Task[] producers = new Task[3];
for (int i = 0; i < 3; i++) {
    producers[i] = Task.Factory.StartNew(() => {
        // create a series of deposits
        for (int j = 0; j < 20; j++) {
            // create the transfer
            Deposit deposit = new Deposit { Amount = 100 };
            // place the transfer in the collection
            blockingCollection.Add(deposit);
        }
    });
};
```

The producers are very straightforward. Each of the three producer `Tasks` creates twenty deposits and calls the `Add()` method to add them to the `BlockingCollection`.

The `Add()` method will block until `BlockingCollection` accepts the new data item. If another `Task` is trying to add or take an item from the collection, your call to `Add()` will block until the other operation has finished, because all operations on `BlockingCollection` are synchronized. If you have created a bounded collection, this can mean that your producer `Task` will not be able to add a new item until the consumers have cleared the backlog.

The `BlockingCollection` class has a number of methods to add items to the collection, including ones which will block until an item is accepted by the collection or a `CancellationToken` is cancelled. All of the methods are described in Table 4-11.

Table 4-11. Members for Adding Items to BlockingCollection.

Member	Description
`Add(T)` `Add(T, CancellationToken)`	Add an item of type T, blocking until the item is added or the `CancellationToken` is cancelled. Throw an exception if `CompleteAdding()` has been called.

`TryAdd(T)`
 `TryAdd(T, int)`
 `TryAdd(T, TimeSpan)`
 `TryAdd(T, int, CancellationToken)`
	Try to add an item of type T, blocking until the item is added or the specified time period has elapsed or the `CancellationToken` is cancelled. Return `true` if the item was added or `false` if the time expired, the token was cancelled, or `CompleteAdding()` has been called.

Creating the Consumer

The producer/consumer model allows for asymmetry between the number of producers and the number of consumers. This can be useful if it takes a different amount of time to create an item than to consume it, for example. Listing 4-19 created a single consumer, as follows:

```
Task consumer = Task.Factory.StartNew(() => {
    while (!blockingCollection.IsCompleted) {
        Deposit deposit;
        // try to take the next item
        if (blockingCollection.TryTake(out deposit)) {
            // update the balance with the transfer amount
            account.Balance += deposit.Amount;
        }
    }
    // print out the final balance
    Console.WriteLine("Final Balance: {0}", account.Balance);
});
```

The consumer `Task` enters a loop while the `BlockingCollection.IsCompleted` property returns `false`. You'll notice that I created a continuation `Task` for the producers in Listing 4-19. The continuation contains one statement of code, as follows:

```
blockingCollection.CompleteAdding();
```

The CompleteAdding() method tells BlockingCollection that we won't be adding any more items. The producers in Listing 4-19 create a finite number of items, in this case, 60 instances of Deposit. When all of the items have been created and added to the BlockingCollection, the producer Tasks finish, and the continuation Task is scheduled.

The IsCompleted property returns true when CompleteAdding() has been called and no items are in the collection, meaning that production and consumption have both been completed. This mechanism is a useful means of allowing the production side of the pattern to signal the consumer side when production ends without having to couple the Tasks together directly. Table 4-12 summarizes the three members available for signaling in this way.

Table 4-12. Members for Signalling the End of Production to BlockingCollection

Member	Description
CompleteAdding()	Signal that production has ended.
IsAddingComplete	Return true if the CompleteAdding() method has been called.
IsCompleted	Return true if CompleteAdding() has been called and there are no items in the collection

While in the loop, the consumer calls TryTake() to retrieve an item from the collection. This method returns true if an item was taken successfully and assigns the item to the out parameter.

We could have used the Take() method, which blocks until an item is available for consumption in the collection. However, there is a race condition when calling Take() on a BlockingCollection if you use the CompleteAdding() method to signal that production has ended. See the "Common Problems and Their Causes" section at the end of this chapter for an example of this.

■ **Caution** Once you have called CompleteAdding(), further calls to Add() or TryAdd() will throw an exception. Equally, once IsCompleted returns true, calls to Take() or TryTake() will also throw an exception.

The BlockingCollection<T>.GetConsumingEnumerable() method returns an IEnumerable<T> instance that blocks until an item is available and allows the BlockingCollection instance to be used as the source in a foreach loop. You can see an example of this in Listing 4-21 in the following section. Table 4-13 summarizes the methods available to take items from BlockingCollection.

Table 4-13. Members for Taking an Item from BlockingCollection

Member	Description
Take() Take(CancellationToken)	Take an item from the collection, blocking until one becomes available or the CancellationToken is cancelled. Throw an exception if CompleteAdding() has been called and there are no items in the collection.
TryTake(out T) TryTake(out T, int) TryTake(out T, TimeSpan) TryTake(out T, int, CancellationToken)	Try to take an item from the collection; assign it to the out parameter, and block until one becomes available, the specified time elapses, or the CancellationToken is cancelled. Return true if an item was taken or false if the time period elapsed, the token was cancelled or CompleteAdding() has been called and are no items are in the collection.
GetConsumingEnumerable() GetConsumingEnumerable(CancellationToken)	Return IEnumerable<T> for the items in the collection that will block until an item is available to be taken, the collection is complete (i.e., CompleteAdding() has been called and there are no items in the collection), or the token has been cancelled.

Combining Multiple Collections

Listing 4-19 used a single instance of BlockingCollection to mediate between the producer and consumer Tasks, but BlockingCollection also contains members that allow multiple instances to be used together seamlessly as a single entity. Table 4-14 describes the members of BlockingCollection<T> that enable combined collections.

Table 4-14. Members for Combining BlockingCollections

Member	Description
AddToAny(BlockingCollection<T>[], T) AddToAny(BlockingCollection<T>[], T, CancellationToken)	Add an item of type T to any one of the BlockingCollection<T>s specified, blocking until the item has been added to a collection or the CancellationToken has been cancelled. Return an int representing the array index of the BlockingCollection to which the item was added. Throw an exception if the item cannot be added to any of the collections.

Member	Description
TryAddToAny(BlockingCollection<T>[], T) TryAddToAny(BlockingCollection<T>[], T, int) TryAddToAny(BlockingCollection<T>[], T, Timespan) TryAddToAny(BlockingCollection<T>[], T, int, CancellationToken)	Add an item of type T to any one of the BlockingCollection<T> instances specified, blocking until the item has been added to a collection, the specified time period has elapsed, or the CancellationToken has been cancelled. Return an int representing the array index of the BlockingCollection to which the item was added, or return -1 if the item could not be added to any of the collections.
TakeFromAny(BlockingCollection<T>[], out T) TakeFromAny(BlockingCollection<T>[], out T, CancellationToken)	Take an item from any one of the BlockingCollection<T>s specified, and assign it to the out parameter. Block until the item is taken and assigned or until the token is cancelled. Return an int representing the array index of the BlockingCollection from which the item was taken. Throw an exception if an item cannot be taken from any of the collections.
TryTakeFromAny(BlockingCollection<T>[], out T) TryTakeFromAny(BlockingCollection<T>[], out T, int) TryTakeFromAny(BlockingCollection<T>[], out T, Timespam) TryTakeFromAny(BlockingCollection<T>[], out T, CancellationToken)	Take an item from any one of the BlockingCollection<T> instances specified, and assign it to the out parameter. Block until the item is taken and assigned, the time period elapses, or until the token is cancelled. Return an int representing the array index of the BlockingCollection from which the item was taken or -1 if an item could not be taken.

There are two common uses for collections combined in this way. The first is when you have a large number of Tasks or a high item-production rate. Adding and taking from the collection involves synchronization, and you may see performance problems if you have a lots of calls being made to Add() or Take(). The second use is when you want to keep items from different producers separate but have them processed by a single set of consumers. Listing 4-20 demonstrates both approaches.

Listing 4-20. Using Multiple BlockingCollection Instances

```
using System;
using System.Collections.Concurrent;
using System.Threading;
using System.Threading.Tasks;

namespace Listing_20 {

    class Listing_20 {
```

```
static void Main(string[] args) {

    // create a pair of blocking collections
    // that will be used to pass strings
    BlockingCollection<string> bc1 = new BlockingCollection<string>();
    BlockingCollection<string> bc2 = new BlockingCollection<string>();

    // create another blocking collection
    // that will be used to pass ints
    BlockingCollection<string> bc3 = new BlockingCollection<string>();

    // create two arrays of the blocking collections
    BlockingCollection<string>[] bc1and2 = {bc1, bc2};
    BlockingCollection<string>[] bcAll   = {bc1, bc2, bc3};

    // create a cancellation token source
    CancellationTokenSource tokenSource = new CancellationTokenSource();


    // create the first set of producers
    for (int i = 0; i < 5; i++) {
        Task.Factory.StartNew(() => {
            while (!tokenSource.IsCancellationRequested) {
                // compose the message
                string message
                    = String.Format("Message from task {0}", Task.CurrentId);
                // add the message to either collection
                BlockingCollection<string>.AddToAny(bc1and2,
                    message, tokenSource.Token);
                // put the task to sleep
                tokenSource.Token.WaitHandle.WaitOne(1000);
            }
        }, tokenSource.Token);
    }

    // create the second set of producers
    for (int i = 0; i < 3; i++) {
        Task.Factory.StartNew(() => {
            while (!tokenSource.IsCancellationRequested) {
                // compose the message
                string warning
                    = String.Format("Warning from task {0}", Task.CurrentId);
                // add the message to either collection
                bc3.Add(warning, tokenSource.Token);
                // put the task to sleep for 500ms
                tokenSource.Token.WaitHandle.WaitOne(500);
            }
        }, tokenSource.Token);
    }
```

```
        // create the consumers
        for (int i = 0; i < 2; i++) {
            Task consumer = Task.Factory.StartNew(() => {
                string item;
                while (!tokenSource.IsCancellationRequested) {
                    // take an item from any collection
                    int bcid = BlockingCollection<string>.TakeFromAny(bcAll,
                        out item, tokenSource.Token);
                    // write out the item to the console
                    Console.WriteLine("From collection {0}: {1}", bcid, item);
                }
            }, tokenSource.Token);
        }

        // prompt the user to press enter
        Console.WriteLine("Press enter to cancel tasks");
        Console.ReadLine();
        // cancel the token
        tokenSource.Cancel();

        // wait for input before exiting
        Console.WriteLine("Press enter to finish");
        Console.ReadLine();
    }
}
}
```

Three `BlockingCollections` are used in this example: two are use by one set of producers (simulating messages being sent) and the third by a different set of producers (simulating warnings being sent).

The first two `BlockingCollections` are used as a single entity by the message producers. Items are added using the static `BlockingCollection<string>.AddToAny()` method. This method takes an array of `BlockingCollections` and checks them in turn to see which will accept an item immediately. Note that the `AddToAny()` method is only available on strongly typed instances of `BlockingCollection`. Therefore, you must call `BlockingCollection<T>.AddtoAny()` and not `BlockingCollection.AddToAny()`, *and* you can't treat differently typed instances of `BlockingCollection` as a single entity.

The consumer treats all three `BlockingCollections` as a single entity by calling the static method `BlockingCollection<string>.TakeFromAny()`, which returns an item from the first collection that has one available. In this way, the consumer is able to receive items from both groups of producers as they become available.

■ **Note** There are no guarantees about the order in which items are taken from `BlockingCollections` when they are being treated as a single entity.

Using a Custom Task Scheduler

The *task scheduler* is the point at which tasks and threads meet, and it is responsible for assigning threads to execute your Tasks and deciding how many Tasks will be executed in parallel and in which order.

As Chapter 1 explained, the TPL is built on the foundation of the classic threading features, and you have to understand these to build a custom scheduler. I am not going to explain the classic features in this book, but I will show you how to use them to create a custom scheduler.

This is an advanced topic, and you don't need to worry if you don't know how to use the classic threads or can't follow the explanation in this section. You can skip this section and still write effective parallel programs, because the .NET Framework's default scheduler is exceptionally sophisticated. In fact, my advice is to use the default scheduler and not implement a custom replacement. It is possible that you will be able to squeeze a little more performance out of your program with a custom scheduler, but the default scheduler is very competent, and any performance gain is likely to be marginal and offset by the need to test and maintain it for every platform to which your application is deployed.

Creating a Custom Scheduler

Custom task schedulers derive from the System.Threading.Tasks.TaskScheduler class. Table 4-15 describes the key members of the TaskScheduler class, but the most important members are the QueueTask() and the TryExecuteTask() methods.

Table 4-15. Key Members of the TaskScheduler Class

Member	Description
QueueTask()	This method is called by the TPL when a Task has been created and requires execution.
TryExecuteTask()	This one is called by the scheduler to (synchronously) execute a Task that has been previously passed to the scheduler via the QueueTask() method. The Task will not be executed if it is already executing or has already been executed. It returns true if the task was executed.
TryExecuteTaskInLine()	This is called by the TPL to request that a Task be executed inline, and returns true if your scheduler executes the Task or false otherwise.
GetScheduledTasks()	This method returns an enumeration of Tasks that are waiting to be executed.
TryDequeue()	Try to remove a Task from the queue with this method, which returns true if the Task was removed.
Current	Static property that returns the TaskScheduler for the current Task. Returns the value from the Default property if called outside of a Task.
Default	This static property returns the default TPL TaskScheduler.

Member	Description
MaximumConcurrencyLevel	This method returns the maximum number of Tasks that the scheduler will execute in parallel.
Id	Returns a unique int identifier for the scheduler with this method.
UnobservedTaskException	This static event \can be used to create a custom exception escalation policy; see Chapter 1 for details.

The QueueTask() method is called by the TPL when a new Task has been created and is ready to be executed. You call the TryExecuteTask() method when your custom scheduler is ready to execute a Task. The purpose of the task scheduler is to implement some kind of policy that determines what happens between the time a Task arrives via QueueTask() and the time it's executed via TryExecuteTask().

Task schedulers use a collection to store Tasks as they arrive from the TPL via the QueueTask() method. One or more System.Threading.Threads polls the collection looking for Tasks, and if one is waiting, the thread takes the Task from the collection and executes it using the TryExecuteTask() method.

The implementation design of the task scheduler determines how many threads are available to execute queued Tasks, and the type of collection determines the order in which the Tasks are executed. For example, a using queue would mean that the tasks are executed in the order in which they arrive, while using a stack would mean that the most recently arrived Task would be executed first.

You don't have to worry about the detail of executing Tasks, handling exceptions or cancellations, looking for continuation or child Tasks, and so on—all of this is taken care of by the TryExecuteTask() method. You just write the code that maps Tasks to the Threads that will call TryExecuteTask().

Listing 4-21 demonstrates a simple custom task scheduler, imaginatively called CustomScheduler. A BlockingCollection stores the queued Tasks, and the default constructor is called, which creates an unbounded BlockingCollection instance that uses a ConcurrentQueue to store items. The CustomScheduler constructor takes an int parameter, which defines how many Tasks the task scheduler will execute at once—the *maximum concurrency* of our scheduler.

We create a number of Threads equal to the maximum concurrency. The Threads call the GetConsumingEnumerable() method of BlockingCollection and use the resulting IEnumerable as the basis for a foreach loop. The GetConsumingEnumerable() method returns an IEnumerable that blocks until there is an item available to be taken from the BlockingCollection or until the collection is complete (the CompleteAdding() method has been called, and no items are in the collection). When a Task is taken from the BlockingCollection, the Thread calls the TryExecuteTask() method.

Since TryExecuteTask() blocks while the Task is executed, the number of Threads limits how many Tasks can be performed simultaneously. A Thread is either free (waiting for a new Task to arrive in the queue) or busy (executing a Task). When all of the Threads are busy, new Tasks remain in the BlockingCollection until one of the Threads becomes free again. The Threads are created and started when the CustomScheduler instance is created but do nothing until Tasks are scheduled using the QueueTask() method.

Our implementation of QueueTask() checks to see if the Task passed, because the method parameter has been created using TaskCreationOptions.LongRunning enumeration value. You may recall from Chapter 2 that this value indicates a Task that is expected to run for a long time to complete (or may never complete). Using the creation values is optional, but it makes the life of the task scheduler simpler.

A long-running Task would tie up one of my execution Threads, effectively reducing the maximum concurrency of our scheduler. If we have carefully worked out that we need, say, four Threads to get the best performance for our program and we end up with three Threads because one has been tied up by a long running Task, we won't get the behavior we had hoped for.

To avoid this problem, we look for the LongRunning value, and if it has been used, we create a dedicated Thread to execute the Task. If the LongRunning value has not been used, we add the Task to the BlockingCollection so that it can be picked up and processed by one of our regular Threads.

■ **Note** The code in Listing 4-21 cannot be executed on its own. See Listing 4-22 for an example of how to use the customer scheduler in Listing 4-21.

Listing 4-21. *A Custom Task Scheduler*

```
using System;
using System.Collections.Concurrent;
using System.Collections.Generic;
using System.Linq;
using System.Threading;
using System.Threading.Tasks;

namespace Listing_21 {

    public class CustomScheduler: TaskScheduler, IDisposable {
        private BlockingCollection<Task> taskQueue;
        private Thread[] threads;

        public CustomScheduler(int concurrency) {
            // initialize the collection and the thread array
            taskQueue = new BlockingCollection<Task>();
            threads = new Thread[concurrency];
            // create and start the threads
            for (int i = 0; i < threads.Length; i++) {
                (threads[i] = new Thread(() => {
                    // loop while the blocking collection is not
                    // complete and try to execute the next task
                    foreach (Task t in taskQueue.GetConsumingEnumerable()) {
                        TryExecuteTask(t);
                    }
                })).Start();
            }
        }

        protected override void QueueTask(Task task) {
            if (task.CreationOptions.HasFlag(TaskCreationOptions.LongRunning)) {
                // create a dedicated thread to execute this task
                new Thread(() => {
                    TryExecuteTask(task);
                }).Start();
            } else {
```

```
            // add the task to the queue
            taskQueue.Add(task);
        }
    }

    protected override bool TryExecuteTaskInline(Task task,
        bool taskWasPreviouslyQueued) {
        // only allow inline execution if the executing thread is one
        // belonging to this scheduler
        if (threads.Contains(Thread.CurrentThread)) {
            return TryExecuteTask(task);
        } else {
            return false;
        }
    }

    public override int MaximumConcurrencyLevel {
        get {
            return threads.Length;
        }
    }

    protected override IEnumerable<Task> GetScheduledTasks() {
        return taskQueue.ToArray();
    }

    public void Dispose() {
        // mark the collection as complete
        taskQueue.CompleteAdding();
        // wait for each of the threads to finish
        foreach (Thread t in threads) {
            t.Join();
        }
    }
}
}
```

The CustomScheduler constructor and QueueTask() method handle the bulk of the scheduling, but they are not the only members required to implement TaskScheduler.

The TryExecuteTaskInline() method is called by the TPL if a Task that is being executed calls Wait() on another Task. Rather than wait until the second Task reaches the head of the queue and is executed (which could take a while), the TPL asks the scheduler if it is willing to let the second Task jump the queue and execute it straight away. This is called *inline execution*, and a Task executed in this way is said to have been *implicitly inlined*. TryExecuteTaskInline() is also called if one Task calls RunSynchronously() on another Task. The second task is said to be *explicitly inlined*.

The arguments to the TryExecuteTaskInline() are the Task that the TPL wants to jump the queue and a bool indicating if the Task has already been passed to the QueueTask() method. The Boolean value will be true for implicitly inlined Tasks and false for explicitly inlined Tasks. The scheduler is not required to execute the Task, but doing so can improve performance by altering the order in which Tasks are executed so that they are performed in the order they are required, rather than the order in which they were created.

In Listing 4-21, we allow inline execution when the request comes from one of our scheduler `Threads`, but not otherwise. For example, when the main application thread calls `Task.Wait()`, the `Task` will not be inlined; instead, it will be put in the queue and dealt with in the usual order.

You don't need to remove a `Task` from your scheduler queue if it has been passed to the `QueueTask()` method and later requested for inline execution. The `TryExecuteTask()` method will only execute a `Task` if it is not already running or has not already been run, so the `Task` will be performed only once.

■ **Tip** Aside from improving performance, inline execution can be used to avoid a common problem with task schedulers. See the "Common Problems and Their Causes" section at the end of this chapter for details.

The `MaximumConcurrencyLevel` property reports the maximum number of `Task`s that will be executed in parallel. In our example, this is the number of `Thread`s that were created. The `GetScheduledTasks()` method returns a list of pending `Task`s in the queue, which we deal with in Listing 4-21 by calling the `BlockingCollection.ToArray()` method.

The final method in Listing 4-21 is `Dispose()`. It's used to finish the collection by calling `CompleteAdding()`, which causes the `Thread`s to finish when all of the `Task`s in the queue have been executed. We wait for each of the `Thread`s using the `Join()` method.

The scheduler in Listing 4-21 is useful for demonstrating how to write a custom scheduler but not much else. You certainly shouldn't use it for your parallel programs. While useable, `CustomScheduler` doesn't have any of the sophisticated features that are required to get the best performance possible; in particular, it doesn't pay any attention to the relationship between `Task`s and doesn't vary the effective concurrency when all of the `Thread`s are busy.

Using a Custom Scheduler

When you schedule a `Task`, either explicitly by calling the `Start()` method or implicitly when calling `Task.Factory.StartNew()`, the TPL will pass the `Task` to the scheduler returned by the static `TaskScheduler.Current` property.

`TaskScheduler.Current` returns the default TPL scheduler if called outside of a `Task`. If the property is called within a `Task`, it returns the scheduler of the `Task` in which the call was made. This means that once you have scheduled a `Task` using a custom scheduler, any new `Task`s you create in the task body will be scheduled using that same custom scheduler.

You can specify the scheduler the TPL should use for a `Task`. All of the methods that allow you to schedule a `Task` (`Task.Start()`, `Task.Factory.StartNew()`, `Task.ContinueWith()`, `Task.Factory.ContinueWhenAll()`, etc.) have a version that lets you specify a scheduler, which can be a custom scheduler or the TPL default. Listing 4-22 demonstrates how to control which scheduler is used for some of these methods.

Listing 4-22. Using a Custom Scheduler

```
using System;
using System.Threading;
using System.Threading.Tasks;
using Listing_21;
```

```
namespace Listing_22 {

    class Listing_22 {

        static void Main(string[] args) {

            // get the processor count for the system
            int procCount = System.Environment.ProcessorCount;

            // create a custom scheduler
            CustomScheduler scheduler = new CustomScheduler(procCount);

            Console.WriteLine("Custom scheduler ID: {0}", scheduler.Id);
            Console.WriteLine("Default scheduler ID: {0}", TaskScheduler.Default.Id);

            // create a cancellation token source
            CancellationTokenSource tokenSource = new CancellationTokenSource();

            // create a task
            Task task1 = new Task(() => {

                Console.WriteLine("Task {0} executed by scheduler {1}",
                        Task.CurrentId, TaskScheduler.Current.Id);

                // create a child task - this will use the same
                // scheduler as its parent
                Task.Factory.StartNew(() => {
                    Console.WriteLine("Task {0} executed by scheduler {1}",
                        Task.CurrentId, TaskScheduler.Current.Id);
                });

                // create a child and specify the default scheduler
                Task.Factory.StartNew(() => {
                    Console.WriteLine("Task {0} executed by scheduler {1}",
                        Task.CurrentId, TaskScheduler.Current.Id);
                }, tokenSource.Token, TaskCreationOptions.None, TaskScheduler.Default);

            });

            // start the task using the custom scheduler
            task1.Start(scheduler);

            // create a continuation - this will use the default scheduler
            task1.ContinueWith(antecedent => {
                Console.WriteLine("Task {0} executed by scheduler {1}",
                    Task.CurrentId, TaskScheduler.Current.Id);
            });
```

```
            // create a continuation using the custom scheduler
            task1.ContinueWith(antecedent => {
                Console.WriteLine("Task {0} executed by scheduler {1}",
                    Task.CurrentId, TaskScheduler.Current.Id);
            }, scheduler);
        }
    }
}
```

Common Problems and Their Causes

Successfully coordinating Tasks requires thought and care and mistakes are common. This section describes and demonstrate some of the most common problems in the hope that you will be able to more quickly determine the cause of a problem when it arises.

Inconsistent/Unchecked Cancellation

Cancellation tokens are used to create antecedent Tasks but not continuations. The continuations are still scheduled, which causes unexpected results and usually leads to unhandled exceptions.

Solution

Either check the status of the antecedent using the Task.Status property, or create antecedents using tokens from the same CancellationTokenSource as the antecedent (in which case the continuation is not performed).

Example

The following example creates a Task that waits until the CancellationToken it has been created with is cancelled. Three continuations are created. The first indicates the problem of not using a cancellation token and not checking the antecedent status; the Result property of the antecedent is read, which cause the continuation Task to throw an unhandled exception. The second continuation uses the same cancellation token source as its antecedent, so it isn't executed when the antecedent is cancelled. The third continuation checks the status of the antecedent and reads the Result property only if the antecedent has not been cancelled.

```
using System;
using System.Threading;
using System.Threading.Tasks;

namespace Inconsistent_Cancellation {
    class Inconsistent_Cancellation {

        static void Main(string[] args) {

            // create a token source
            CancellationTokenSource tokenSource
                = new CancellationTokenSource();
```

```
            // create the antecedent task
            Task<int> task1 = new Task<int>(() => {
                // wait for the token to be cancelled
                tokenSource.Token.WaitHandle.WaitOne();
                // throw the cancellation exception
                tokenSource.Token.ThrowIfCancellationRequested();
                // return the result - this code will
                // never be reached but is required to
                // satisfy the compiler
                return 100;
            }, tokenSource.Token);

            // create a continuation
            // *** BAD CODE ***
            Task task2 = task1.ContinueWith((Task<int> antecedent) => {
                // read the antecedent result without checking
                // the status of the task
                Console.WriteLine("Antecedent result: {0}", antecedent.Result);
            });

            // create a continuation, but use a token
            Task task3 = task1.ContinueWith((Task<int> antecedent) => {
                // this task will never be executed
            }, tokenSource.Token);

            // create a continuation that checks the status
            // of the antecedent
            Task task4 = task1.ContinueWith((Task<int> antecedent) => {
                if (antecedent.Status == TaskStatus.Canceled) {
                    Console.WriteLine("Antecedent cancelled");
                } else {
                    Console.WriteLine("Antecedent Result: {0}", antecedent.Result);
                }
            });

            // prompt the user and cancel the token
            Console.WriteLine("Press enter to cancel token");
            Console.ReadLine();
            tokenSource.Cancel();

            // wait for input before exiting
            Console.WriteLine("Press enter to finish");
            Console.ReadLine();
        }
    }
}
```

Assuming Status on Any-To-One Continuations

The `Task.WaitAny()` method triggers the continuation `Task` when one of the antecedents completes, but completion can include cancellation or an exception being thrown. A common problem arises when a continuation `Task` doesn't check the state of the antecedent.

Solution

This problem is a variation on the previous one, and the solution is similar. Check to see if the antecedent that has triggered the continuation has completed properly, and use common cancellation token sources.

Example

The following example ensures that a cancelled `Task` is the antecedent to a many-to-one continuation that reads the `Result` property without checking the antecedent status. This results in an unhandled exception.

```
using System;
using System.Threading;
using System.Threading.Tasks;

namespace Assuming_WaitAny_Status {
    class Assuming_WaitAny_Status {
        static void Main(string[] args) {

            // create a cancellation token source
            CancellationTokenSource tokenSource
                = new CancellationTokenSource();

            Task<int>[] tasks = new Task<int>[2];

            tasks[0] = new Task<int>(() => {
                while (true) {
                    // sleep
                    Thread.Sleep(100000);
                }
            });

            tasks[1] = new Task<int>(() => {
                // wait for the token to be cancelled
                tokenSource.Token.WaitHandle.WaitOne();
                // throw a cancellation exceptioon
                tokenSource.Token.ThrowIfCancellationRequested();
                // return a result to satisfy the compiler
                return 200;
            }, tokenSource.Token);
```

```
        Task.Factory.ContinueWhenAny(tasks, (Task<int> antecedent) => {
            Console.WriteLine("Result of antecedent is {0}",
                antecedent.Result);
        });

        // start the tasks
        tasks[1].Start();
        tasks[0].Start();

        // prompt the user and cancel the token
        Console.WriteLine("Press enter to cancel token");
        Console.ReadLine();
        tokenSource.Cancel();

        // wait for input before exiting
        Console.WriteLine("Press enter to finish");
        Console.ReadLine();
    }
    }
}
```

Trying to Take Concurrently

A common problem when consuming items from a `BlockingCollection` is to enter a loop while the `IsCompleted` property returns `false` and call the blocking `Take()` method to remove items from the collection. This creates a potential race condition, such that:

- No items waiting to be processed.

- The consumer checks the `IsCompleted` property and gets `false`.

- The producer calls the `CompleteAdding()` method.

- The consumer calls `Take()`.

This sequence causes an exception to be thrown. Between the call to `IsCompleted` and `Take()`, the producer has completed the collection and attempts to `Take()` from a completed collection result in an exception.

Solution

Use the `TryTake()` method. See Listing 4-19 for an example.

Example

The following example demonstrates the race condition:

```
using System;
using System.Collections.Concurrent;
using System.Threading.Tasks;

namespace Trying_To_Take_Concurrently {
```

```
class Trying_To_Take_Concurrently {
    static void Main(string[] args) {

        // create a blocking collection
        BlockingCollection<int> blockingCollection
            = new BlockingCollection<int>();

        // create and start a producer
        Task.Factory.StartNew(() => {
            // put items into the collectioon
            for (int i = 0; i < 1000; i++) {
                blockingCollection.Add(i);
            }
            // mark the collection as complete
            blockingCollection.CompleteAdding();
        });

        // create and start a producer
        Task.Factory.StartNew(() => {
            while (!blockingCollection.IsCompleted) {
                // take an item from the collection
                int item = blockingCollection.Take();
                // print out the item
                Console.WriteLine("Item {0}", item);
            }
        });

        // wait for input before exiting
        Console.WriteLine("Press enter to finish");
        Console.ReadLine();
    }
}
}
```

Reusing Objects in Producers

A frequently used optimization in C# is to reuse objects. This is done to avoid the overhead of creating and subsequently disposing of new instances. No issues arise when this technique is applied to a consumer taking items from a `BlockingCollection`, but it cannot be safely applied to a producer. Doing so adds the same instance to the collection again and again, and each time the producer changes the fields of the object, the change applies to every reference currently unprocessed in the collection.

Solution

Don't reuse objects in a producer.

Example

The following example shows how reusing objects in the producer causes odd behavior in the consumer:

```csharp
using System;
using System.Collections.Concurrent;
using System.Threading.Tasks;

namespace Reusing_Objects_in_Producers {

    class DataItem {

        public int Counter {
            get;
            set;
        }
    }

    class Reusing_Objects_in_Producers {
        static void Main(string[] args) {

            // create a blocking collection
            BlockingCollection<DataItem> blockingCollection
                = new BlockingCollection<DataItem>();

            // create and start a consumer
            Task consumer = Task.Factory.StartNew(() => {
                // define a data item to use in the loop
                DataItem item;
                while (!blockingCollection.IsCompleted) {
                    if (blockingCollection.TryTake(out item)) {
                        Console.WriteLine("Item counter {0}", item.Counter);
                    }
                }
            });

            // create and start a producer
            Task.Factory.StartNew(() => {
                // create a data item to use in the loop
                DataItem item = new DataItem();
                for (int i = 0; i < 100; i++) {
                    // set the numeric value
                    item.Counter = i;
                    // add the item to the collection
                    blockingCollection.Add(item);
                }
                // mark the collection as finished
                blockingCollection.CompleteAdding();
            });

            // wait for the consumer to finish
            consumer.Wait();
```

```
                // wait for input before exiting
                Console.WriteLine("Press enter to finish");
                Console.ReadLine();
            }
        }
    }
}
```

Using BlockingCollection as IEnumerable

The `BlockingCollection` class can be used with `foreach` loops to allow consumers to safely take items from the collection. However, the input to the loop must be the result of the `BlockingCollection.GetConsumingEnumerable` method and not the collection itself.

If the collection is used, the `foreach` loop will immediately exit if it is executed before the first item has been added to the collection by the producer. The `BlockingCollection` class implements the `IEnumerable<>` interface, so the compiler will not generate an error for this problem.

Solution

Either use the `IsComplete` and `TryTake()` members, or ensure that the enumeration for `foreach` loops always comes from the `GetConsumingEnumerable()` method.

Example

The following example delays the production of items by 500 milliseconds to ensure that the consumer calls `foreach` before the first item is added to the collection. The loop in the consumer `Task` body returns, and the consumer does not process any of the items that are subsequently added to the collection.

```
using System;
using System.Collections.Concurrent;
using System.Threading.Tasks;

namespace Using_BlockingCollection_as_IEnum {
    class Using_BlockingCollection_as_IEnum {
        static void Main(string[] args) {

            // create a blocking collection
            BlockingCollection<int> blockingCollection
                = new BlockingCollection<int>();

            // create and start a producer
            Task.Factory.StartNew(() => {
                // put the producer to sleep
                System.Threading.Thread.Sleep(500);
                for (int i = 0; i < 100; i++) {
                    // add the item to the collection
                    blockingCollection.Add(i);
                }
                // mark the collection as finished
                blockingCollection.CompleteAdding();
            });
```

```
            // create and start a consumer
            Task consumer = Task.Factory.StartNew(() => {
                // use a foreach loop to consume the blocking collection
                foreach (int i in blockingCollection) {
                    Console.WriteLine("Item {0}", i);
                }
                Console.WriteLine("Collection is fully consumed");
            });


            // wait for the consumer to finish
            consumer.Wait();

            // wait for input before exiting
            Console.WriteLine("Press enter to finish");
            Console.ReadLine();

        }
    }
}
```

Deadlocked Task Scheduler

Custom task schedulers are often written with no means of expanding the number of threads available. This causes deadlock when there are more Task dependencies than free threads.

Solution

Task schedulers should either allow inline execution or be able to add to the set of regular execution threads to cope with complex waiting relationships.

Example

The following demonstrates a custom task scheduler that maintains a fixed number of threads and does not allow inline execution. The code that tests the scheduler will cause a deadlock, because there are more waiting Tasks than there are working threads.

```
using System;
using System.Collections.Concurrent;
using System.Collections.Generic;
using System.Threading;
using System.Threading.Tasks;

namespace Deadlocked_Task_Scheduler {

    class Deadlocked_Task_Scheduler: TaskScheduler, IDisposable {
        private BlockingCollection<Task> taskQueue;
        private Thread[] threads;
```

```
public Deadlocked_Task_Scheduler(int concurrency) {
    // initialize the collection and the thread array
    taskQueue = new BlockingCollection<Task>();
    threads = new Thread[concurrency];
    // create and start the threads
    for (int i = 0; i < threads.Length; i++) {
        (threads[i] = new Thread(() => {
            // loop while the blocking collection is not
            // complete and try to execute the next task
            foreach (Task t in taskQueue.GetConsumingEnumerable()) {
                TryExecuteTask(t);
            }
        })).Start();
    }
}

protected override void QueueTask(Task task) {
    if (task.CreationOptions.HasFlag(TaskCreationOptions.LongRunning)) {
        // create a dedicated thread to execute this task
        new Thread(() => {
            TryExecuteTask(task);
        }).Start();
    } else {
        // add the task to the queue
        taskQueue.Add(task);
    }
}

protected override bool TryExecuteTaskInline(Task task,
    bool taskWasPreviouslyQueued) {

    // disallow all inline execution
    return false;
}

public override int MaximumConcurrencyLevel {
    get {
        return threads.Length;
    }
}

protected override IEnumerable<Task> GetScheduledTasks() {
    return taskQueue.ToArray();
}
```

```csharp
    public void Dispose() {
        // mark the collection as complete
        taskQueue.CompleteAdding();
        // wait for each of the threads to finish
        foreach (Thread t in threads) {
            t.Join();
        }
    }
}


class Test_Deadlocked_Task_Scheduler {
    static void Main(string[] args) {

        // create the scheduler
        Deadlocked_Task_Scheduler scheduler
            = new Deadlocked_Task_Scheduler(5);

        // create a token source
        CancellationTokenSource tokenSource =
            new CancellationTokenSource();

        Task[] tasks = new Task[6];

        for (int i = 0; i < tasks.Length; i++) {
            tasks[i] = Task.Factory.StartNew((object stateObj) => {
                int index = (int)stateObj;
                if (index < tasks.Length - 1) {
                    Console.WriteLine("Task {0} waiting for {1}", index, index + 1);
                    tasks[index + 1].Wait();
                }
                Console.WriteLine("Task {0} complete", index);
            }, i, tokenSource.Token, TaskCreationOptions.None, scheduler);
        }

        Task.WaitAll(tasks);
        Console.WriteLine("All tasks complete");

        // wait for input before exiting
        Console.WriteLine("Press enter to finish");
        Console.ReadLine();
    }
}
}
```

Summary

In this chapter, we have seen how the basic building blocks of the TPL can be used to create sophisticated parallel programs. Continuations and child tasks allow you to connect together pieces of work that are performed only when your criteria are met. We also looked at some of the more advanced synchronization techniques. These are tools that you will use again and again to ensure predictable execution of your code.

This chapter also introduced the parallel consumer/producer pattern, which is one of the most useful and flexible techniques available in parallel programming and mastering its use will help you build more reliable and better performing applications. It can take a while to get your head around this pattern, but it is time well spent.

We finished up by looking at how to write a customer scheduler. I included this because it gives a good demonstration of how the TPL is built on top of the legacy threading support. If you didn't understand how the scheduler worked, or just weren't that interested, and don't worry. You are extremely unlikely to need to write your own scheduler for most projects.

The theme of building complex functionality out of basic building blocks continues in the next chapter when we turn our attention to parallel loops. These are implemented using the classes and techniques you have seen in this and previous chapters and can be extremely useful.

CHAPTER 5

■ ■ ■

Parallel Loops

Listing 5-1. A Parallel For Loop

```csharp
using System;
using System.Threading.Tasks;

namespace Listing_01 {

    class Listing_01 {

        static void Main(string[] args) {

            // create the arrays to hold the data and the results
            int[] dataItems = new int[100];
            double[] resultItems = new double[100];

            // create the data items
            for (int i = 0; i < dataItems.Length; i++) {
                dataItems[i] = i;
            }

            // process the data in a parallel for loop
            Parallel.For(0, dataItems.Length, (index) => {
                resultItems[index] =  Math.Pow(dataItems[index],2);
            });

            // wait for input before exiting
            Console.WriteLine("Press enter to finish");
            Console.ReadLine();
        }
    }
}
```

Parallel vs. Sequential Loops

For and foreach loops are cornerstones of C# development, and it doesn't take long for a new
programmer to reach the point where they become a frequently used (and sometimes abused!) tool. The

for and foreach keywords create *sequential loops*, so called because an iteration isn't started until the previous iteration has completed.

The TPL contains support for *parallel loops*; that is to say, loops in which the iterations are performed with some degree of concurrency. You can see a simple example in Listing 5-1, which calculates the squares of 100 integer values. Because this is a parallel loop, some of the calculations will be performed in parallel.

In this chapter, I'll show you how to create and use parallel loops, starting with basic loops like the one in Listing 5-1 and working up to more complex permutations. This topic is a strange, because parallel loops are a convenience abstraction, built out of the features we have explored in the previous chapters. Once you have mastered them, you will find parallel loops convenient, easy to use, and often simpler than Tasks for some types of programming problem. But in order to attain that simplicity, there is a lot of information to take in. Table 5-1 summarizes the key sections of this chapter.

Table 5-1. Parallel Loops and Actions

Problem	Solution	Listing
Perform actions concurrently.	Use the `Parallel.Invoke()` method.	5-2
Concurrently iterate over a series of integer values.	Use the `Parallel.For()` method.	5-1 and 5- 3
Concurrently process a series of items in an array or collection.	Use the `Parallel.ForEach()` method.	5-4
Iterate over a series of stepped integer values.	Use the `yield` keyword to create a custom `IEnumerable<>` that produced stepped integer results. Use with the `Parallel.ForEach()` method.	5-5
Limit concurrency for parallel loops or specify a custom task scheduler.	Create an instance of `ParallelOptions`, set the appropriate properties, and pass it as an argument to `Parallel.For()` or `Parallel.ForEach()`.	5-6
Break out of a parallel loop.	Create an instance of `ParallelLoopState`, pass it as an argument to `Parallel.For()` or `Parallel.ForEach()`, and call either the `Break()` or `Stop()` methods.	5-7 and 5-8
Check loop status.	Check the properties of the `ParallelLoopResult` instance returned as the result from the `Parallel.For()` and `Parallel.ForEach()` methods.	5-9
Cancel a parallel loop.	Create an instance of `ParallelOptions`, and set the `CacellationToken` property. Pass the options as an argument to `Parallel.For()` or `Parallel.ForEach()`, and cancel the token.	5-10

Problem	Solution	Listing
Use thread-local storage in a parallel loop.	Use the versions of `Parallel.For()` or `Parallel.Foreach()`, which allow a thread-local variable to be initialized and processed with each iteration of the loop.	5-11 and 5-12
Performing loops with chain dependencies.	Use a combination of sequential and parallel loops.	5-13
Partition data into chunks.	Use the static `Partition.Create()` method.	5-15 and 5-16
Partition data using a custom strategy.	Derive from the `Partition` or `OrderablePartition` classes.	5-17 to 5-26

The Parallel Class

Parallel loops are made possible through the `System.Threading.Tasks.Parallel` class, which will be the focus for much of this chapter. There are no parallel equivalents to the `for` and `foreach` keywords, so parallel loops are performed using methods of the `Parallel` class.

Parallel loops create and manage `Tasks` on your behalf. Knowing how to create and coordinate `Tasks`, you could create your own parallel loops to process data. But you don't need to; the `System.Threading.Tasks.Parallel` class provides some very useful convenience methods that take care of this for you. In this section, I'll take you through how to use this class to achieve useful and effective parallel loops.

Invoking Actions

The most basic feature of the `Parallel` class is the ability to perform actions concurrently via the `Invoke()` method; this feature forms the basis for the parallel `for` and `foreach` loops that we cover in the "Using Parallel Loops" section. Listing 5-2 demonstrates the use of the `Invoke()` method, which takes an array of `System.Actions` to execute. The listing demonstrates `Actions` that are defined anonymously inline and explicitly in an array; it also demonstrates the equivalent statements using the `Task` class explicitly.

Listing 5-2. Performing Actions Using the Parallel.Invoke() Method

```
using System;
using System.Threading.Tasks;

namespace Listing_02 {

    class Listing_02 {

        static void Main(string[] args) {
```

```
            // invoke actions described by lambda expressions
            Parallel.Invoke(
                () => Console.WriteLine("Action 1"),
                () => Console.WriteLine("Action 2"),
                () => Console.WriteLine("Action 3"));

            // explicitly create an array of actions
            Action[] actions = new Action[3];
            actions[0] = new Action(() => Console.WriteLine("Action 4"));
            actions[1] = new Action(() => Console.WriteLine("Action 5"));
            actions[2] = new Action(() => Console.WriteLine("Action 6"));

            // invoke the actions array
            Parallel.Invoke(actions);

            // create the same effect using tasks explicitly
            Task parent = Task.Factory.StartNew(() => {
                foreach (Action action in actions) {
                    Task.Factory.StartNew(action, TaskCreationOptions.AttachedToParent);
                }
            });
            // wait for the task to finish
            parent.Wait();

            // wait for input before exiting
            Console.WriteLine("Press enter to finish");
            Console.ReadLine();
        }
    }
}
```

The `Invoke()` method blocks until all of the `Actions` have been performed, which is equivalent to creating attached child `Tasks`. Any exceptions thrown by the `Actions` are packaged up into a `System.AggregateException`, which is thrown by the `Invoke()` method (see Chapter 2 for details of how to handle `AggregateExceptions`). Given that you have mastered the use of `Tasks` in the previous chapters, you won't use `Parallel.Invoke()` very often—if at all—but, this method does provide the backbone of the much more useful feature of the `Parallel` class, parallel loops.

■ **Tip** You can specify options to control the execution of the `Actions` using the `ParallelOptions` class; see the "Setting Parallel Loop Options" section of this chapter for details.

Using Parallel Loops

If you have done any programming, you will have encountered **for** and **foreach** loops, such as the following.

```
for (int i = 0; i < 100; i++) {
    // ... loop body...
    // do the ith item of work
}

int[] dataItems = new int[100];
foreach (int i in dataItems) {
    // ... loop body...
    // process the ith data item
}
```

The **for** loop executes a set of code statements (the loop body) a specified number of times; the loop body can determine which iteration is being performed by using the loop counter, which is the variable **i** in the code fragment.

The **foreach** loop executes the statements in the loop body for each item in a type that implements the **System.Collection.IEnumerable** or **System.Collections.Generic.IEnumerable<T>** interfaces. There are lots of types that implement these interfaces, including collection classes and arrays. In the code fragment, the loop body will be executed for each element in the **int** array, and the loop body is passed each item from the array in turn via the variable **i**.

Both of these loops are *sequential*, which is to say that one execution of the loop body finishes before the next one is started. The **Parallel** class provides features that let us create *parallel loops*, where the loop body is executed concurrently so that different values can be processed simultaneously.

Creating a Basic Parallel *For* Loop

Creating a basic parallel **for** loop is a simply a matter of calling the **Parallel.For()** method, and supplying three arguments. The first argument is the start index, the second argument is the end index and the third item is the **System.Action<int>**, representing the loop body that should be executed for each index value. The **int** passed to the **Action** is the index value for the current iteration. Listing 5-3 demonstrates a basic parallel **for** loop.

Listing 5-3. A Basic Parallel for Loop

```
using System;
using System.Threading.Tasks;

namespace Listing_03 {

    class Listing_03 {

        static void Main(string[] args) {

            Parallel.For(0, 10, index => {
                Console.WriteLine("Task ID {0} processing index: {1}",
                    Task.CurrentId, index);
            });
```

```
        // wait for input before exiting
        Console.WriteLine("Press enter to finish");
        Console.ReadLine();
    }
  }
}
```

The loop body prints out the ID of the Task performing the Action and the index of the current iteration. Running Listing 5-3 produces the following output, although you may see slight variations:

```
Task ID 1 processing index: 0

Task ID 4 processing index: 6

Task ID 3 processing index: 4

Task ID 3 processing index: 5

Task ID 3 processing index: 9

Task ID 3 processing index: 3

Task ID 1 processing index: 1

Task ID 5 processing index: 8

Task ID 2 processing index: 2

Task ID 4 processing index: 7

Press any key to continue . . .
```

There are some points to note. The start index value is *inclusive*, meaning that the value you specify for this argument will be processed using the loop body. The end index is *exclusive*, meaning that the value you specify for this argument will *not* be processed using the loop body. That means that start and end indexes used in the listing (0 and 10, respectively) are equivalent to a sequential loop such as the following:

```
for (int i = 0; i < 10; i++) {
    //...loop body...
}
```

You can see from the results that Tasks are used to process more than one index value. For example, the Task with the ID of three processed index values 4, 5, 9, and 3. You will also see that the index values were not processed in order. As is the case with much of the TPL, you cannot rely on a specific processing order.

Creating a Basic Parallel *ForEach* Loop

Parallel **for** loops can be useful, but they are somewhat limited by the fact that the loop body receives only the index from the **Parallel** class. That's super if you need to do something with the actual numeric values, but otherwise, you need to read some external data to which the index value is the key, as in Listing 5-1 at the start of this chapter—the index value is used to get some source data from one array and put the processed value into a another.

The parallel **foreach** loop is more flexible. It will process any set of items that are available through an **IEnumerable**. You create a parallel **foreach** loop by using the **Parallel.ForEach()** method, and the basic form takes an **IEnumerable<T>** implementation and an **Action<T>** which is used to process each item. The obvious application of this feature is to parallel process the elements in a collection, as illustrated by Listing 5-4.

Listing 5-4. Processing a Collection Using Parallel.ForEach()

```
using System;
using System.Collections.Generic;
using System.Threading.Tasks;

namespace Listing_04 {

    class Listing_04 {

        static void Main(string[] args) {

            // create a collection of strings
            List<string> dataList = new List<string> {
                "the", "quick", "brown", "fox", "jumps", "etc"
            };

            // process the elements of the collection
            // using a parallel foreach loop
            Parallel.ForEach(dataList, item => {
                Console.WriteLine("Item {0} has {1} characters",
                    item, item.Length);
            });

            // wait for input before exiting
            Console.WriteLine("Press enter to finish");
            Console.ReadLine();
        }
    }
}
```

One of the limitations of `Parallel.For` is that all index values are processed, making it impossible to create a parallel equivalent of a sequential loop such as this one, which increments the loop counter by two per iteration to create a stepped index:

```
for (int i = 0; i < 10; i +=2) {
    //...loop body...
}
```

Fortunately, we can achieve the same effect by using `Parallel.ForEach()` and creating an `IEnumerable` that contains only the stepped values, as illustrated by Listing 5-5.

Listing 5-5. Creating a Stepped Loop

```
using System;
using System.Collections.Generic;
using System.Threading.Tasks;

namespace Listing_05 {
    class Listing_05 {

        static IEnumerable<int> SteppedIterator(int startIndex,
            int endEndex, int stepSize) {
            for (int i = startIndex; i < endEndex; i += stepSize) {
                yield return i;
            }
        }

        static void Main(string[] args) {

            Parallel.ForEach(SteppedIterator(0, 10, 2), index => {
                Console.WriteLine("Index value: {0}", index);
            });

            // wait for input before exiting
            Console.WriteLine("Press enter to finish");
            Console.ReadLine();
        }
    }
}
```

The static `SteppedIterator()` method creates an `IEnumerable<int>` that contains the values between `startIndex` and `endIndex` with a step of `stepSize`. This is then used as the input to the `Parallel.ForEach()` method, which executes the `Action` for each value in the enumeration. Running Listing 5-5 produces the following results:

```
Index value: 0

Index value: 4

Index value: 8

Index value: 2

Index value: 6

Press enter to finish
```

Setting Parallel Loop Options

You can influence the behavior of parallel loops by supplying an instance of the `ParallelOptions` class as an argument to `Parallel.For()` or `Parallel.ForEach()`. There are three properties in `ParallelOptions`, and they are described in Table 5-2.

Table 5-2. *Properties of the System.Threading.Tasks.ParallelOptions class*

Property	Description
CancellationToken	Get or set a `CancellationToken` (see the "Canceling Parallel Loops" section later in this chapter).
MaxDegreeOfParallelism	Get or set the maximum concurrency for a parallel loop. Setting this property to `-1` means no concurrency limit is set.
TaskScheduler	Get or set the scheduler that will be used for the `Tasks` created in a parallel loop. Setting this property to null will cause the default scheduler to be used.

The three properties in Table 5-2 are the only members of the `ParallelOptions` class. The `CancellationToken` property is discussed later in this chapter. The `TaskScheduler` property lets you specify a custom task scheduler that will be applied to the `Tasks` created by the parallel loop; we covered creating and using custom schedulers in the previous chapter.

The remaining property, `MaxDegreeOfParallelism`, allows you to limit the number of `Tasks` that are executed concurrently to perform a parallel loop. Setting a high limit does not increase the degree of parallelism; all you can do with this property is set a limit for the concurrency. Specifying a value of `0` (i.e., no concurrency at all) will cause `Parallel.For()` and `Parallel.ForEach()` to throw an exception.

Both `Parallel.For` and `Parallel.ForEach` have overloaded versions that take an instance of `ParallelOptions` as an argument. Listing 5-6 shows both methods being used with a `ParallelOptions` instance that limits concurrency to one `Task`—effectively sequential execution.

Listing 5-6. Setting Options for a Parallel Loop

```csharp
using System;
using System.Collections.Generic;
using System.Threading;
using System.Threading.Tasks;

namespace Listing_06 {

    class Listing_06 {

        static void Main(string[] args) {

            // create a ParallelOptions instance
            // and set the max concurrency to 1
            ParallelOptions options
                = new ParallelOptions() { MaxDegreeOfParallelism = 1 };

            // perform a parallel for loop
            Parallel.For(0, 10, options, index => {
                Console.WriteLine("For Index {0} started", index);
                Thread.Sleep(500);
                Console.WriteLine("For Index {0} finished", index);
            });

            // create an array of ints to process
            int[] dataElements = new int[] { 0, 2, 4, 6, 8 };

            // perform a parallel foreach loop
            Parallel.ForEach(dataElements, options, index => {
                Console.WriteLine("ForEach Index {0} started", index);
                Thread.Sleep(500);
                Console.WriteLine("ForEach Index {0} finished", index);
            });

            // wait for input before exiting
            Console.WriteLine("Press enter to finish");
            Console.ReadLine();
        }
    }
}
```

Breaking and Stopping Parallel Loops

Sequential loops don't always run to completion, and the same holds true for parallel loops. Imagine that we have a collection of strings, and we want to find one that contains the letter k. We might write a sequential loop as follows:

```
List<string> dataItems
    = new List<string>() { "an", "apple", "a", "day",
        "keeps", "the", "doctor", "away" };

foreach (string item in dataItems) {
    if (item.Contains("k")) {
        Console.WriteLine("Hit: {0}", item);
        break;
    } else {
        Console.WriteLine("Miss: {0}", item);
    }
}
```

This loop works through the collection item by item until it reaches the word **keeps**, at which point the **break** keyword terminates the loop. You can't use **break** with parallel loops, but you can get the same effect using the `ParallelLoopState` class.

The `Parallel.For()` and `Parallel.ForEach()` methods have overloaded versions where the **Action** parameter is `Action(int, ParalllelLoopState)` (for `Parallel.For()`) and `Action(T, ParallelLoopState)` where T is the type of the IEnumerable used with `Parallel.ForEach()`. The following fragment demonstrates both forms:

```
Parallel.For(0, 100, (int index, ParallelLoopState loopState) => {
    // ...loop body...
});

string[] dataItems = new string[] { "an", "apple", "a" };

Parallel.ForEach(dataItems, (string item, ParallelLoopState loopState) => {
    // ...loop body...
}
```

The instance of `ParallelLoopState` is created automatically by the `Parallel` class and passed to your **Action**. I find it easier to declare the type of the variable in the lambda expression so that Visual Studio IntelliSense works properly, because Visual Studio doesn't know what type the argument is otherwise. The `ParallelLoopState` class contains the `Stop()` and `Break()` methods, which can be used to stop a parallel loop from completing. These methods and the other members of the `ParallelLoopState` class are summarized in Table 5-3.

Table 5-3. *Members of the System.Threading.Tasks.ParallelLoopStateclass*

Member	Description
Stop()	Request that the loop stop execution as possible.
Break()	Request that loop stop execution of iterations beyond the current iteration as soon as possible.
IsExceptional	Return true if any iteration of the loop has thrown an exception.
IsStopped	Return true if any iteration has called Stop().
LowestBreakIteration	Return the index of the lowest iteration in which Break() was called.
ShouldExitCurrentIteration	Return true if this iteration should exit.

The Stop() method is useful when you are looking for a specific result, as in the sequential loop where we looked for a word containing the letter k. When you call Stop(), the Parallel class doesn't stop any new iterations. However, iterations that are already running may continue to be performed, and as you saw earlier, Tasks are used to process more than one iteration value, so some of your data items may continue to be processed even after you have called Stop().

The Break() method is slightly different . If you call Break() in the tenth iteration, no further iterations will be started except those that are required to process the first to ninth items. Other iterations may be already running (including those that are processing later items) and will complete, which means that you are guaranteed to get *at least* the first ten items processed but may end up with more.

If Stop() and Break() seem a bit woolly, it is because the items in a parallel loop are not processed in sequence. This statement may seem obvious, but the trade-off inherent in a parallel loop is that the concurrent performance improvement comes at a cost of a lack of precision when you want to terminate the loop early. Listing 5-7 demonstrates a parallel loop that uses Stop(); this is the parallel implementation of looking for a word with the letter k.

Listing 5-7. Using Stop() in a Parallel Loop

```
using System;
using System.Collections.Generic;
using System.Threading.Tasks;

namespace Listing_07 {
    class Program {
        static void Main(string[] args) {

            List<string> dataItems
                = new List<string>() { "an", "apple", "a", "day",
                    "keeps", "the", "doctor", "away" };

            Parallel.ForEach(dataItems, (string item, ParallelLoopState state) => {
```

```
                if (item.Contains("k")) {
                    Console.WriteLine("Hit: {0}", item);
                    state.Stop();
                } else {
                    Console.WriteLine("Miss: {0}", item);
                }
            });

            // wait for input before exiting
            Console.WriteLine("Press enter to finish");
            Console.ReadLine();
        }
    }
}
```

Running Listing 5-7 produces the following result:

```
Miss: an

Miss: day

Miss: the

Miss: apple

Miss: doctor

Miss: a

Hit: keeps

Miss: away

Press enter to finish
```

Notice that all of the items in the collection have been processed even through a match was found. This illustrates the slightly unpredictable nature of stopping a parallel loop. Listing 5-8 demonstrates a parallel loop that uses the **Break()** method, which is called when the square of the index is greater than 100.

Listing 5-8. Using Break() in a Parallel Loop

```
using System;
using System.Collections.Generic;
using System.Threading.Tasks;

namespace Listing_08 {
```

```
class Listing_08 {
    static void Main(string[] args) {

        ParallelLoopResult res = Parallel.For(0, 100,
            (int index, ParallelLoopState loopState) => {

            // calculate the square of the index
            double sqr = Math.Pow(index, 2);
            // if the square value is > 100 then break
            if (sqr > 100) {
                Console.WriteLine("Breaking on index {0}", index);
                loopState.Break();
            } else {
                // write out the value
                Console.WriteLine("Square value of {0} is {1}", index, sqr);
            }
        });

        // wait for input before exiting
        Console.WriteLine("Press enter to finish");
        Console.ReadLine();
    }
}
}
```

Running the listing produces the results that follow. See how the range of index values has been broken down so that Tasks can start processing at different points ? The values produced by squaring the index exceed our threshold, so those iterations terminated immediately.

```
Square value of 0 is 0

Breaking on index 25

Square value of 2 is 4

Square value of 3 is 9

Square value of 4 is 16

Square value of 5 is 25


Square value of 6 is 36

Square value of 7 is 49

Square value of 8 is 64
```

```
Square value of 9 is 81

Square value of 10 is 100

Breaking on index 11

Breaking on index 75

Square value of 1 is 1

Breaking on index 50

Press enter to finish
```

When, as in this example, `Break()` is called more than once, the `Parallel` class ensures that all of the items prior to the lowest index where `Break()` was called are processed. In Listing 5-8, `Break()` was called on indices 11, 25, 75, and 50. In this case, the lowest break occurred at index 11; therefore, all items prior to 11 will be processed.

The three `ParallelLoopState` properties `IsStopped`, `LowestBreakIteration`, and `ShouldExitCurrentIteration` allow you to improve the responsiveness of a parallel loop by checking the overall state of the loop from within your iteration. Checking these values, especially in iterations that will take a long time to complete, will reduce the amount of unwanted processing after `Break()` or `Stop()` has been called.

■ **Tip** See the "Getting Loop Results" section for details of how to determine if `Break()` or `Stop()` was called from outside of the `Parallel.For()` and `Parallel.ForEach()` methods.

Handling Parallel Loop Exceptions

If an exception is thrown in a sequential loop, the loop stops, and no further iterations are performed. If an exception is thrown in a parallel loop, no new iterations are started, but iterations that are already in progress are allowed to complete.

You can detect if an exception has been thrown in another iteration by checking the `IsExceptional` property of the `ParallelLoopState` class (this class is described in the previous section).

The exceptions thrown by iterations are gathered and packaged into a `System.AggregateException`, which is thrown by the `Parallel.For()` and `Parallel.ForEach()` methods. See Chapter 2 for details of how to process an `AggregateException`.

■ **Tip** See the "Getting Loop Results" section for details of how to determine if an exception was thrown inside of the `Parallel.For()` and `Parallel.ForEach()` methods.

Getting Loop Results

The result returned by the `Parallel.For()` and `Parallel.ForEach()` methods is an instance of the `System.Threading.Tasks.ParallelLoopResult` structure. `ParallelLoopResult` contains two properties that you can use to determine if `Break()` or `Stop()` was called. Table 5-4 summarizes the properties.

Table 5-4. Properies of the System.Threading.Tasks.ParallelLoopResult structure

Member	Description
IsCompleted	Return **true** if all of the loop iterations were completed without **Stop()** and **Break()** being called.
LowestBreakIteration	Return the index of the lowest iteration in which the **Break()** method was called.

Listing 5-9 shows the use of the `ParallelLoopResult`, produced by a loop in which one of the iterations calls the `ParallelLoopState.Stop()` method.

Listing 5-9. Using the ParallelLoopResult Structure

```
using System;
using System.Threading;
using System.Threading.Tasks;

namespace Listing_09 {
    class Listing_09 {
        static void Main(string[] args) {

            // run a parallel loop in which one of
            // the iterations calls Stop()
            ParallelLoopResult loopResult =
                Parallel.For(0, 10, (int index, ParallelLoopState loopState) => {
                    if (index == 2) {
                        loopState.Stop();
                    }
                });

            // get the details from the loop result
            Console.WriteLine("Loop Result");
            Console.WriteLine("IsCompleted: {0}", loopResult.IsCompleted);
            Console.WriteLine("BreakValue: {0}", loopResult.LowestBreakIteration.HasValue);

            // wait for input before exiting
            Console.WriteLine("Press enter to finish");
            Console.ReadLine();
        }
    }
}
```

If `IsCompleted` returns `false` and `LowestBreakIteration.HasValue()` also returns `false`, we know that the `Stop()` method has been called. Table 5-5 summarizes the permutations of the property results and what they mean.

Table 5-5. Using the ParallelLoopResult structure to determine loop status

IsCompleted	LowestBreakIteration.HasValue()	Description
true	false	Neither `Stop()` nor `Break()` has been called.
false	false	`Stop()` was called.
false	true	`Break()` was called.

Canceling Parallel Loops

The `Parallel.For()` and `Parallel.ForEach()` methods will monitor a `CancellationToken` supplied through an instance of the `ParallelOptions` class. See the "Setting Parallel Loop Options" section earlier in the chapter for details, and see Chapter 2 for more generation information about the standardized cancellation mechanisms.

When the `CancellationTokenSource` from which the token was obtained is cancelled, the `Parallel` class will not start any new loop iterations, but any that are running will be allowed to complete. When all of the running iterations have completed, the `Parallel.For()` or `Parallel.ForEach()` method will throw an `OperationCancellationException`.

Listing 5-10 demonstrates how to cancel a parallel loop. Note that in the example, the cancellation is performed by a `Task`, because the `Parallel.For()` method blocks the main application thread. So either the parallel loop or the cancellation needs to be performed by a separate `Task`.

Listing 5-10. Cancelling a Parallel Loop

```
using System;
using System.Threading;
using System.Threading.Tasks;

namespace Listing_10 {
    class Listing_10 {
        static void Main(string[] args) {

            // create a cancellation token source
            CancellationTokenSource tokenSource
                = new CancellationTokenSource();
            // start a task that will cancel the token source
            // after a few seconds sleep
            Task.Factory.StartNew(() => {
                // sleep for 5 seconds
                Thread.Sleep(5000);
                // cancel the token source
                tokenSource.Cancel();
```

```
                    // let the user know
                    Console.WriteLine("Token cancelled");
            });

            // create loop options with a token
            ParallelOptions loopOptions =
                new ParallelOptions() {
                    CancellationToken = tokenSource.Token
                };

            try {
                // perform a parallel loop specifying the options
                // make this a loop that will take a while to complete
                // so the user has time to cancel
                Parallel.For(0, Int64.MaxValue, loopOptions, index => {
                    // do something just to occupy the cpu for a little
                    double result = Math.Pow(index, 3);
                    // write out the current index
                    Console.WriteLine("Index {0}, result {1}", index, result);
                    // put the thread to sleep, just to slow things down
                    Thread.Sleep(100);
                });
            } catch (OperationCanceledException) {
                Console.WriteLine("Caught cancellation exception...");
            }

            // wait for input before exiting
            Console.WriteLine("Press enter to finish");
            Console.ReadLine();

        }
    }
}
```

Using Thread Local Storage in Parallel Loops

Chapter 3 described thread local storage (TLS), where each thread has its own isolated version of a variable. The `Parallel.For()` and `Parallel.ForEach()` methods have versions that support TLS, which you can use to efficiently share data between parallel loop iterations and to get a single result value from a parallel loop.

A simple parallel loop that requires synchronization follows. The `total` variable is shared between the iterations of the loop and, since the iterations may be performed concurrently, there is the potential for a data race.

```
int total = 0;

Parallel.For(0, 100, index => {
    Interlocked.Add(ref total, index);
});
```

To avoid the data race, we use the System.Threading.Interlocked class to safely add the current iteration index to the total. Because there are 100 steps in the parallel loop, the Interlocked class will be called 100 times, and as you know, synchronization has an overhead—so we incur that overhead 100 times.

Listing 5-11 shows the preceding loop rewritten to use loop TLS.

Listing 5-11. A Parallel for Loop with TLS

```
using System;
using System.Threading;
using System.Threading.Tasks;

namespace Listing_11 {
    class Listing_11 {
        static void Main(string[] args) {

            int total = 0;

            Parallel.For(
                0,
                100,
                () => 0,
                (int index, ParallelLoopState loopState, int tlsValue) => {
                    tlsValue += index;
                    return tlsValue;
                },
                value => Interlocked.Add(ref total, value));

            Console.WriteLine("Total: {0}", total);

            // wait for input before exiting
            Console.WriteLine("Press enter to finish");
            Console.ReadLine();
        }
    }
}
```

In Listing 5-11, the first and second arguments to Parallel.For() are the start and end index values. The third argument is a delegate that initializes an instance of the thread-local type. In our example, this is an int with a value of 0.

When you use a parallel loop, your data is broken down into a series of blocks (known as *chunks* or *partitions*), which are processed concurrently. The detail of how your data is partitioned depends on the *partitioning strategy* applied to your loop, and I explain how to select a strategy later in the chapter. The TLS initialization delegate is called once for each data partition. In our example, it creates an int with a value of 0. You don't need to worry about the details of partitioning when using TLS, other than to know that the delegate may be called several times.

The fourth argument is the loop body, an Action which has three arguments: the current iteration index, the ParallelLoopState for the loop, and the current value of the thread-local variable. This Action is called once per index value and must return a result that is the same type as the thread-local variable. In the example, we add the current index to the thread-local variable and return the result.

The final argument is an `Action` that is passed the TLS value and is called once per data partition. This action is the complement of the TLS initialization delegate. In the example, we use the `Interlocked` class to safely update the overall total.

The benefit of using TLS in a loop is that you don't need to synchronize access to the variable in your loop body. In Listing 5-11, the `Interlocked` class is only used once per data partition. On my test system, the default practitioner usually breaks up the data in Listing 5-11 into four partitions, resulting in 96 fewer calls to `Interlocked` than the original loop. The exact savings depends on the source data and the partition strategy used; the greater the number of iterations, the greater the savings in overhead.

Listing 5-12 illustrates a `Parallel.ForEach()` loop with TLS and shows that you can use any of the synchronization techniques described in Chapter 3 to coordinate the TLS value with variables outside of the parallel loop.

Listing 5-12. A Parallel foreach Loop with TLS

```
using System;
using System.Threading;
using System.Threading.Tasks;

namespace Listing_12 {
    class Listing_12 {
        static void Main(string[] args) {

            // create a running total of matched words
            int matchedWords = 0;

            // create a lock object
            object lockObj = new object();

            // define the source data
            string[] dataItems
                = new string[] { "an", "apple", "a", "day",
                    "keeps", "the", "doctor", "away" };

            // perform a parallel foreach loop with TLS
            Parallel.ForEach(
                dataItems,
                () => 0,
                (string item, ParallelLoopState loopState, int tlsValue) => {
                    // increment the tls value if the item
                    // contains the letter 'a'
                    if (item.Contains("a")) {
                        tlsValue++;
                    }
                    return tlsValue;
                },
                tlsValue => {
                    lock (lockObj) {
                        matchedWords += tlsValue;
                    }
                });
```

```
        Console.WriteLine("Matches: {0}", matchedWords);

        // wait for input before exiting
        Console.WriteLine("Press enter to finish");
        Console.ReadLine();
      }
    }
  }
```

Performing Parallel Loops with Dependencies

The parallel loops so far in this chapter have been examples of what is known as *embarrassingly parallel* problems. This is an unfortunate name, but it means that the work being done is extremely easy to parallelize, because each data element can be processed independently of every other element; that allows the items to be processes in any order and with any degree of concurrency. In other words, these problems are perfect for demonstrating the new .NET parallel programming features, and they appear at one end of a spectrum of dependency between items.

At the other end of the spectrum are problems where there is a very high degree of dependency between data items, for example, generating Fibonacci numbers, where each item is the sum of the previous two items (with 0 and 1 as seed values), a problem that is best solved sequentially.

In the middle are problems where there is some degree of dependence between some items. Generally, such problems are best approached using the techniques from Chapters 3 and 4 to coordinate and synchronize a set of Tasks. There is one situation, however, where we can mix sequential and parallel loops to process data with a particular type of dependency.

The dependency I have in mind is where the first value in a region of data depends on the last value of the previous region, as illustrated in Figure 5-1. The nth region of data cannot be completed until the $(n-1)$ region has been processed, but the items within the region can be processed in parallel.

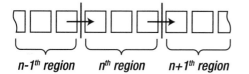

$n-1^{th}$ region n^{th} region $n+1^{th}$ region

Figure 5-1. *Chain dependency*

Listing 5-13 demonstrates this situation. A series of bank account transactions must be processed in order to determine the final balance for each month of the year, where each month contains 10,000 transactions. To determine the balance for the end of one month, we need to know the balance of the previous month. Aside from that dependency, we are able to process a month's transactions concurrently.

Listing 5-13 solves the dependency issue by mixing sequential and parallel loops. The outer loop is sequential and iterates through each monthly region in turn. The inner loop is parallel and sums the individual transactions. The result of the parallel loop for one month becomes the seed value for the following month.

Listing 5-13. Mixing Synchronous and Parallel Loops

```
using System;
using System.Threading.Tasks;

namespace Listing_13 {

    class Transaction {
        public int Amount {
            get;
            set;
        }
    }

    class Listing_13 {

        static void Main(string[] args) {

            // create a random number generator
            Random rnd = new Random();

            // set the number of items created
            int itemsPerMonth = 100000;

            // create the source data
            Transaction[] sourceData = new Transaction[12 * itemsPerMonth];
            for (int i = 0; i < 12 * itemsPerMonth; i++) {
                sourceData[i] = new Transaction() { Amount = rnd.Next(-400, 500) };
            }

            // create the results array
            int[] monthlyBalances = new int[12];

            for (int currentMonth = 0; currentMonth < 12; currentMonth++) {
                // perform the parallel loop on the current month's data
                Parallel.For(
                    currentMonth * itemsPerMonth,
                    (currentMonth + 1) * itemsPerMonth,
                    new ParallelOptions(),
                    () => 0,
                    (index, loopstate, tlsBalance) => {
                        return tlsBalance += sourceData[index].Amount;
                    },
                    tlsBalance => monthlyBalances[currentMonth] += tlsBalance);
                // end of parallel for
                // add the previous month's balance
```

```
        if (currentMonth > 0) monthlyBalances[currentMonth]
            += monthlyBalances[currentMonth - 1];
    }

    for (int i = 0; i < monthlyBalances.Length; i++) {
        Console.WriteLine("Month {0} - Balance: {1}", i, monthlyBalances[i]);
    }

    // wait for input before exiting
    Console.WriteLine("Press enter to finish");
    Console.ReadLine();
      }
   }
}
```

By mixing sequential and parallel loops in this way, we get a good degree of concurrency and still benefit from the simplicity of using a `Parallel.For()` loop. You may be tempted to replace the sequential loop with synchronization to achieve a similar effect; see the "Common Problems and Their Causes" section later in this chapter for an often-encountered pitfall.

Selecting a Partitioning Strategy

When you use a parallel loop, the data you supply is broken into *partitions* which are processed concurrently. Partitioning is a performance optimization – if the `Task`s performing a parallel loop had to get each item individually from the data source, the synchronization required to avoid the same item being taken and processed by multiple `Task`s would outweigh any parallel performance gains. Instead, partitioning means the `Task`s go to the data source and ask for multiple items at once, reducing the amount of synchronization required.

A *partitioner* breaks up a data source into partitions. There are lots of different ways to perform partitioning and the technique that is used can have an impact on the performance of your parallel loops. The TPL includes default partitioner strategies that offer good performance on a wide range of data sources and of hardware configurations. You may, however, find that you can get better performance from your parallel loop by using a partitioning strategy that is tailored to your data source.

This section will explain how the default partitioner works, show you how to improve performance for small loop bodies using a technique called *chunking*, and how to create and use a custom partitioner.

Partitions are passed to consumers, who take items from the partition and process them. In the case of parallel loops, the consumers are the `Task`s: they request a partition from the partitioner, take items one by one from the partition, and invoke the loop body to process the items.

There are two kinds of partitioner: *static* and *dynamic*. We'll look at static partitioners when we investigate PLINQ in Chapter 6, so for now, we'll focus on dynamic partitioners, which are what parallel loops use. A dynamic partitioner doesn't know in advance how many partitions are going to be requested, so it needs to be able to divide up the data dynamically. A common approach to handling this is to break the data down into small *blocks*.

When a dynamic partition is created, the partitioner gives it one block of data to begin servicing the consumer with. When the consumer has taken all of the items in the first block, the partitioner gives the partition another. This continues until all of the blocks have been used.

If there is one consumer, and therefore one partition, all of the blocks will be passed to the same partition, and all of the items will be processed by the same consumer. If there is more than one consumer, there will be more than one partition, and the blocks will be shared out between them so that each consumer receives and processes a portion of the data items.

For example, the default TPL partitioner used in the `Parallel.ForEach()` method starts off by creating small blocks, which is to say blocks containing relatively few data items. Small blocks give the best performance for data sources with small numbers of items, because the items can be spread across the available cores or CPUs to increase concurrency. For example, if you have a collection of ten items and the partitioner created blocks of ten items in size, all of the items would go into one block, which would be consumed by one `Task`, and the work in your parallel loop would be bound to one CPU or core. By contrast, if each block contained, say, two items, up to five cores could be usefully engaged in processing items concurrently.

The default `ForEach()` partitioner doubles the size of the block it gives to a partition every time it has given that partition three blocks; this means that the block size grows in relation to the number of items in the data source and that the largest block sizes will be reached when processing the largest amounts of data. Large blocks give the best performance for large data sources.

The default partitioner used in the `Parallel.For()` method works in a different way. It breaks down the range of values that are to be iterated through into ranges, which can then be executed in parallel. This strategy is very similar to chunking, which I discuss in the following section.

Using the Chunking Partitioning Strategy

By starting with small blocks and increasing their size as the number of data items processed increases, the default partitioner tries to give balanced performance whatever size data source is used. As a general approach, the default partitioner is excellent, but there are times when a different approach can give better results, particularly when the performance problem isn't with the data source at all.

A problem with parallel **for** loops arises when the loop body is very small and doesn't take much time to process a data element. In such situations, the amount of time required to invoke the `System.Action` for each element becomes a disproportionate overhead. Consider the first parallel loop in Listing 5-14, which has a very small loop body; it simply calculates the square of the index value and assigns the result to an array.

Listing 5-14. A Parallel Loop with a Very Small Body

```
using System;
using System.Threading.Tasks;

namespace Listing_14 {
    class Listing_14 {

        delegate void ProcessValue(int value);
        static double[] resultData = new double[10000000];

        static void Main(string[] args) {

            // perform the parallel loop
            Parallel.For(0, resultData.Length, (int index) => {
                // compuute the result for the current index
                resultData[index] = Math.Pow(index, 2);
            });
```

```
            // perform the loop again, but make the delegate explicit
            Parallel.For(0, resultData.Length, delegate(int index) {
                resultData[index] = Math.Pow((double)index, 2);
            });

            // perform the loop once more, but this time using
            // a declared delegate and action
            ProcessValue pdel = new ProcessValue(computeResultValue);
            Action<int> paction = new Action<int>(pdel);
            Parallel.For(0, resultData.Length, paction);

            // wait for input before exiting
            Console.WriteLine("Press enter to finish");
            Console.ReadLine();
        }

        static void computeResultValue(int indexValue) {
            resultData[indexValue] = Math.Pow(indexValue, 2);
        }
    }
}
```

When using lambda expressions, it is easy to forget that the compiler is creating an anonymous **delegate** in which to wrap the code statements, and this delegate must be invoked to process every item in a parallel loop. In fact, the second loop in Listing 5-13 is what the C# compiler produces when it compiles the first loop.

The final loop in Listing 5-13 uses an explicit **delegate** to call the **computeResultValue()** method. The point to note is that all three loops are identical, and the **delegate** is invoked 10,000,000 times. The work required by the runtime to invoke the delegate is huge in proportion to the work required to perform the trivial loop body.

We can counter this problem through a partitioning technique called *chunking*. Rather than using a **Parallel.For()** loop that invokes the delegate for each index value, we transform the index range into a series of **System.Tuple<int, int>** instances, where each **Tuple** represents a chunk or range of index values. These ranges are then processed by a **Parallel.ForEach()** loop. Listing 5-15 shows this technique in action.

Listing 5-15. Using a Chunking Partitioner

```
using System;
using System.Collections.Concurrent;
using System.Threading.Tasks;

namespace Listing_15 {

    class Listing_15 {

        static void Main(string[] args) {

            // create the results array
            double[] resultData = new double[10000000];
```

```
        // created a partioner that will chunk the data
        OrderedPartitioner<Tuple<int, int>> chunkPart
            = Partitioner.Create(0, resultData.Length, 10000);

        // perform the loop in chunks
        Parallel.ForEach(chunkPart, chunkRange => {
            // iterate through all of the values in the chunk range
            for (int i = chunkRange.Item1; i < chunkRange.Item2; i++) {
                resultData[i] = Math.Pow(i, 2);
            }
        });

        // wait for input before exiting
        Console.WriteLine("Press enter to finish");
        Console.ReadLine();
    }
  }
}
```

We can perform chunking using the static `Create()` method of the `System.Collections.Concurrent.Partitioner` class. This method takes a start index, an end index, and optionally the range of index values that each chunk should represent. Table 5-6 summarizes the different method versions.

Table 5-6. The Partitioner.Create() Method Versions

Method Overload	Description
Create(int, int) Create(long, long)	Chunk a range of values using the default range size.
Create(int, int, int) Create(long, long, long)	Chunk a range of values using a specified range size.

If you do not specify the size of each chunk, then the default will be used; this is currently the number of items divided by three times the number of processor cores available. For example, for 1,000 index values on a four-way machine, each chunk will have a range of 1000 / (3 × 4) values, which rounds down to eight values per chunk. The default may be calculated differently in future releases, so you shouldn't code in the expectation of this value.

The `Partitioner.Create()` method returns an instance of `System.Collections.Concurrent.OrderablePartitioner`. I'll explain the purpose of this class in the next section, but for now, it is enough to know that you can pass this as an argument to the `Parallel.ForEach()` method, along with a loop body that processes instances of `Tuple<int, int>`. The `Tuple.Item1` value is the inclusive start index of the range, and the `Tuple.Item2` value is the exclusive end index of the range. This means that, instead of the loop body processing individual items, we create a sequential loop in which a range of values are processed, like this:

```
// perform the loop in chunks
Parallel.ForEach(chunkPart, chunkRange => {
    // iterate through all of the values in the chunk range
    for (int i = chunkRange.Item1; i < chunkRange.Item2; i++) {
        resultData[i] = Math.Pow(i, 2);
    }
});
```

By breaking 10,000,000 index values into chunks of 10,000, we reduce the number of times that the delegate is invoked to 1,000 and improve the ratio of overhead versus index processing.

Using the Ordered Default Partitioning Strategy

When you use the `Parallel.ForEach()` method, the default partitioning strategy will be applied unless the first argument you provide is an instance of the `Partitioner` or `OrderablePartitioner` classes in the `System.Collections.Concurrent` namespace. In the previous example, we applied the chunking strategy by creating an instance of `OrderablePartitioner` and passing it to `Parallel.ForEach()`. But now, it is time for me to admit that I fudged things slightly to make the example simpler.

The `OrdereablePartitioner` class extends `Partitioner`. When I called `Parallel.ForEach()` in the previous example, I used a version of the method that implicitly treated the argument as an instance of the base class, `Partitioner`. I did this because the feature that `OrderablePartitioner` adds over the base `Partitioner` doesn't have any relevance when chunking.

Any partitioner, be it implemented using `Partitioner` or `OrderablePartitioner`, is free to arrange the items in whatever order it wants to in each partition. This is fine when items are self-contained, such as `Tuples` representing index ranges. In such situations, you can use `Partitioner` either directly by extending the class or implicitly as I did in the previous example. But, if the data items have some kind of order, and you need to preserve that order, you need to use `OrderablePartitioner` instead. Listing 5-16 demonstrates the difference.

Listing 5-16. Using an Orderable Partitioner

```
using System;
using System.Collections.Concurrent;
using System.Collections.Generic;
using System.Threading.Tasks;

namespace Listing_15 {
    class Listing_15 {
        static void Main(string[] args) {

            // create the source data
            IList<string> sourceData
                = new List<string>() { "an", "apple", "a", "day",
                    "keeps", "the", "doctor", "away" };

            // create an array to hold the results
            string[] resultData = new string[sourceData.Count];

            // create an orderable partitioner
            OrderablePartitioner<string> op = Partitioner.Create(sourceData);
```

```
        // perform the parallel loop
        Parallel.ForEach(op, (string item, ParallelLoopState loopState, long index) => {
            // process the item
            if (item == "apple") item = "apricot";
            // use the index to set the result in the array
            resultData[index] = item;
        });

        // print out the contents of the result array
        for (int i = 0; i < resultData.Length; i++) {
            Console.WriteLine("Item {0} is {1}", i, resultData[i]);
        }

        // wait for input before exiting
        Console.WriteLine("Press enter to finish");
        Console.ReadLine();
    }
  }
}
```

The difference is that the loop body is passed an additional argument, which is the numeric key for the item being processed. If we use a version of `Parallel.ForEach()` that treats the partitioner as an instance of `Partitioner` rather than `OrderablePartitioner`, we lose that information and would not be able to reconstruct the order of the items after they have been processed. Table 5-7 shows the static methods of the `Partitioner` class that can be used to explicitly create instances of `OrderablePartitioner` using the default strategy.

Table 5-7. The Partitioner.Create() Method Versions

Method Overload	Description
Create(IEnumerable<T>)	Create an OrderablePartitioner using an IEnumerable<T> as the source.
Create(T[], bool)	Create an OrderablePartitioner using an array as the source. The **bool** argument determines if the partitioner will support dynamic partitions; this must always be **true** for use in parallel loops.
Create(IList<T>, bool)	Create an OrderablePartitioner using an IList<T> as the source. The **bool** argument determines if the partitioner will support dynamic partitions; this must always be **true** for use in parallel loops.

Creating a Custom Partitioning Strategy

If the default or chunking strategies don't suit your needs, you can implement your own partitioning strategy. You do this by deriving from the `Partitioner` or `OrderablePartitioner` classes in the `System.Collections.Concurrent` namespace.

`Partitioner` is the basic class, and subclasses can support either dynamic or static partitions. `OrderablePartitioner` extends `Partitioner`. The difference between them is that `OrderablePartitioner` provides the consumer with the data items *and* their index in the sequence of data items. Given that a partitioner can reorder the data items in any way it wants, providing the index number along with each item can be useful if the order of the items needs to be restored later.

I'll show you how to implement custom partition strategies using both classes.

Writing a Contextual Partitioner

The default partitioner and the chunking partitioner both operate on any data type. One advantage of writing a customer partitioner is that you can tailor your strategy to the data type that you need to process. This section will demonstrate how to implement a *contextual* partitioner and, in doing so, explain how to extend the `Partitioner` class to implement a custom technique.

To start our partitioner, we need a context—some data type with characteristics that we are going to specialize. I have defined the class `WorkItem` in Listing 5-17.

■ **Note** Listings 5-17 through 5-25 contains fragments that won't compile on their own; they need to be assembled together. If you have downloaded the source code from `www.apress.com`, you will find all of code fragments already assembled for you in the project called `Listing_17-25`.

Listing 5-17. The WorkItem Class

```
class WorkItem {

    public int WorkDuration {
        get; set;
    }

    public void performWork() {
        // simulate work by sleeping
        Thread.Sleep(WorkDuration);
    }
}
```

The `WorkItem` has a property that reports how long processing an instance will take and a method that simulates the processing by sleeping. This is a conveniently simple example, but it is representative of many situations where you are able to make an estimate of how long it will take to process an instance based on some other characteristic, for example, encrypting a message based on the number of characters.

The objective for our partitioner is to use the estimated duration of each item to create chunks of items that take the same amount of time to process. The result will be chunks with varying lengths. The effect of focusing on the amount of processing required will be to evenly distribute the workload across the cores in the system.

Listing 5-18 shows how we will use our partitioner, called `ContextualPartitioner`. To create the source data for the parallel loop, we create an instance of `System.Random` and use it to generate pseudo-random values between one and ten, which we use to set the `WorkDuration` property of 10,000 instances of `WorkItem`.

Listing 5-18. Using the ContextPartitioner Class

```
class ContextTest {
    static void Main(string[] args) {

        // create a random number source
        Random rnd = new Random();

        // create the source data
        WorkItem[] sourceData = new WorkItem[10000];
        for (int i = 0; i < sourceData.Length; i++) {
            sourceData[i]
            = new WorkItem() { WorkDuration = rnd.Next(1, 11) };
        }

        // created the contextual partitioner
        Partitioner<WorkItem> cPartitioner
            = new ContexPartioner(sourceData, 100);

        // create the parallel
        Parallel.ForEach(cPartitioner, item => {
            // perform the work item
            item.performWork();
        });

        // wait for input before exiting
        Console.WriteLine("Press enter to finish");
        Console.ReadLine();

    }
}
```

After creating the data source, we then create the partitioner, and the arguments passed to the constructor are the WorkItem array and the target total processing timer per chunk. The example specifies a target value of 100. The partitioner is passed as an argument to a Parallel.ForEach() loop, the body of which simply calls the performWork() method of each WorkItem instance that is processed.

Now that you have seen the WorkItem definition and how the partitioner is used, we can turn our attention to the partitioner itself. To create a partitioner, you must override the members listed in Table 5-8.

Table 5-8. Required Overrides of the Partitioner Class

Member	Description
SupportsDynamicPartitions	Return true if the partitioner supports dynamic partitioning. Returning false from this property will cause an exception if the partitioner is used in a Parallel.ForEach() loop.
GetPartitions(int)	Break up the data into a fixed number of partitions. No further partitions will be requested; the partitioner is free to allocate data as it wishes to each partition.
GetDynamicPartitions()	Return an object which creates new partitions when its GetEnumerator() method is called.

The complete partitioner class is shown in Listing 5-19.

Listing 5-19. A Contextual Partitioner

```
class ContextPartitioner : Partitioner<WorkItem> {
    // the set of data items to partition
    protected WorkItem[] dataItems;
    // the target sum of values per chunk
    protected int targetSum;
    // the first unchunked item
    private long sharedStartIndex = 0;
    // lock object to avoid index data races
    private object lockObj = new object();
    // the object used to create enumerators
    private EnumerableSource enumSource;

    public ContextPartitioner(WorkItem[] data, int target) {
        // set the instance variables from the parameters
        dataItems = data;
        targetSum = target;
        // create the enumerable source
        enumSource = new EnumerableSource(this);
    }

    public override bool SupportsDynamicPartitions {
        get {
            // dynamic partitions are required for
            // parallel foreach loops
            return true;
        }
    }
}
```

```
public override IList<IEnumerator<WorkItem>> GetPartitions(int partitionCount) {
    // create the list which will be the result
    IList<IEnumerator<WorkItem>> partitionsList = new List<IEnumerator<WorkItem>>();
    // get the IEnumerable that will generate dynamic partitions
    IEnumerable<WorkItem> enumObj = GetDynamicPartitions();
    // create the required number of partitions
    for (int i = 0; i < partitionCount; i++) {
        partitionsList.Add(enumObj.GetEnumerator());
    }
    // return the result
    return partitionsList;
}

public override IEnumerable<WorkItem> GetDynamicPartitions() {
    return enumSource;
}

private Tuple<long, long> getNextChunk() {
    // create the result tuple
    Tuple<long, long> result;
    // get an exclusive lock as we perform this operation
    lock (lockObj) {
        // check that there is still data available
        if (sharedStartIndex < dataItems.Length) {
            int sum = 0;
            long endIndex = sharedStartIndex;
            while (endIndex < dataItems.Length && sum < targetSum) {
                sum += dataItems[endIndex].WorkDuration;
                endIndex++;
            }
            result = new Tuple<long, long>(sharedStartIndex, endIndex);
            sharedStartIndex = endIndex;
        } else {
            // there is no data available
            result = new Tuple<long, long>(-1, -1);
        }
    }
    // end of locked region
    // return the result
    return result;
}

class EnumerableSource : IEnumerable<WorkItem> {
    ContextPartitioner parentPartitioner;

    public EnumerableSource(ContextPartitioner parent) {
        parentPartitioner = parent;
    }

    IEnumerator IEnumerable.GetEnumerator() {
        return ((IEnumerable<WorkItem>)this).GetEnumerator();
    }
```

```
        IEnumerator<WorkItem> IEnumerable<WorkItem>.GetEnumerator() {
            return new ChunkEnumerator(parentPartitioner).GetEnumerator();
        }
    }

    class ChunkEnumerator {
        private ContextPartitioner parentPartitioner;

        public ChunkEnumerator(ContextPartitioner parent) {
            parentPartitioner = parent;
        }

        public IEnumerator<WorkItem> GetEnumerator() {
            while (true) {
                // get the indices of the next chunk
                Tuple<long, long> chunkIndices = parentPartitioner.getNextChunk();
                // check that we have data to deliver
                if (chunkIndices.Item1 == -1 && chunkIndices.Item2 == -1) {
                    // there is no more data
                    break;
                } else {
                    // enter a loop to yield the data items
                    for (long i = chunkIndices.Item1; i < chunkIndices.Item2; i++) {
                        yield return parentPartitioner.dataItems[i];
                    }
                }
            }
        }
    }
}
```

Let's go through the class in fragments so you can better understand how it fits together. The constructor, shown in Listing 5-20, takes the array of `WorkItems` and our chunk processing target and assigns them to the instance variables `dataItems` and `targetSum` respectively. It also creates an instance of `EnumerableSource`, which we'll get to in due course.

Listing 5-20. The Constructor and Property of the ContextPartitioner Class

```
class ContextPartitioner : Partitioner<WorkItem> {
    // the set of data items to partition
    protected WorkItem[] dataItems;
    // the target sum of values per chunk
    protected int targetSum;
    // the first unchunked item
    private long sharedStartIndex = 0;
    // lock object to avoid index data races
    private object lockObj = new object();
    // the object used to create enumerators
    private EnumerableSource enumSource;
```

```
    public ContextPartitioner(WorkItem[] data, int target) {
        // set the instance variables from the parameters
        dataItems = data;
        targetSum = target;
        // create the enumerable source
        enumSource = new EnumerableSource(this);
    }

    public override bool SupportsDynamicPartitions {
        get {
            // dynamic partitions are required for
            // parallel foreach loops
            return true;
        }
    }
}
```

The `SupportsDynamicPartitions` property must always return **true** for partitioners used in `Parallel.For()` loops. Static partitioners can be used with PLINQ however (see Chapter 6 for details). The `GetDynamicPartitions()` method returns an object that implements the `IEnumerable<WorkItem>` interface and will create a new partition each time that the `GetEnumerator()` call is made on it. In our case, shown in Listing 5-21, we return the instance of the `EnumerableSource` class we created in the constructor.

Listing 5-21. The ContextPartitioner.GetDynamicPartitions() Method

```
public override IEnumerable<WorkItem> GetDynamicPartitions() {
    return enumSource;
}
```

The `GetPartitions()` method is used to generate static partitions; this task is easy for a dynamic partitioner, as you can simply create the required number of dynamic partitions. The result from the `GetPartitions()` method is an `IList` of `IEnumerator<WorkItem>`s ; each of these is a static partition. In our implementation, shown in Listing 5-22, you can see that we do this using the result from the `GetDynamicPartitions()` method.

Listing 5-22. The ContextPartitioner.GetPartitions() Method

```
public override IList<IEnumerator<WorkItem>> GetPartitions(int partitionCount) {
    // create the list which will be the result
    IList<IEnumerator<WorkItem>> partitionsList = new List<IEnumerator<WorkItem>>();
    // get the IEnumerable that will generate dynamic partitions
    IEnumerable<WorkItem> enumObj = GetDynamicPartitions();
    // create the required number of partitions
    for (int i = 0; i < partitionCount; i++) {
        partitionsList.Add(enumObj.GetEnumerator());
    }
    // return the result
    return partitionsList;
}
```

The most interesting method in the `ContextPartitioner` class is `getNextChunk()`, shown in Listing 5-23. This is the method that implements our partitioning strategy, creating chunks that will take roughly the target amount of time to process. I say "roughly" because this method iterates through the data items until the target is exceeded, so the amount of processing time per chunk can be slightly more than the target. This variation is acceptable for our example, but you could be a lot more rigorous if required.

There are a couple of key design decisions to note with this method. First, observe that the result from this method is a `System.Tuple<long,long>`. The `Tuple` values represent the inclusive start index and exclusive end index into the `WorkItem` array that the chunk represents. We don't copy the data into a dedicated array, but rather share the main array between each of the partitions—you'll see how this works shortly.

Second, you'll see that we used the `sharedStartIndex` variable to track the index of the first unchunked `WorkItem` in the data array. We use synchronization to protect this variable to ensure we don't create multiple chunks with the same index values, leading to `WorkItems` being processed more than once (the `lock` keyword is used for simplicity, but any of the primitives discussed in Chapter 4 would work).

Listing 5-23. The ContextPartitioner.getNextChunk() Method

```
private Tuple<long, long> getNextChunk() {
    // create the result tuple
    Tuple<long, long> result;
    // get an exclusive lock as we perform this operation
    lock (lockObj) {
        // check that there is still data available
        if (sharedStartIndex < dataItems.Length) {
            int sum = 0;
            long endIndex = sharedStartIndex;
            while (endIndex < dataItems.Length && sum < targetSum) {
                sum += dataItems[endIndex].WorkDuration;
                endIndex++;
            }
            result = new Tuple<long, long>(sharedStartIndex, endIndex);
            sharedStartIndex = endIndex;
        } else {
            // there is no data available
            result = new Tuple<long, long>(-1, -1);
        }
    }
    // end of locked region
    // return the result
    return result;
}
```

If there is no data left, we return a `Tuple` whose values are both `-1`, which signals the partition that requested the chunk that no more data will be forthcoming. You'll see how this works when we get to the `ChunkEnumerator` class shortly. Before we get there, we have to cover the `EnumerableSource` class, as shown in Listing 5-24.

Listing 5-24. The ContextPartitioner.EnumerableSource Class

```
class EnumerableSource : IEnumerable<WorkItem> {
    ContextPartitioner parentPartitioner;

    public EnumerableSource(ContextPartitioner parent) {
        parentPartitioner = parent;
    }

    IEnumerator IEnumerable.GetEnumerator() {
        return ((IEnumerable<WorkItem>)this).GetEnumerator();
    }

    IEnumerator<WorkItem> IEnumerable<WorkItem>.GetEnumerator() {
        return new ChunkEnumerator(parentPartitioner).GetEnumerator();
    }
}
```

This class doesn't do very much other than act as a bridge between `ContextPartitioner` and `ChunkEnumerator`, but it exists for an important reason. If the `ContextPartitioner` class implements the `IEnumerable<WorkItem>` interface and returns an instance of itself when the `GetDynamicPartitions()` method is called, we create ambiguity with the `Parallel.ForEach()` method, which has separate versions that accept classes derived from `Partitioner` and that implement `IEnumerable<>`. The ambiguity requires that the user of `ContextPartitioner` cast instances of the class to `Partitioner`. If `ContextPartitioner` is cast to an implementation of `IEnumerable<>`, the default partitioner will be used to partition our partitioner, which is obviously not the effect we are striving for. To that end, `EnumerableSource` is the result from the `ContextPartitioner.CreateDynamicPartitions()` method to separate out the base class from the interface implementation.

As described in Table 5-8, the object returned from the `ContextPartitioner.CreateDynamicPartitions()` must create new partitions when the `GetEnumerator()` method is called. `EnumerableSource` does this by creating a new instance of `ChunkEnumerator` and returning the result from its `GetEnumerator()` method. The `ChunkEnumerator` class is shown in Listing 5-25.

Listing 5-25. The ContextPartitioner.ChunkEnumerator Class

```
class ChunkEnumerator {
    private ContextPartitioner parentPartitioner;

    public ChunkEnumerator(ContextPartitioner parent) {
        parentPartitioner = parent;
    }

    public IEnumerator<WorkItem> GetEnumerator() {
        while (true) {
            // get the indices of the next chunk
            Tuple<long, long> chunkIndices = parentPartitioner.getNextChunk();
```

```
        // check that we have data to deliver
        if (chunkIndices.Item1 == -1 && chunkIndices.Item2 == -1) {
            // there is no more data
            break;
        } else {
            // enter a loop to yield the data items
            for (long i = chunkIndices.Item1; i < chunkIndices.Item2; i++) {
                yield return parentPartitioner.dataItems[i];
            }
        }
      }
    }
  }
}
```

This class works in a very simple manner. The `GetEnumerator()` method enters a loop that requests chunks via the `ContextPartitioner.getNextChunk()` method. If it receives a `Tuple` with both items set to -1, it breaks out of the loop. This happens when there is no unchunked data left. Otherwise, the `yield` keyword is used to return items from the main data array, using the index values of the `Tuple` returned from `getNextChunk()`,

And that's our contextual partitioner and an explanation of how to implement a custom partitioning strategy by extending the `Partitioner` class.

Writing an Orderable Contextual Partitioner

Having written a regular partitioner, it is a simple matter to create an orderable version. We won't go through this example member by member, because it is so similar to the previous listings. In fact, only four key things need to change to make our `Partioner` into an `OrderablePartitioner`.

The first thing we have to change is the return types. Instead of returning enumerations of `WorkItem`, we are required to operate around instances of `KeyValuePair<long, WorkItem>`, where the `long` value is the key associated with the `WorkItem` value. In our scenario, this key is the index into the source data array.

The second change is in the set of methods that we have to override. We have to provide implementations of the members described in Table 5-9. These methods work in the same way as the required overrides in the base class, but they work on `KeyValuePairs` to include the index information. The `OrderablePartition` class provides default implementations for the `GetPartitions()` and `GetDynamicPartitions()` methods of the base `Partition` class; the implementations call `GetOrderablePartitions()` and `GetOrderableDynamicPartitions()` and strip out the index information to return the `WorkItems`.

Table 5-9. Required Overrides of the Partitioner Class

Member	Description
SupportsDynamicPartitions	Return true if the partitioner supports dynamic partitioning. Returning false from this property will cause an exception if the partitioner is used in a Parallel.ForEach() loop.
GetOrderablePartitions(int)	Break up the data into a fixed number of partitions. No further partitions will be requested; the partitioner is free to allocate data as it wishes to each partition.
GetOrderableDynamicPartitions()	Return an object which creates new partitions when the GetEnumerator() method is called.

The third change is to alter the base for our class from Partitioner to OrderablePartitioner. In doing this, we inherit a new constructor that requires us to provide three bool values when a new instance of our partitioner is created. These values relate to three properties in the OrderablePartitioner class, which are described in Table 5-10.

Table 5-10. OrderablePartitioner Properties

Property	Description
KeysOrderedInEachPartition	Return true if the elements within a partition are ordered in increasing key value. This is the first bool required by the base constructor.
KeysOrderedAcrossPartitions	Return true if the elements across partitions are ordered in increasing key value. This means that the keys in the *n*th partition are less than in the (n + 1) partition. This is the second bool required by the base constructor.
KeysNormalized	Return true if the key values are distinct integers. This is the third bool required by the base constructor.

These properties can be used by the consumer of the partitions, but they don't affect us directly when implementing our strategy. However, it is important to set the values correctly to reflect your strategy since your partitioner may be used in ways you did not originally expect.

The final change is in the ChunkEnumerator class, where the change from working with WorkItems to working with KeyValuePair<long, WorkItem> takes real effect. Instead of yielding items, we must now **yield** items and their key, and we can do this easily because the key is simply the array index, as follows:

```
yield return new KeyValuePair<long, WorkItem>(i, parentPartitioner.dataItems[i]);
```

So we have easily transformed our Partitioner into an OrderablePartitioner. I tend to create OrderablePartitioners by default when I can easily determine the key values in a data source, and I recommend that you do the same. Listing 5-26 shows the transformed partitioner class.

Listing 5-26. An orderable (and Contextual) Partitioner

```
using System;
using System.Collections;
using System.Collections.Concurrent;
using System.Collections.Generic;
using System.Threading;
using System.Threading.Tasks;


namespace Listing_26 {

    class ContextPartitioner : OrderablePartitioner<WorkItem> {
        // the set of data items to partition
        protected WorkItem[] dataItems;
        // the target sum of values per chunk
        protected int targetSum;
        // the first un-chunked item
        private long sharedStartIndex = 0;
        // lock object to avoid index data races
        private object lockObj = new object();
        // the object used to create enumerators
        private EnumerableSource enumSource;

        public ContextPartitioner(WorkItem[] data, int target) : base(true, false, true) {
            // set the instance variables from the parameters
            dataItems = data;
            targetSum = target;
            // create the enumerable source
            enumSource = new EnumerableSource(this);
        }

        public override bool SupportsDynamicPartitions {
            get {
                // dynamic partitions are required for
                // parallel foreach loops
                return true;
            }
        }

        public override IList<IEnumerator<KeyValuePair<long, WorkItem>>>
            GetOrderablePartitions(int partitionCount) {

            // create the list which will be the result
            IList<IEnumerator<KeyValuePair<long, WorkItem>>> partitionsList
                = new List<IEnumerator<KeyValuePair<long, WorkItem>>>();
            // get the IEnumerable that will generate dynamic partitions
            IEnumerable<KeyValuePair<long, WorkItem>> enumObj
                = GetOrderableDynamicPartitions();
```

```
        // create the required number of partitions
        for (int i = 0; i < partitionCount; i++) {
            partitionsList.Add(enumObj.GetEnumerator());
        }
        // return the result
        return partitionsList;
    }

    public override IEnumerable<KeyValuePair<long, WorkItem>>
        GetOrderableDynamicPartitions() {

        return enumSource;
    }

    private Tuple<long, long> getNextChunk() {
        // create the result tuple
        Tuple<long, long> result;
        // get an exclusive lock as we perform this operation
        lock (lockObj) {
            // check that there is still data available
            if (sharedStartIndex < dataItems.Length) {
                int sum = 0;
                long endIndex = sharedStartIndex;
                while (endIndex < dataItems.Length && sum < targetSum) {
                    sum += dataItems[endIndex].WorkDuration;
                    endIndex++;
                }
                result = new Tuple<long, long>(sharedStartIndex, endIndex);
                sharedStartIndex = endIndex;
            } else {
                // there is no data available
                result = new Tuple<long, long>(-1, -1);
            }
        }
        // end of locked region
        // return the result
        return result;
    }

    class EnumerableSource : IEnumerable<KeyValuePair<long, WorkItem>> {
        ContextPartitioner parentPartitioner;

        public EnumerableSource(ContextPartitioner parent) {
            parentPartitioner = parent;
        }

        IEnumerator IEnumerable.GetEnumerator() {
            return ((IEnumerable<WorkItem>)this).GetEnumerator();
        }
```

```
        IEnumerator<KeyValuePair<long, WorkItem>>
            IEnumerable<KeyValuePair<long, WorkItem>>.GetEnumerator() {

            return new ChunkEnumerator(parentPartitioner).GetEnumerator();
        }
    }

    class ChunkEnumerator {
        private ContextPartitioner parentPartitioner;

        public ChunkEnumerator(ContextPartitioner parent) {
            parentPartitioner = parent;
        }

        public IEnumerator<KeyValuePair<long, WorkItem>> GetEnumerator() {
            while (true) {
                // get the indices of the next chunk
                Tuple<long, long> chunkIndices = parentPartitioner.getNextChunk();
                // check that we have data to deliver
                if (chunkIndices.Item1 == -1 && chunkIndices.Item2 == -1) {
                    // there is no more data
                    break;
                } else {
                    // enter a loop to yield the data items
                    for (long i = chunkIndices.Item1; i < chunkIndices.Item2; i++) {
                        yield return new
                            KeyValuePair<long, WorkItem>(i,
                            parentPartitioner.dataItems[i]);
                    }
                }
            }
        }
    }
}

class ContextTest {
    static void Main(string[] args) {

        // create a random number source
        Random rnd = new Random();

        // create the source data
        WorkItem[] sourceData = new WorkItem[10000];
        for (int i = 0; i < sourceData.Length; i++) {
            sourceData[i] = new WorkItem() { WorkDuration = rnd.Next(1, 11) };
        }

        // create the result data array
        WorkItem[] resultData = new WorkItem[sourceData.Length];
```

213

```
        // created the contextual partitioner
        OrderablePartitioner<WorkItem> cPartitioner
            = new ContextPartitioner(sourceData, 100);

        // create the parallel
        Parallel.ForEach(cPartitioner,
            (WorkItem item, ParallelLoopState loopState, long index) => {

            // perform the work item
            item.performWork();
            // place the work item in the result array
            resultData[index] = item;
        });

        // compare the source items to the result items
        for (int i = 0; i < sourceData.Length; i++) {
            if (sourceData[i].WorkDuration != resultData[i].WorkDuration) {
                Console.WriteLine("Discrepancy at index {0}", i);
                break;
            }
        }

        // wait for input before exiting
        Console.WriteLine("Press enter to finish");
        Console.ReadLine();
        }
    }
}
```

I have included some code to test the ordering of the partitioner items at the end of Listing 5-26 to demonstrate how to use the keys and confirms that the keys generated by the partitioner match the innate order of the data items in the source array.

Common Problems and Their Causes

Take a look at the following sections for the common problems with parallel loops and their solutions.

Synchronization in Loop Bodies

A synchronization primitive is used to coordinate access to a shared variable, typically a result. Performance is significantly reduced because the tasks performing the loop body must wait to acquire the primitive on each loop body iteration.

Solution

Use TLS instead of a synchronization primitive as shown in Listing 5-11.

Example

The following example uses the **lock** keyword to synchronize access to a **double** value used to keep a running total shared between iterations of the loop body:

```
using System;
using System.Threading.Tasks;

namespace Synchronization_in_Loop_Bodies {
    class Synchronization_in_Loop_Bodies {
        static void Main(string[] args) {

            // create the shared data value
            double total = 0;
            // create a lock object
            object lockObj = new object();

            // perform a parallel loop
            Parallel.For(
                0,
                100000,
                item => {
                    // get the lock on the shared value
                    lock (lockObj) {
                        // add the square of the current
                        // value to the running total
                        total += Math.Pow(item, 2);
                    }
                });
        }
    }
}
```

Loop Body Data Races

A variation of the previous problem is to share data in the loop body *without* synchronization. This doesn't have the performance impact of using synchronization but creates a data race instead.

Solution

Use TLS as shown in Listing 5-11.

Example

The following example shows a data race where an unexpected result is generated by sharing a data value across iterations of the loop body.

```
using System;
using System.Threading.Tasks;

namespace Loop_Body_Data_Races {
```

```
class Loop_Body_Data_Races {
    static void Main(string[] args) {

        // create the shared data value
        double total = 0;

        // perform a parallel loop
        Parallel.For(
            0,
            100000,
            item => {
                // add the square of the current
                // value to the running total
                total += Math.Pow(item, 2);
            });

        Console.WriteLine("Expected result: 333328333350000");
        Console.WriteLine("Actual result: {0}", total);
    }
}
}
```

Using Standard Collections

Results generated from a parallel loop body are placed in a normal collection, as opposed to one from the System.Collections.Concurrent namespace. These collections are liable to suffer from data races when used in parallel programming and will either throw exceptions or contain unexpected results.

Solution

Always use collections from the System.Collections.Concurrent namespace.

Example

The following example illustrates this problem by using a loop body that adds items to an instance of System.Collections.Generic.List. Running the example will either result in an unexpected number of items in the result collection or an exception when the state of the list is modified by two Tasks at once.

```
using System;
using System.Collections.Generic;
using System.Threading.Tasks;

namespace Using_Standard_Collections {
    class Using_Standard_Collections {
        static void Main(string[] args) {
```

```
            // create some source data
            int[] sourceData = new int[10000];
            for (int i = 0; i < sourceData.Length; i++) {
                sourceData[i] = i;
            }

            // create a list to hold the results
            List<int> resultData = new List<int>();

            Parallel.ForEach(sourceData, item => {
                resultData.Add(item);
            });

            Console.WriteLine("Results {0}", resultData.Count);

            // wait for input before exiting
            Console.WriteLine("Press enter to finish");
            Console.ReadLine();
        }
    }
}
```

Using Changing Data

A parallel loop is used to consume data that is still being produced or modified. Unexpected results will occur because not all of the data items or unexpected values will be processed.

Solution

Avoid working with data that is being changed elsewhere. If you need to process data as it is being produced, you must implement a custom partitioner that will continue to push data to the parallel loop Tasks as it becomes available.

Example

The following example shows a Task that periodically adds an item to a List. A Parallel.ForEach loop processes the same List. However, because the contents are partitioned when the parallel loop starts, any items that the Task adds after that point are not processed.

```
using System;
using System.Collections.Generic;
using System.Threading;
using System.Threading.Tasks;

namespace Using_Changing_Data {
    class Using_Changing_Data {
        static void Main(string[] args) {
```

```
// create some source data
List<int> sourceData = new List<int>();
for (int i = 0; i < 10; i++) {
    sourceData.Add(i);
}

// start a task that adds items to the list
Task.Factory.StartNew(() => {
    int counter = 10;
    while (true) {
        Thread.Sleep(250);
        Console.WriteLine("Adding item {0}", counter);
        sourceData.Add(counter++);
    }
});

// run a parallel loop on the list
Parallel.ForEach(sourceData, item => {
    Console.WriteLine("Processing item {0}", item);
});

// wait for input before exiting
Console.WriteLine("Press enter to finish");
Console.ReadLine();
        }
    }
}
```

Summary

I hope that this chapter has shown you that parallel loops are a useful way to introduce parallelism into your programs. I also hope that you have seen the way that parallel loops use the TPL to build a set of features that are rich, flexible, robust, and easy to use.

One of the things I like most about the new parallel programming features is that you can get a lot done without having to dig into the details. In the next chapter, you'll see another excellent example of this philosophy—Parallel LINQ.

CHAPTER 6

Parallel LINQ

Listing 6-1. A Parallel LINQ Query

```
using System;
using System.Collections.Generic;
using System.Linq;

namespace Listing_01 {
    class Listing_01 {
        static void Main(string[] args) {

            int[] sourceData = new int[100];
            for (int i = 0; i < sourceData.Length; i++) {
                sourceData[i] = i;
            }

            IEnumerable<int> results =
                from item in sourceData.AsParallel()
                where item % 2 == 0
                select item;

            foreach (int item in results) {
                Console.WriteLine("Item {0}", item);
            }

            // wait for input before exiting
            Console.WriteLine("Press enter to finish");
            Console.ReadLine();
        }
    }
}
```

LINQ, But Parallel

Language Integrated Query, or LINQ (pronounced "link") adds native data querying features to .NET. Parallel LINQ, known as PLINQ, is a parallel implementation of LINQ to objects that allows the programmer to perform LINQ queries in parallel, so that multiple data items are processed concurrently.

This chapter assumes that you already know how to use LINQ, which is a topic worthy of a book by itself. In fact, if you are not familiar with LINQ, I gently point you in the direction of *Pro LINQ: Language Integrated Query in C# 2010*, which I coauthored with Joseph Rattz and which is also published by Apress.

PLINQ works with the same data sources that LINQ to Objects does, namely IEnumerable<> and IEnumerable. PLINQ doesn't work as a parallel equivalent with the other kinds of LINQ, such as LINQ to XML and LINQ to SQL. However, since the end result of most LINQ queries is an IEnumerable<>, then PLINQ can be used to parallel process the results from queries on those kinds of data.

If you know how to perform a certain kind of query with LINQ to Objects, the chances are good that you will be able to implement a parallel version without too much difficulty or even too many changes to your code.

As an example, take a look at Listing 6-1 at the start of this chapter, which shows a PLINQ query that selects even numbers from an array of integers. Aside from the call to AsParallel() on the data source, this could be a normal LINQ query.

That similarity can be beguiling; it allows a programmer familiar with LINQ to make parallel queries quickly and easily. But there are pitfalls in the details, and care and consideration are required to make PLINQ queries perform and behave properly.

This chapter will show you the different features of PLINQ, demonstrating how to make different kinds of queries and how to control and customize the way that a query is executed. Table 6-1 summarizes the topics in this chapter.

Table 6-1. PLINQ Tasks

Problem	Solution	Listing
Create a PLINQ query.	Use the AsParallel() extension method to create a ParallelQuery instance and apply LINQ features.	6-1 to 6-4
Preserve the order of PLINQ results.	Apply the AsOrdered() extension method to a ParallelQuery instance.	6-5 and 6-6
Preserve or discard ordering for PLINQ subqueries.	Apply the AsOrdered() and AsUnordered() extension methods to a ParallelQuery instance.	6-7
Perform a no-result query.	Apply the ForAll() method to a ParallelQuery instance.	6-8
Force immediate query execution.	Use the ToArray(), ToDictionary(), or ToList() extension methods.	6-9 and 6-10
Control query concurrency.	Use the WithExecutionMode() method and/or the WithDegreeOfParallelism() method.	6-11 and 6-12
Disable query concurrency.	Use the AsSequential() extension method	6-13
Handle PLINQ exceptions.	Catch System.AggregateException instances in the code that causes the query to be executed	6-14
Cancel a PLINQ query.	Use the WithCancellation() extension method	6-15

Problem	Solution	Listing
Control the rate at which results are made available to the PLINQ consumer.	Use the `WithMergeOptions()` extension method	6-16
Use a custom data partitioner.	Use the version of the `AsParallel()` method that takes an instance of `System.Collections.Concurrent.Partitioner`.	6-17 and 6-18
Create a custom aggregation.	Use the PLINQ-specific `Aggregate()` method.	6-19
Create a parallel range or repeating sequence.	Use the `ParallelEnumeration.Range()` or `ParallelEnumeration.Repeat()` method.	6-20

The public part of LINQ consists of two types in the `System.Linq` namespace: the `Enumerable` class, which contains extension methods that operate on the second type, and the `IEnumerable` interface. (There are a lot more LINQ classes, but they are hidden away behind the scenes and you won't need to use them directly). If you are not familiar with extension methods, see the "Using Custom Aggregation" section in this chapter for a brief overview.

C# contains some keywords that are specific to LINQ, such as `from`, `where`, and `select`. These keywords are mapped to extension methods in the `Enumerable` class, so that a query such as the following

```
IEnumerable<int> result =
    from item in sourceData
    where (item % 2 == 0)
    select item;
```

is mapped to something like this, where the extension methods are called directly:

```
IEnumerable<int> result =
    sourceData
    .Where(item => item % 2 == 0)
    .Select(item => item)
```

For more complex queries, using the extension methods instead of the keywords in your code can be handy, because you can use full lambda expressions. The extension methods are often referred to as the standard query operators and using them as applying the *dot-notation*.

PLINQ also has two public classes: `ParallelEnumerable` and `ParallelQuery`. The `ParallelEnumerable` class contains extension methods that operate on the `ParallelQuery` type. `ParallelEnumerable` contains methods to match each of those in `Enumerable`, plus some others that allow you to create instances of `ParallelQuery` from `IEnumerables`.

Because the methods in `ParallelEnumerable` are parallel implementations of those in `Enumerable`, once you have created a `ParallelQuery`, the magic of extension methods means that your LINQ query will use methods from `ParallelEnumerable`, rather than `Enumerable`, and you will be using PLINQ.

This neat integration extends to the C# keywords. If you apply them to an instance of `ParallelQuery`, the query will be executed using PLINQ. I'll show you how to do this in the next section.

Table 6-2 summarizes the key methods in `ParallelEnumerable`; these are the methods that you will use to convert between `IEnumerable` and `ParallelQuery` and to control the execution of a PLINQ query. All of the other methods in `ParallelEnumerable` are parallel implementations of LINQ features found in the `Enumerable` class.

Table 6-2. *Key members of the System.Linq.ParallelEnumerable class*

Member	Description
AsParallel()	Convert a `ParallelQuery` from an `IEnumerable`.
AsSequential()	Convert an `IEnumerable` from a `ParallelQuery`.
AsOrdered()	Modify a `ParallelQuery` to preserve item ordering.
AsUnordered()	Modify a `ParallelQuery` to discard item ordering.
WithCancellation()	Modify a `ParallelQuery` to monitor a cancellation token.
WithDegreeOfParallelism()	Modify a `ParallelQuery` to set an upper limit on the number of Tasks used to execute a the query.
WithExecutionMode()	Modify a `ParallelQuery` to specify either forced parallel execution or leaving the decision to PLINQ as to selecting parallel or sequential execution.
WithMergeOptions()	Modify a `ParallelQuery` to buffer the results produced by the parallel Tasks.

The first method, `AsParallel()`, is, as you will see, the key to using PLINQ. `AsSequential()` is the counter to `AsParallel()` and lets us selectively apply parallelism in a complex query. The remaining methods configure instances of `ParallelQuery` produced by `AsParallel()` to change the way that a query is executed or behaves. The following sections show you how to use these methods and other techniques to take full control of PLINQ.

Using PLINQ Queries

To use PLINQ, we must create a `ParallelQuery` instance by calling the `AsParallel()` method on an instance of `IEnumerable` and use it as the basis for applying LINQ features. Listing 6-2 shows a LINQ query and its PLINQ alternative. The queries in Listing 6-2 are *projections*; each item in a collection is processed to produce a result, and there are as many result values as there are source data items. The results are available in the `IEnumerable<double>`s that the queries produce.

Listing 6-2. LINQ and PLINQ Queries

```
using System;
using System.Collections.Generic;
using System.Linq;

namespace Listing_02 {
    class Listing_02 {
        static void Main(string[] args) {

            // create some source data
            int[] sourceData = new int[10];
            for (int i = 0; i < sourceData.Length; i++) {
                sourceData[i] = i;
            }

            // define a sequential linq query
            IEnumerable<double> results1 =
                from item in sourceData
                select Math.Pow(item, 2);

            // enumerate the results of the sequential query
            foreach (double d in results1) {
                Console.WriteLine("Sequential result: {0}", d);
            }

            // define a parallel linq query
            IEnumerable<double> results2 =
                from item in sourceData.AsParallel()
                select Math.Pow(item, 2);

            // enumerate the results of the parallel query
            foreach (double d in results2) {
                Console.WriteLine("Parallel result: {0}", d);
            }

            // wait for input before exiting
            Console.WriteLine("Press enter to finish");
            Console.ReadLine();
        }
    }
}
```

You can see that one small change creates a PLINQ query from a LINQ query. By using the `AsParallel()` extension method, we have asked the PLINQ runtime to consider processing the data items concurrently.

Notice that I said we *asked* PLINQ to *consider* concurrency. By design, LINQ and PLINQ hide a lot of complexity away from the programmer. When you write a PLINQ expression, you are specifying *what* you want to happen; the PLINQ engine analyzes your query and determines *how* to do it. In Listing 6-2, we have effectively added parallel execution to the range of options that PLINQ can consider when determining how to execute the query, but the query may still be performed sequentially if that's what the runtime decides is best. PLINQ will try to save you from situations where the cost of parallelization will create a parallel query that takes longer to perform than a sequential query. Later in the chapter, I'll show you how to force parallel execution, even if it is likely to offer poorer performance.

I mentioned that you can call the LINQ and PLINQ extension methods directly. This is how I tend to use LINQ and PLINQ when I write code. Listing 6-3 shows the queries from Listing 6-1 expressed using extension methods. I'll switch between approaches freely in the examples in this chapter to make the listings as clear as possible.

Listing 6-3. Creating Queries Using Extension Methods

```
using System;
using System.Collections.Generic;
using System.Linq;

namespace Listing_03 {
    class Listing_03 {
        static void Main(string[] args) {

            // create some source data
            int[] sourceData = new int[10];
            for (int i = 0; i < sourceData.Length; i++) {
                sourceData[i] = i;
            }

            // define a sequential linq query
            IEnumerable<double> results1 =
                sourceData.Select(item => Math.Pow(item, 2));

            // enumerate the results of the sequential query
            foreach (double d in results1) {
                Console.WriteLine("Sequential result: {0}", d);
            }

            // define a parallel linq query
            var results2 = sourceData.AsParallel()
                    .Select(item => Math.Pow(item,2));

            // enumerate the results of the parallel query
            foreach (var d in results2) {
                Console.WriteLine("Parallel result: {0}", d);
            }

            // wait for input before exiting
            Console.WriteLine("Press enter to finish");
            Console.ReadLine();
        }
    }
}
```

Listing 6-3 defines the result type of the PLINQ query to be **var**, meaning that we want the compiler to infer the type. This technique is commonly used with LINQ and is invaluable when generating types on the fly, as demonstrated in the "Ordering Query Results" section later in this chapter. I'll explicitly type the results from PLINQ queries in this chapter for clarity.

Using PLINQ Query Features

You may have noticed that there is little difference between a PLINQ projection and a parallel loop— each and every value in a data source is projected to a corresponding result.

This is true, but the power of PLINQ is that it builds on the rich feature set of LINQ to allow you to do things that would be extremely cumbersome in parallel loops. A common example is *filtering*, where a subset of items from the source data are processed. Listing 6-4 demonstrates a simple PLINQ filtering query, which projects results for even numbers only.

Listing 6-4. A PLINQ Filtering Query

```
using System;
using System.Collections.Generic;
using System.Linq;

namespace Listing_04 {
    class Listing_04 {
        static void Main(string[] args) {

            // create some source data
            int[] sourceData = new int[100000];
            for (int i = 0; i < sourceData.Length; i++) {
                sourceData[i] = i;
            }

            // define a filtering query using keywords
            IEnumerable<double> results1
                = from item in sourceData.AsParallel()
                  where item % 2 == 0
                  select Math.Pow(item, 2);

            // enumerate the results
            foreach (var d in results1) {
                Console.WriteLine("Result: {0}", d);
            }

            // define a filtering query using extension methods
            IEnumerable<double> results2
                = sourceData.AsParallel()
                .Where(item => item % 2 == 0)
                .Select(item => Math.Pow(item, 2));
```

```
        // enumerate the results
        foreach (var d in results2) {
            Console.WriteLine("Result: {0}", d);
        }

        // wait for input before exiting
        Console.WriteLine("Press enter to finish");
        Console.ReadLine();
    }
  }
}
```

PLINQ is not a solution to every parallel problem, but the breadth of features it inherits from LINQ puts it into consideration for many situations. Of special value is the ability to easily parallelize an existing LINQ query, a quick and easy way to introduce parallelism into existing .NET programs.

Ordering Query Results

If we run compile and run the code in Listing 6-2, we get the following results:

```
Sequential result: 0

Sequential result: 1

Sequential result: 4

Sequential result: 9

Sequential result: 16

Sequential result: 25

Sequential result: 36

Sequential result: 49

Sequential result: 64

Sequential result: 81

Parallel result: 9

Parallel result: 36

Parallel result: 64

Parallel result: 0
```

```
Parallel result: 16

Parallel result: 49

Parallel result: 81

Parallel result: 1

Parallel result: 25

Parallel result: 4

Press enter to finish
```

You can see that the results produced by the parallel query are not in the same order as those of the sequential query. Much as with the parallel loops we covered in the previous chapter, PLINQ partitions source data to improve efficiency in the Tasks that are used behind the scenes to execute the query and this breaks up the natural order of items.

You can preserve order in a PLINQ query by using the AsOrdered() extension method, which modifies the ParallelQuery instance that we get by calling the AsParallel() method. Listing 6-5 demonstrates this feature.

Listing 6-5. Preserving Order in a Parallel Query

```
using System;
using System.Collections.Generic;
using System.Linq;

namespace Listing_05 {
    class Listing_05 {
        static void Main(string[] args) {

            // create some source data
            int[] sourceData = new int[10];
            for (int i = 0; i < sourceData.Length; i++) {
                sourceData[i] = i;
            }

            // preserve order with the AsOrdered() method
            IEnumerable<double> results =
                from item in sourceData.AsParallel().AsOrdered()
                select Math.Pow(item, 2);

            // enumerate the results of the parallel query
            foreach (double d in results) {
                Console.WriteLine("Parallel result: {0}", d);
            }
```

```
            // wait for input before exiting
            Console.WriteLine("Press enter to finish");
            Console.ReadLine();
        }
    }
}
```

Compiling and running the code in Listing 6-4 gives us the same results, in the same order as if we had performed a sequential query, but with the benefits of parallel execution. Well, almost.

We lost ordering in the original PLINQ query because the data was partitioned to improve performance, so it follows that there is a performance cost to restore the order with the `AsOrdered()` method.

You should only use the `AsOrdered()` method if the order of the results in relation to the source data is important (i.e., you need the *n*th result item to be the result of processing the *n*th source item). In such situations, creating a dynamic type that preserves this relationship is often more efficient. Listing 6-6 shows the common misuse of `AsOrdered()` and a more efficient alternative.

Listing 6-6. Misusing the AsOrdered() Extension Method

```
using System;
using System.Collections.Generic;
using System.Linq;

namespace Listing_06 {
    class Listing_06 {
        static void Main(string[] args) {

            // create some source data
            int[] sourceData = new int[5];
            for (int i = 0; i < sourceData.Length; i++) {
                sourceData[i] = i;
            }

            // preserve order with the AsOrdered() method
            IEnumerable<double> results1 =
                from item in sourceData.AsParallel().AsOrdered()
                select Math.Pow(item, 2);

            // create an index into the source array
            int index = 0;

            // enumerate the results
            foreach (double d in results1) {
                Console.WriteLine("Bad result {0} from item {1}", d, index++);
            }
```

```
            // perform the query without ordering the results
            var results2 =
                from item in sourceData.AsParallel()
                select new {
                    sourceValue = item,
                    resultValue = Math.Pow(item, 2)
                };

            // enumerate the results
            foreach (var v in results2) {
                Console.WriteLine("Better result {0} from item {1}",
                    v.resultValue, v.sourceValue);
            }

            // wait for input before exiting
            Console.WriteLine("Press enter to finish");
            Console.ReadLine();
        }
    }
}
```

Compiling and running the code in Listing 6-6 gives us the following results. You can see that using dynamic types allows us to preserve the relationship between source and result data items without having to force ordering.

```
Bad result 0 from item 0

Bad result 1 from item 1

Bad result 4 from item 2

Bad result 9 from item 3

Bad result 16 from item 4

Better result 0 from item 0

Better result 4 from item 2

Better result 9 from item 3

Better result 16 from item 4

Better result 1 from item 1

Press enter to finish
```

■ **Tip** One situation when you must be sure to use `AsOrdered()` is when you are modifying existing code to parallelize a LINQ query and the consumer of the results expects the results to be in order.

Using Ordered Subqueries

Once you have called `AsOrdered()`, each subsequent PLINQ operation that you perform preserves order, which means that order is lost and then reconstructed, with the associated performance hit, for each part of a multistep query.

You can control ordering from one part of a query to the next by combing the `AsOrdered()` and `AsUnordered()` extension methods. The `AsUnordered()` method does the exact opposite to `AsOrdered()`, and tells PLINQ that order need not be preserved.

Listing 6-7 shows you how to do so. In the example, the first ten items are taken from the data source after the `AsParallel()` method is called. For this part of the query, the items are ordered. The taken items are then used as the basis for a call to `Select()`, which can be performed without ordering, so we call the `AsUnordered()` method.

Listing 6-7. Combining Ordered and Unordered Queries

```
using System;
using System.Collections.Generic;
using System.Linq;
using System.Text;

namespace Listing_07 {
    class Listing_07 {
        static void Main(string[] args) {

            // create some source data
            int[] sourceData = new int[10000];
            for (int i = 0; i < sourceData.Length; i++) {
                sourceData[i] = i;
            }

            // define a query that has an ordered subquery
            var result =
                sourceData.AsParallel().AsOrdered()
                .Take(10).AsUnordered()
                .Select(item => new {
                    sourceValue = item,
                    resultValue = Math.Pow(item, 2)
                });

            foreach (var v in result) {
                Console.WriteLine("Source {0}, Result {1}",
                    v.sourceValue, v.resultValue);
            }
```

```
            // wait for input before exiting
            Console.WriteLine("Press enter to finish");
            Console.ReadLine();

        }
    }
}
```

The effect of calling AsOrdered() or AsUnordered() carries through into further subqueries, so in the case of Listing 6-6 any additional subqueries would be unordered.

Performing a No-Result Query

The ForAll() extension method performs a System.Action on each item in a ParallelQuery. This may seem oddly duplicative of a parallel loop, and it is. But this feature means that you can take advantage of other PLINQ features such as filtering. Listing 6-8 demonstrates using ForAll() to print even valued data items and their second power to the console.

Listing 6-8. Using the ForAll() Extension Method

```
using System;
using System.Linq;

namespace Listing_08 {
    class Listing_08 {
        static void Main(string[] args) {

            // create some source data
            int[] sourceData = new int[50];
            for (int i = 0; i < sourceData.Length; i++) {
                sourceData[i] = i;
            }

            // filter the data and call ForAll()
            sourceData.AsParallel()
                .Where(item => item % 2 == 0)
                .ForAll(item => Console.WriteLine("Item {0} Result {1}",
                    item, Math.Pow(item, 2)));

            // wait for input before exiting
            Console.WriteLine("Press enter to finish");
            Console.ReadLine();
        }
    }
}
```

The ForAll() method can be a surprisingly useful way to take advantage of the rich LINQ features in parallel code; the main limitation is that you can't return a result from the Action which ForAll() invokes.

Managing Deferred Query Execution

PLINQ queries are not executed until the results are required, which is known as *deferred* or *lazy execution*. This is the same model as for LINQ, and the idea is that you don't incur the cost of performing a query if you don't use the results. Listing 6-9 demonstrates how this works.

Listing 6-9. Deferred PLINQ Execution

```
using System;
using System.Collections.Generic;
using System.Linq;
using System.Threading;

namespace Listing_09 {
    class Listing_09 {
        static void Main(string[] args) {

            // create some source data
            int[] sourceData = new int[10];
            for (int i = 0; i < sourceData.Length; i++) {
                sourceData[i] = i;
            }

            Console.WriteLine("Defining PLINQ query");
            // define the query
            IEnumerable<double> results =
                sourceData.AsParallel().Select(item => {
                    Console.WriteLine("Processing item {0}", item);
                    return Math.Pow(item, 2);
                });

            Console.WriteLine("Waiting...");
            Thread.Sleep(5000);

            // sum the results - this will trigger
            // execution of the query
            Console.WriteLine("Accessing results");
            double total = 0;
            foreach (double d in results) {
                total += d;
            }
            Console.WriteLine("Total {0}", total);

            // wait for input before exiting
            Console.WriteLine("Press enter to finish");
            Console.ReadLine();

        }
    }
}
```

Compiling and running the code in the listing produces the results shown following. The query is defined but not executed until the `foreach` loop starts to read the results.

```
Defining PLINQ query

Waiting...

Accessing results

Processing item 0

...

Processing item 9

Total 285

Press enter to finish
```

For most situations, deferred execution is fine, but sometimes, you want to ensure that a query is performed as soon as it is defined. In such cases, you can force immediate execution by calling the `ToArray()`, `ToDictionary()`, or `ToList()` extension methods as the last element in a PLINQ query. Listing 6-10 demonstrates how this can be applied to our previous example.

Listing 6-10. Forcing Immediate Query Execution

```csharp
using System;
using System.Collections.Generic;
using System.Linq;
using System.Threading;

namespace Listing_10 {
    class Listing_10 {
        static void Main(string[] args) {

            // create some source data
            int[] sourceData = new int[10];
            for (int i = 0; i < sourceData.Length; i++) {
                sourceData[i] = i;
            }

            Console.WriteLine("Defining PLINQ query");
            // define the query
            IEnumerable<double> results =
                sourceData.AsParallel().Select(item => {
                    Console.WriteLine("Processing item {0}", item);
                    return Math.Pow(item, 2);
                }).ToArray();
```

```
        Console.WriteLine("Waiting...");
        Thread.Sleep(5000);

        // sum the results - this will trigger
        // execution of the query
        Console.WriteLine("Accessing results");
        double total = 0;
        foreach (double d in results) {
            total += d;
        }
        Console.WriteLine("Total {0}", total);

        // wait for input before exiting
        Console.WriteLine("Press enter to finish");
        Console.ReadLine();

    }
  }
}
```

When we compile and run this code, we get the following results, which demonstrate that the query is executed immediately:

```
Defining PLINQ query

Processing item 0

...

Processing item 9

Waiting...

Accessing results

Total 285

Press enter to finish
```

Controlling Concurrency

I mentioned earlier in this chapter that PLINQ analyses your query to determine the best way to execute it and may, as a consequence, decide that sequential execution will offer better performance. As with all parallel programming features, there is an overhead associated with creating and managing the concurrent workload.

In general, you should leave PLINQ to determine the most effective strategy, but if you are not getting the performance you expect (or if you just can't leave well alone), some options are available for controlling the concurrency used to perform your query.

Forcing Parallelism

You can request that a query be performed concurrently by using the `WithExecutionMode()` extension method, which takes a value from the `ParallelExecutionMode` enumeration as an argument. The values of the enumeration are shown in Table 6-3.

Table 6-3. Values of the System.Linq.ParallelExecutionMode enumeration

Enumeration Value	Description
Default	The PLINQ runtime will determine whether to execute a query sequentially or in parallel.
ForceParallelism	The query will be parallelized, even if the overhead of parallel execution is likely to outweigh the benefit of concurrency..

The `WithExecutionMode()` method modifies an instance of `ParallelQuery`; Listing 6-11 demonstrates the use of this method.

Listing 6-11. Forcing Parallel Execution of a Query

```
using System;
using System.Collections.Generic;
using System.Linq;

namespace Listing_11 {
    class Listing_11 {
        static void Main(string[] args) {

            // create some source data
            int[] sourceData = new int[10];
            for (int i = 0; i < sourceData.Length; i++) {
                sourceData[i] = i;
            }

            // define the query and force parallelism
            IEnumerable<double> results =
                sourceData.AsParallel()
                .WithExecutionMode(ParallelExecutionMode.ForceParallelism)
                .Where(item => item % 2 == 0)
                .Select(item => Math.Pow(item, 2));
```

```
        // enumerate the results
        foreach (double d in results) {
            Console.WriteLine("Result {0}", d);
        }

        // wait for input before exiting
        Console.WriteLine("Press enter to finish");
        Console.ReadLine();

        }
    }
}
```

Limiting Parallelism

You can request an upper limit to the number of Tasks that will be used to perform your LINQ query by using the WithDegreeOfParallelism() extension method. The PLINQ engine may choose to use fewer Tasks than you specify with this method. Listing 6-12 demonstrates the use of this method to specify a maximum of two Tasks.

Listing 6-12. Limiting the Degree of Parallelism for a Query

```
using System;
using System.Collections.Generic;
using System.Linq;

namespace Listing_12 {
    class Listing_12 {
        static void Main(string[] args) {

            // create some source data
            int[] sourceData = new int[10];
            for (int i = 0; i < sourceData.Length; i++) {
                sourceData[i] = i;
            }

            // define the query and force parallelism
            IEnumerable<double> results =
                sourceData.AsParallel()
                .WithDegreeOfParallelism(2)
                .Where(item => item % 2 == 0)
                .Select(item => Math.Pow(item, 2));

            // enumerate the results
            foreach (double d in results) {
                Console.WriteLine("Result {0}", d);
            }
```

```
            // wait for input before exiting
            Console.WriteLine("Press enter to finish");
            Console.ReadLine();


        }
    }
}
```

Forcing Sequential Execution

The AsSequential() extension method takes a ParallelQuery and returns a regular, sequential
IEnumerable. This method is the opposite of AsParallel(). You can use AsSequential() to enable and
disable parallelism in subqueries, and this technique can be useful if you want to explicitly avoid the
overhead of parallel execution for part of a multistep query, for example. Listing 6-13 demonstrates the
use of this method. The first part of the query squares the source values in parallel, and the second part
of the query, where the squared values are then doubled, is performed sequentially.

Listing 6-13. Using the AsSequential() Extension Method

```
using System;
using System.Collections.Generic;
using System.Linq;

namespace Listing_13 {
    class Listing_13 {
        static void Main(string[] args) {

            // create some source data
            int[] sourceData = new int[10];
            for (int i = 0; i < sourceData.Length; i++) {
                sourceData[i] = i;
            }

            // define the query and force parallelism
            IEnumerable<double> results =
                sourceData.AsParallel()
                .WithDegreeOfParallelism(2)
                .Where(item => item % 2 == 0)
                .Select(item => Math.Pow(item, 2))
                .AsSequential()
                .Select(item => item * 2);

            // enumerate the results
            foreach (double d in results) {
                Console.WriteLine("Result {0}", d);
            }
```

```
            // wait for input before exiting
            Console.WriteLine("Press enter to finish");
            Console.ReadLine();
        }
    }
}
```

Handling PLINQ Exceptions

Any exceptions thrown in a PLINQ query will be packaged in a `System.AggregateException`. See Chapter 2 for details of how to work with `AggregateException` instances.

The `AggregateException` is thrown when the query is executed; this is usually when the results are enumerated because execution of the query is typically deferred until that happens. If you have forced immediate execution, or have used the `ForAll()` method, the exceptions will be thrown at those points in your code.

Listing 6-14 demonstrates how to catch and process an exception that is thrown in a `select` clause of a PLINQ query when a specific source data value is encountered.

Listing 6-14. Handling Exceptions in a PLINQ Query

```
using System;
using System.Collections.Generic;
using System.Linq;

namespace Listing_14 {
    class Listing_14 {
        static void Main(string[] args) {

            // create some source data
            int[] sourceData = new int[100];
            for (int i = 0; i < sourceData.Length; i++) {
                sourceData[i] = i;
            }

            // define the query and force parallelism
            IEnumerable<double> results =
                sourceData.AsParallel()
                .Select(item => {
                    if (item == 45) {
                        throw new Exception();
                    }
                    return Math.Pow(item, 2);
                });
```

```
            // enumerate the results
            try {
                foreach (double d in results) {
                    Console.WriteLine("Result {0}", d);
                }
            } catch (AggregateException aggException) {
                aggException.Handle(exception => {
                    Console.WriteLine("Handled exception of type: {0}",
                        exception.GetType());
                    return true;
                });
            }

            // wait for input before exiting
            Console.WriteLine("Press enter to finish");
            Console.ReadLine();
        }
    }
}
```

PLINQ may continue to process data after an exception has been thrown, which means that you should not use exceptions to manually terminate a PLINQ query.

Cancelling PLINQ Queries

PLINQ supports cancellation using the `CancellationTokens` you have seen throughout this book. You associate a token with a query using the `WithCancellation()` extension method. Listing 6-15 demonstrates cancellation by using a token that is cancelled by a `Task` while the results of a query are being enumerated.

Listing 6-15. Cancelling PLINQ Queries

```
using System;
using System.Collections.Generic;
using System.Linq;
using System.Threading;
using System.Threading.Tasks;

namespace Listing_15 {
    class Listing_15 {
        static void Main(string[] args) {

            // create a cancellation token source
            CancellationTokenSource tokenSource
                = new CancellationTokenSource();
```

```
// create some source data
int[] sourceData = new int[1000000];
for (int i = 0; i < sourceData.Length; i++) {
    sourceData[i] = i;
}

// define a query that supports cancellation
IEnumerable<double> results = sourceData
    .AsParallel()
    .WithCancellation(tokenSource.Token)
    .Select(item => {
        // return the result value
        return Math.Pow(item, 2);
    });

// create a task that will wait for 5 seconds
// and then cancel the token
Task.Factory.StartNew(() => {
    Thread.Sleep(5000);
    tokenSource.Cancel();
    Console.WriteLine("Token source cancelled");
});

try {
    // enumerate the query results
    foreach (double d in results) {
        Console.WriteLine("Result: {0}", d);
    }
} catch (OperationCanceledException) {
    Console.WriteLine("Caught cancellation exception");
}

// wait for input before exiting
Console.WriteLine("Press enter to finish");
Console.ReadLine();
        }
    }
}
```

If a query is cancelled, a System.OperationCanceledException is thrown, and you should catch this in the code that has caused the query to be executed. It will usually be the statements in which you enumerate the results or in the ForAll() method. PLINQ may continue to process some items after a cancellation has been performed, so you must not assume that cancellation will terminate your query immediately.

Setting Merge Options

When you execute a PLINQ query, Tasks are assigned to process blocks of source data to produce a series of results, which are then consumed—typically by a sequential enumeration. You can control how the results are passed from the Tasks to the consumer by using the WithMergeOptions() method on an instance of `ParallelQuery`. This method takes a value from the `ParallelMergeOptions` enumeration, which is summarized in Table 6-4.

Table 6-4. Values of the System.Linq.ParallelMergeOptions Enumeration

Enumeration Value	Description
`Default` `AutoBuffered`	Use the default merge option, which is to buffer a number of results selected by the runtime.
`NotBuffered`	Each result is passed to the consumer as soon as it has been produced.
`FullyBuffered`	All of the results are produced before any of them are passed to the consumer.

Specifying a merge option can be useful when you have a PLINQ query that takes a significant amount of time to generate each result item. With the default or fully buffered options, the consumer will not receive any results for an extended period of time. Listing 6-16 shows how to set the merge option.

Listing 6-16. A Fully Buffered PLINQ Query

```
using System;
using System.Collections.Generic;
using System.Linq;

namespace Listing_16 {
    class Listing_16 {
        static void Main(string[] args) {

            // create some source data
            int[] sourceData = new int[5];
            for (int i = 0; i < sourceData.Length; i++) {
                sourceData[i] = i;
            }

            // define a fully buffered query
            IEnumerable<double> results =
                sourceData.AsParallel()
                .WithMergeOptions(ParallelMergeOptions.FullyBuffered)
                .Select(item => {
                    double resultItem = Math.Pow(item, 2);
                    Console.WriteLine("Produced result {0}", resultItem);
                    return resultItem;
                });

            // enumerate the query results
            foreach (double d in results) {
                Console.WriteLine("Enumeration got result {0}", d);
            }
```

```
        // wait for input before exiting
        Console.WriteLine("Press enter to finish");
        Console.ReadLine();
    }
  }
}
```

Compiling and running the code in Listing 6-16 produces the output that follows. You can see that all of the results are generated before any of them are made available for enumeration by the **foreach** loop.

```
Produced result 16

Produced result 9

Produced result 0

Produced result 4

Produced result 1

Enumeration got result 0

Enumeration got result 1

Enumeration got result 4

Enumeration got result 9

Enumeration got result 16

Press enter to finish
```

Using Custom Partitioning

PLINQ uses the same partitioning approach that you saw in the previous chapter. You can specify a customer partitioner for your PLINQ query by using the version of the **AsParallel()** method that takes an instance of the **System.Collections.Concurrent.Partitioner** class as an argument. The previous chapter showed you how to create a custom dynamic partitioner, where the number of partitions is not known in advance. Parallel loops support only dynamic partitioners. PLINQ supports the simpler static partitioners, which are much easier to write, since you can simply break up the data into blocks. Listing 6-17 shows a simple static partitioner that works on arrays; see the previous chapter for details of the methods that are required to implement a partitioner.

Listing 6-17. A Simple Static Partitioner

```
using System;
using System.Collections;
using System.Collections.Concurrent;
using System.Collections.Generic;

namespace Listing_17 {

    public class StaticPartitioner<T> : Partitioner<T> {
        private T[] Data;

        public StaticPartitioner(T[] data) {
            Data = data;
        }

        public override bool SupportsDynamicPartitions {
            get {
                return false;
            }
        }

        public override IList<IEnumerator<T>> GetPartitions(int partitionCount) {
            // create the list to hold the enumerators
            IList<IEnumerator<T>> list = new List<IEnumerator<T>>();
            // determine how many items per enumerator
            int itemsPerEnum = Data.Length / partitionCount;
            // process all but the last partition
            for (int i = 0; i < partitionCount - 1; i++) {
                list.Add(CreateEnum(i * itemsPerEnum, (i + 1) * itemsPerEnum));
            }
            // handle the last, potentially irregularly sized, partition
            list.Add(CreateEnum((partitionCount - 1) * itemsPerEnum,
                Data.Length));
            // return the list as the result
            return list;
        }

        IEnumerator<T> CreateEnum(int startIndex, int endIndex) {
            int index = startIndex;
            while (index < endIndex) {
                yield return Data[index++];
            }
        }
    }
}
```

The `StaticPartitioner` class in Listing 6-17 breaks up the array of objects into partitions that are roughly the same size to ensure that each `Task` that PLINQ assigns to process data receives about the same amount of data to work on. Listing 6-18 demonstrates how to use a custom partitioner with PLINQ.

Rather than call AsParallel() on the source data, we call it on an instance of the partitioner, in this case, the StaticPartitioner class from the Listing 6-17.

Listing 6-18. Using a Custom Partitioner

```
using System;
using System.Collections;
using System.Collections.Concurrent;
using System.Collections.Generic;
using System.Linq;

namespace Listing_18 {
    class Listing_18 {
        static void Main(string[] args) {


            // create some source data
            int[] sourceData = new int[10];
            for (int i = 0; i < sourceData.Length; i++) {
                sourceData[i] = i;
            }

            // create the partitioner
            StaticPartitioner<int> partitioner = new StaticPartitioner<int>(sourceData);

            // define a query
            IEnumerable<double> results =
                partitioner.AsParallel()
                .Select(item => Math.Pow(item, 2));

            // enumerate the query results
            foreach (double d in results) {
                Console.WriteLine("Enumeration got result {0}", d);
            }

            // wait for input before exiting
            Console.WriteLine("Press enter to finish");
            Console.ReadLine();


        }
    }
}
```

If you wish to preserve order in PLINQ results with a custom partitioner, your class must derive from OrderablePartitioner; see the previous chapter for details of this class and how it differs from Partitioner.

Using Custom Aggregation

Aggregation is where many data items are processed to produce a single result. Some aggregations are used so frequently that there are dedicated LINQ/PLINQ methods to support them—Sum(), Average(), Count(), and so on.

The ParallelEnumerable class supports a version of the Aggregate() extension method that is unique to PLINQ and provides support for custom parallel aggregation. The PLINQ Aggregate() method version takes four functions or lambda expressions as arguments. Here's what these functions do:

- *Define the initial value for the result*: this is executed once for the aggregation.

- *Process each data value*: When the data value is processed, the function takes the subtotal for the current Task and the present data item as arguments. This is executed for each data value.

- *Process each per-Task subtotal*: When the data value is processed, take the subtotal and the overall total as arguments. This is executed for each Task assigned to perform the aggregation.

- *Process the final result*: This is executed once for the aggregation.

The best way of understanding the Aggregation() is with an example. Listing 6-19 demonstrates a simple aggregation, which calculates half the sum of the squares of the first 10,000 integer values.

Listing 6-19. PLINQ Custom Aggregation

```
using System;
using System.Linq;

namespace Listing_19 {
    class Listing_19 {
        static void Main(string[] args) {

            // create some source data
            int[] sourceData = new int[10000];
            for (int i = 0; i < sourceData.Length; i++) {
                sourceData[i] = i;
            }

            // perform a custom aggregation
            double aggregateResult = sourceData.AsParallel().Aggregate(
                // 1st function - initialize the result
                0.0,
                // 2nd function - process each item and the per-Task subtotal
                (subtotal, item) => subtotal += Math.Pow(item, 2),
                // 3rd function - process the overall total and the per-Task total
                (total, subtotal) => total + subtotal,
                // 4th function - perform final processing
                total => total/2);

            // write out the result
            Console.WriteLine("Total: {0}", aggregateResult);
```

```
            // wait for input before exiting
            Console.WriteLine("Press enter to finish");
            Console.ReadLine();
        }
    }
}
```

For the first function, we initialize the result, which is a **double**. We use lambda expressions in the listing, so to create a new double with a value of 0, we simply call this:

```
// 1st function - initialize the result
0.0,
```

The second function allows me to process each data value and add it to the running total for the current **Task**. If we want to add the square of the current data value to the total, we call the following:

```
// 2nd function - process each item and the per-Task subtotal
(subtotal, item) => subtotal += Math.Pow(item, 2),
```

The subtotal is a **double** (the type of the result), and the item is an **int** (the type of the source data array). The third function is called when each **Task** finishes processing data; it allows us to combine the result value generated by each **Task** with the overall result. We want to sum the per-**Task** results together, so we call the following function:

```
// 3rd function - process the overall total and the per-Task total
(total, subtotal) => total + subtotal,
```

The arguments **total** and **subtotal** are both **doubles**. Finally, we have the chance to do any final processing of the overall result before it is returned as the aggregated result. In the case of the example, we want to return only half of the total, so we call this:

```
// 4th function - perform final processing
total => total/2
```

If you read the example again, you will see that it shares some characteristics with the use of TLS in parallel loops; see the previous chapter for details. Although creating custom parallel aggregations can be confusing at first glance, the ability to do so can be a useful and powerful tool—much like PLINQ overall.

Generating Parallel Ranges

Although the most common way of creating instances of **ParallelQuery** is through the **AsParallel()** extension method, two other means are available: the **ParallelEnumerable.Range()** and **ParallelEnumerable.Repeat()** methods. The **Range()** method generates a sequence of stepped integer values, whereas the **Repeat()** method generates a sequence that contains the same value repeated over and over. These methods do the same thing as the equivalent methods in the **Enumerable** class, but since they return **ParallelQuery** instances as their results, any processing that you do on them will be handled using PLINQ. Listing 6-20 demonstrates PLINQ queries using these methods.

Listing 6-20. Using Parallel Ranges and Repeating Sequences

```
using System;
using System.Collections.Generic;
using System.Linq;

namespace Listing_20 {
    class Listing_20 {
        static void Main(string[] args) {

            // use PLINQ to process a parallel range
            IEnumerable<double> result1 =
                from e in ParallelEnumerable.Range(0, 10)
                where e % 2 == 0
                select Math.Pow(e, 2);

            // use PLINQ to process a parallel repeating sequence
            IEnumerable<double> result2 =
                ParallelEnumerable.Repeat(10, 100)
                .Select(item => Math.Pow(item, 2));

            // wait for input before exiting
            Console.WriteLine("Press enter to finish");
            Console.ReadLine();
        }
    }
}
```

Common Problems and Their Causes

Take a look at the following sections for common PLINQ problems and their solutions.

Forgetting the PLINQ Basics

Two related items are not calling `AsParallel()` on the source data to switch from LINQ to PLINQ and defining the PLINQ query without enumerating the results, which means that the query is never executed. I have grouped these two together into one problem because I fall foul of them often. I have lost count of the number of times just in writing this chapter that I have not gotten the result or performance that I was expecting, and the problem turned out to be a lack of parallelism or, worse, a lack of any data being processed.

Solution

I find that a daily multivitamin supplement seems to help me maintain attention when writing code for long periods. Otherwise, I think the best hope is for some kind of cure for aging and the forgetfulness that comes with it.

Creating Race Conditions

A common trick with LINQ is to use the where clause to filter items from the source data while some external value has a specified value and is modified inside the where clause itself. This presents a data race with PLINQ because multiple Tasks can be reading and modifying the value at once.

Solution

Perform the filter sequentially before processing the data in parallel. Or find a PLINQ method that will work safely with multiple threads (e.g., the Take() method would be a suitable alternative to the example code for this problem). As a last resort, use a synchronization primitive to control access to the shared value.

Example

The following example uses a shared value to limit the number of items that the where clause filters for processing and so suffers from a race condition:

```
using System;
using System.Linq;

namespace Creating_Race_Conditions {
    class Creating_Race_Conditions {
        static void Main(string[] args) {

            // create some source data
            int[] sourceData = new int[10000];
            for (int i = 0; i < sourceData.Length; i++) {
                sourceData[i] = i;
            }

            // create a counter - this will be shared
            int counter = 1000;

            // create a plinq query that uses the shared value
            var result = from e in sourceData.AsParallel()
                        where (counter-- > 0)
                        select e;

            Console.WriteLine("Expected {0} items", counter);
            Console.WriteLine("Got {0} items", result.ToArray().Length);
        }
    }
}
```

Confusing Ordering

A common problem is confusing the use of the AsOrderable() and OrderBy() methods. AsOrderable() preserves the order of the query results so that the nth result is the result of processing the nth item in the source data. The OrderBy() method sorts the items rather than preserve their natural order.

Solution

Pay close attention to how you order the source data.

Example

The following example demonstrates the two different ordering techniques:

```
using System;
using System.Linq;

namespace Confusing_Ordering {
    class Confusing_Ordering {
        static void Main(string[] args) {

            string[] sourceData = new string[] {
                "an", "apple", "a", "day", "keeps",
                "the", "doctor", "away"};

            // create an AsOrdered() query
            var result1 = sourceData.AsParallel()
                .AsOrdered()
                .Select(item => item);

            // enumerate the results
            foreach (var v in result1) {
                Console.WriteLine("AsOrdered() - {0}", v);
            }

            // create an OrderBy() query
            var result2 = sourceData.AsParallel()
                .OrderBy(item => item)
                .Select(item => item);

            // enumerate the results
            foreach (var v in result2) {
                Console.WriteLine("OrderBy() - {0}", v);
            }
        }
    }
}
```

Sequential Filtering

When adapting exiting LINQ filtering queries to PLINQ, a common error is to apply the `AsParallel()` method to the results of the filtering expression rather than to the source data. This means that the filtering is performed sequentially, and the remainder of the query performed in parallel, as opposed to the entire query being performed in parallel.

Solution

Apply the AsParallel() method to the source data.

Example

The following example demonstrates inadvertent sequential filtering in an otherwise parallel query:

```
using System;
using System.Linq;

namespace Sequential_Filtering {
    class Sequential_Filtering {
        static void Main(string[] args) {

            // create some source data
            int[] source1 = new int[100];
            for (int i = 0; i < source1.Length; i++) {
                source1[i] = i;
            }

            // perform the query - but note
            // where the AsParallel call is
            var result = source1
                .Where(item => item % 2 == 0)
                .AsParallel()
                .Select(item => item);

            // wait for input before exiting
            Console.WriteLine("Press enter to finish");
            Console.ReadLine();
        }
    }
}
```

Summary

PLINQ, like parallel loops, lets you take advantage of parallel programming with minimum changes to your program design. There are pitfalls, of course, as you learned in this chapter, but the ease with which you can parallelize LINQ to Objects queries is something to behold. I already liked LINQ enough to write a book about it, and seeing the new parallel execution support in PLINQ was like receiving a gift.

If you already use LINQ, you will find PLINQ creeping into your projects pretty quickly. And, if you don't use LINQ, I strongly encourage you to look closely at the examples in this chapter and give some thought as to how you might apply this feature to simplify and parallelize data-centric applications.

CHAPTER 7

■ ■ ■

Testing and Debugging

Listing 7-1. A Simple Deadlock

```csharp
using System;
using System.Threading.Tasks;
using System.Diagnostics;

namespace Listing_01 {
    class Listing_01 {
        static void Main(string[] args) {

            Task[] tasks = new Task[2];

            tasks[0] = Task.Factory.StartNew(() => {
                tasks[1].Wait();
            });

            tasks[1] = Task.Factory.StartNew(() => {
                tasks[0].Wait();
            });

            Console.WriteLine("Waiting for tasks to complete.");
            Task.WaitAll(tasks);
        }
    }
}
```

Making Things Better When Everything Goes Wrong

Parallel programming can create complex problems. Sometimes, the problems relate to performance ("that's too slow") and sometimes to correctness ("that's the wrong answer"). This chapter gives you a brief overview of the tools available to help you understand the performance and the behavior of your application.

I say a "brief" overview, because fixing performance and correctness problems depends very much on the nature of the problem and the design of the parallel application. One of the biggest aids to solving problems is, inconveniently, prior experience in solving similar problems; it can be hard to understand what is going wrong, until you have reached a critical mass of time spent debugging. You should be able to recognize the problem in Listing 7-1, but it is rare that problems are so easy to spot in real projects. But debugging does get easier, an, while you will never stop creating bugs, you *will* get better at finding them and fixing them.

Measuring Parallel Performance

The very point of parallel programming is to improve performance. Why else would we be trying to distribute work across multiple cores and processors? One of the questions you will ask yourself again and again as you write parallel programs is, "Can I make it faster?"

The answer to that question depends on the problem you are solving and the way you have written your code, but the first step in any optimization process is measurement. Unless you know what you are starting with, you have no means of assessing the impact of any changes you make.

Using Good Coding Strategies

In general, there are some basic tips that will help you get good performance from your parallel code.

Using Synchronization Sparingly

Every synchronization primitive is effectively a bottleneck; multiple Tasks will have to wait while they acquire the lock on a primitive. As the ratio of Tasks to synchronization primitives increases, the more waiting there will be. Each time you add synchronization to your program, you will reduce the performance, so you should use synchronization as little as possible.

Using Synchronization Readily

Of course, if you don't use synchronization at all, you will cause data races, and we know where that leads. So, the goal is to use just enough synchronization to ensure the correct behavior of your program without having an unnecessary impact on overall performance. Don't avoid using synchronization where you really need it—just don't use it as a belt-and-braces solution because you don't want to work out where the data races arise in your code.

Partitioning Work Evenly

As a rule of thumb, the more evenly you are able to spread you work across Tasks, the more evenly work will be assigned to cores and better the performance of your parallel program will be. If one Task has to perform 90 percent of the work, for example, the opportunities for other cores or processors to speed up execution are limited to the remaining 10 percent of the work.

When using parallel loop or PLINQ, you can control how work is divided up by selecting a specific partitioning strategy or providing your own custom partitioner. See Chapters 5 and 6 for details and examples.

Avoiding Parallelizing Small Work Loads

Setting up and managing Tasks, PLINQ queries or a parallel loop incurs a degree of overhead. For small workloads, that overhead outweighs the performance gains that parallel execution can deliver. Don't automatically parallelize everything in your program; sequential execution can sometimes offer the best performance.

Measure Different Degrees of Concurrency

Performance can change drastically with different degrees of concurrency—not just in the obvious way of having more or fewer cores available. The effects (or lack of effect) of synchronization can become apparent, different kinds of data race can appear, and assumptions made about program structure and execution can be easily undermined.

Always measure the effect of changing concurrency, especially if your target platform is configured differently from your development platform. You can alter concurrency by configuring the task scheduler (see Chapter 4) or by setting options for parallel loops and PLINQ (see chapters 5 and 6).

Making Simple Performance Comparisons

You will often want to compare different approaches to solving a problem. For example, you might want to see how using a different synchronization primitive changes performance, compare PLINQ to a parallel loop, or alter the degree of concurrency of your parallel program. In such cases, the System.Diagnostics.Stopwatch class is your friend.

Stopwatch is a very accurate timer that you can use to measure performance. Table 7-1 summarizes the key methods of the Stopwatch class.

Table 7-1. Key Members of the System.Diagnostics.Stopwatch Class

Member	Description
Start()	Start timing.
StartNew()	This static convenience method returns a new instance of Stopwatch on which the Start() method has been called.
Stop()	Stop timing.
Reset()	Stop timing, and reset the elapsed time.
Restart()	Reset the elapsed time, and start timing.
IsRunning	Return true if the Stopwatch is currently timing.
Elapsed	Return a TimeSpan representing the elapsed time recorded by the Stopwatch.
ElapsedMilliseconds	Return the number of elapsed milliseconds recorded by the Stopwatch.
ElapsedTicks	Return the number of timer ticks recorded by the Stopwatch.

The Stopwatch class is easy to use and can give a good indication as to the relative performance of different techniques. However, you must make sure that you repeat the work you are measuring several times. If you measure the work only once, you run the risk of including overhead associated with the .NET runtime, such as just-in-time compilation. Listing 7-2 demonstrates how to use the Stopwatch class to measure different degrees of concurrency in a parallel loop.

Listing 7-2. Using Stopwatch to Measure Parallel Loop Concurrency

```
using System;
using System.Diagnostics;
using System.Threading.Tasks;

namespace Listing_02 {
    class Listing_02 {
        static void Main(string[] args) {

            // create some source data
            Random rnd = new Random();
            int[] sourceData = new int[100000000];
            for (int i = 0; i < sourceData.Length; i++) {
                sourceData[i] = rnd.Next(0, int.MaxValue);
            }

            // define the measurement variables
            int numberOfIterations = 10;
            int maxDegreeOfConcurrency = 16;

            // define the lock object for updating the shared result
            object lockObj = new object();

            // outer loop is degree of concurrency
            for (int concurrency = 1;
                concurrency <= maxDegreeOfConcurrency;
                concurrency++) {

                // reset the stopwatch for this concurrency degree
                Stopwatch stopWatch = Stopwatch.StartNew();

                // create the loop options for this degree
                ParallelOptions options = new ParallelOptions()
                    { MaxDegreeOfParallelism = concurrency };

                // inner loop is repeated iterations with same concurrency
                for (int iteration = 0;
                    iteration < numberOfIterations;
                    iteration++) {

                    // define the (shared) result
                    double result = 0;

                    // perform the work
                    Parallel.ForEach(
                        sourceData,
                        options,
                        () => 0.0,
                        (int value,
                            ParallelLoopState loopState,
```

```
                    long index,
                    double localTotal) => {
                        return localTotal + Math.Pow(value, 2);
                    },
                localTotal => {
                    lock (lockObj) {
                        result += localTotal;
                    }
                });
        }
        // stop the stopwatch
        stopWatch.Stop();

        // write out the per-iteration time for this degree of concurrency
        Console.WriteLine("Concurrency {0}: Per-iteration time is {1} ms",
            concurrency,
            stopWatch.ElapsedMilliseconds/numberOfIterations);
    }

    // wait for input before exiting
    Console.WriteLine("Press enter to finish");
    Console.ReadLine();
    }
  }
}
```

The loop is performed ten times for each degree of concurrency in order to smooth out the results. Figure 7-1 shows the results that were obtained from my development machine.

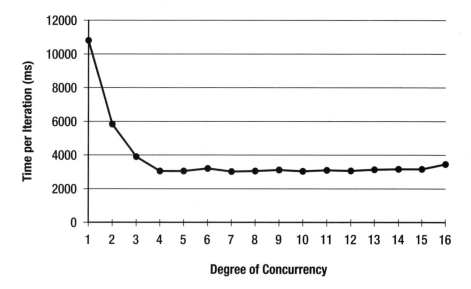

Figure 7-1. Varying concurrency in a parallel loop

You can see that performance increases as the degree of concurrency increases, until we reach a limit of four concurrent Tasks. By this stage, it will be no surprise to you that my development machine has four cores. Increasing the degree of concurrency beyond this level for the parallel loop in Listing 7-2 offers no additional performance gain.

Performing Parallel Analysis with Visual Studio

Visual Studio 2010 includes the Concurrency Visualizer, which allows you to examine the behavior of your parallel program, albeit it with some significant limitations and frustrations.

To use the Concurrency Visualizer, Visual Studio must be started with Administrator privileges. To do this, find Visual Studio in your Start menu, right-click it, and select "Run as administrator". Load your project, and select Start Performance Analysis from the Debug menu.

■ **Note** If you are running Windows 64-bit, you will be prompted to disable executive paging and reboot before you can use the Concurrency Visualizer.

When the Performance Wizard appears, select the Concurrency option, and ensure that the two boxes underneath are checked, as shown in Figure 7-2.

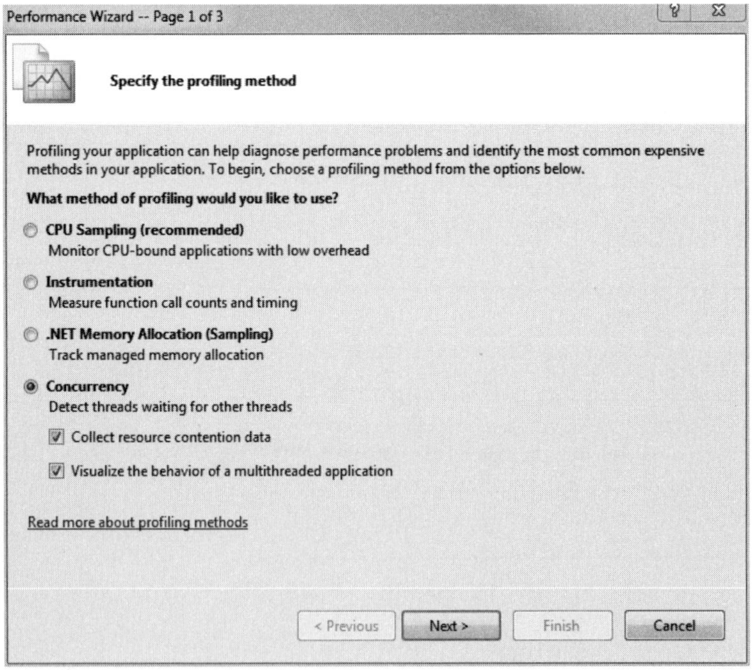

Performance Wizard -- Page 1 of 3

Specify the profiling method

Profiling your application can help diagnose performance problems and identify the most common expensive methods in your application. To begin, choose a profiling method from the options below.

What method of profiling would you like to use?

○ **CPU Sampling (recommended)**
Monitor CPU-bound applications with low overhead

○ **Instrumentation**
Measure function call counts and timing

○ **.NET Memory Allocation (Sampling)**
Track managed memory allocation

◉ **Concurrency**
Detect threads waiting for other threads

☑ Collect resource contention data

☑ Visualize the behavior of a multithreaded application

Read more about profiling methods

[< Previous] [Next >] [Finish] [Cancel]

Figure 7-2. Selecting the concurrent options in the profiler

Click the Next button; select the project you wish to profile, and click Next again. Ensure that the option to profile immediately after the wizard closes is checked, and click Finish. Visual Studio will run and profile your application and then generate a report and display it to you.

At this point, you will encounter the first frustrating aspect of the profiler. It is slow—slow to start, slow to execute your program, and slow to analyze the results. However, to be fair, it is doing a lot of work. The Concurrency Visualizer is not a tool you use lightly; I tend to start it and then go make some coffee. By the time that I have ground the beans, boiled the water, and let the coffee percolate, the Concurrency Visualizer has usually finished—usually; sometimes, I get to drink the coffee, read a book, and perform small errands as well.

Listing 7-3 shows a simple parallel program that has some problems. We'll use this as the basis to explore the views that the Concurrency Visualizer can produce.

Listing 7-3. A Problematic Parallel Program

```csharp
using System;
using System.Threading.Tasks;

namespace Listing_03 {
    class Listing_03 {

        static void Main(string[] args) {

            // create a lock object
            object lockObj = new object();

            // create a sequence of tasks that acquire
            // the lock in order to perform a
            // time-expensive function over and over
            Task[] tasks = new Task[10];
            for (int i = 0; i < tasks.Length; i++) {
                tasks[i] = Task.Factory.StartNew(() => {
                    // acquire the lock
                    lock (lockObj) {
                        // perform some work
                        for (int index = 0; index < 50000000; index++) {
                            Math.Pow(index, 2);
                        }
                    }
                });
            }

            // wait for the tasks to complete
            Task.WaitAll(tasks);
        }
    }
}
```

In the listing, ten `Tasks` are created to perform a body that contains a critical region, and this region performs a series of calculations. Since the calculations are performed inside the critical region, only one `Task` can be performing work at any given time. If we run the Concurrency Visualizer on Listing 7-3, we get the report summary show in Figure 7-3.

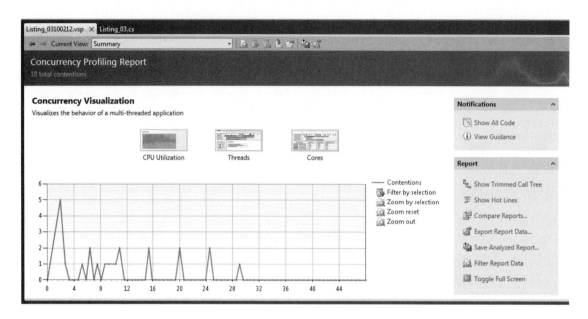

Figure 7-3. Report summary for visualizing Listing 7-3

We are interested in three detailed reports, and they are accessible by clicking the CPU Utilization, Threads, and Cores buttons on the report summary screen. Let's start with CPU Utilization, which is shown in Figure 7-4.

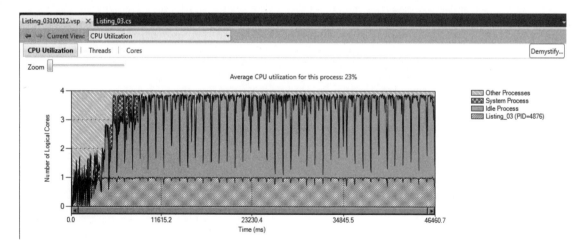

Figure 7-4. The CPU Utilization report for Listing 7-3

The chart might be hard to make out on the printed page, but the striped area that fills the bottom quarter of the plot is the CPU consumed executing Listing 7-3. The other areas represent CPU consumed by the system and other running processes (including Visual Studio). The bulk of the chart shows idle CPU time. This chart shows the problem with Listing 7-3—we are not taking advantage of the cores available, because the poor use of synchronization has created a sequential application.

Parallel programs should be using more than one core, and, in general, the more cores, the better. The most common limitation on using cores is the need to coordinate Tasks using synchronization. Even a well-designed and well-written parallel application will struggle to use all of the capacity of all of the available cores if synchronization is required, and it will be required in most real-world applications. So, use this report view with caution, and don't expect 100 percent CPU utilization.

If you click the Threads button at the top of the graph window, you see a detailed breakdown of what each classic thread did during the profiling section, as shown in Figure 7-5. This is the second area of frustration with the Concurrency Visualizer—this report view is not Task-centric, and threads that are not directly related to executing your code will be displayed. Further, given that a thread can be used to execute multiple Tasks, getting a detailed understanding of what is happening can be a painful process. For a broad overview, however, this view can be quite handy, once you have excluded all of the threads that .NET has created in order to load and execute your classes. In the report shown in Figure 7-5, I have filtered out everything but the threads used to perform the Tasks in Listing 7-3. You can see the stack trace for a given thread at a given moment by clicking n a horizontal bar and looking at the "Current stack" tab. You can hide a thread by right-clicking the name of the thread and selecting Hide.

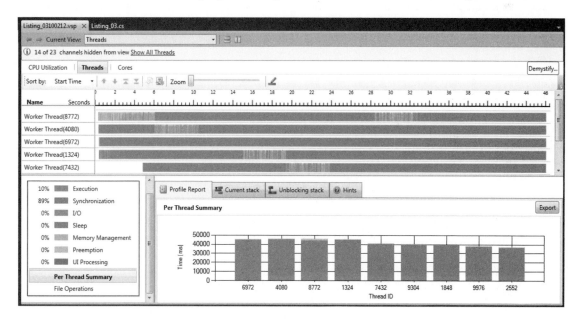

Figure 7-5. Thread analysis for Listing 7-3

The large dark blocks in Figure 7-5 show synchronization, and the smaller areas show execution. You can see that at most one thread is executing at a given moment—another signifier that we have created a program in Listing 7-3 that is effectively sequential.

The Cores report view shows how threads were executed by each available core, as shown in Figure 7-6. This view can be useful to ensure that work is being divided up evenly, when writing a custom partitioner, for example.

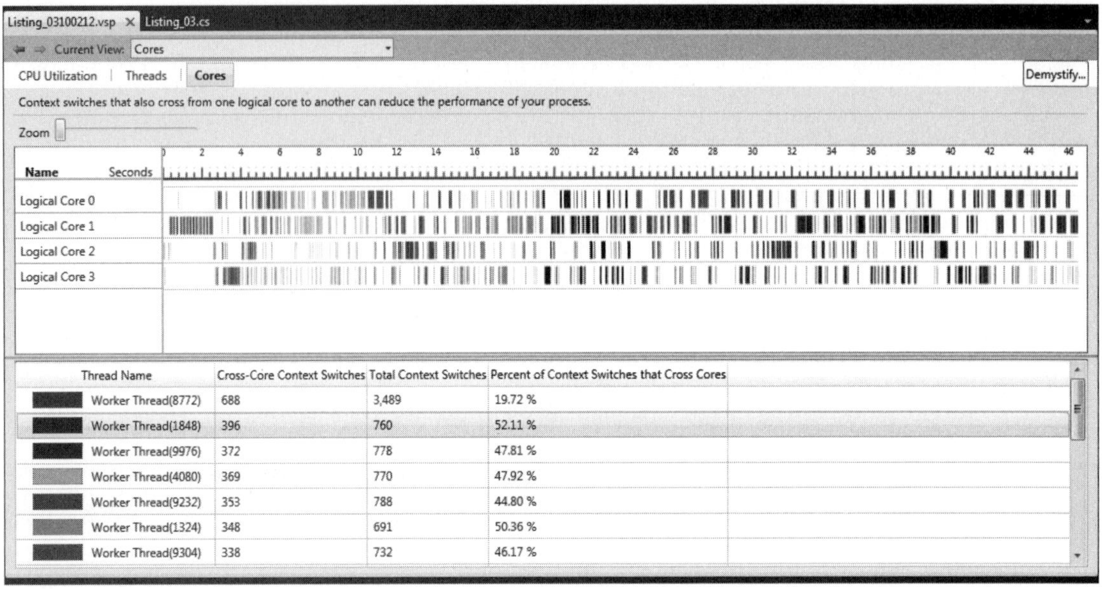

Figure 7-6. Core analysis for Listing 7-3

While the Concurrency Visualizer can be useful, it has some major limitations when you're trying to dig into the performance of a TPL program. It is a general Windows concurrency tool and not really tailored for task-oriented .NET programming. Still, with some care and effort, it can be used to give an overview of how your program is executed.

Finding Parallel Bugs

The problem with debugging parallel programs is that changes you make to figure out the problem can change the way the problem occurs, and this makes many of the tricks you have learned to debug sequential applications less useful.

For example, printing out messages with `Console.WriteLine()` is a very common way to figure out what is happening; I do it all the time. The problem is that the code that the `WriteLine()` method calls is synchronized to prevent strings from being written at the same time and becoming garbled. So, by using `Console.WriteLine()` for debugging, you inadvertently introduce a synchronization primitive, which changes the way that your `Task`s interact and which can change or hide the problem you are looking for—this is especially true for race conditions.

A *slightly* better solution is to use a decoupled console, such as the example shown in the next chapter. This allows you to write debug messages but reduces the impact that doing so has on the behavior of your application by using the Parallel Producer/Consumer pattern. This solution is still not ideal, but it is useable for finding simple problems.

Debugging Program State

The best approach is to use the Visual Studio debugger, which contains some very useful new parallel features to support parallel programming.

To look at these features, we are going to use the code in Listing 7-4. This program has no useful value other than it causes a number of Tasks to call a number of methods to demonstrate the debugger features. The CountDownEvent is used so that the main application thread can wait until all of the Tasks have been created and scheduled. The SemaphoreSlims are included so that two Tasks can gain access to the critical regions in TerminalMethodA() and TerminalMethodB().

Listing 7-4 throws an exception, because I want to be able to include code for you to download or reproduce that will behave exactly as described here. Usually, I would set a breakpoint by right-clicking in Visual Studio and selecting Breakpoint ➤ Insert Breakpoint.

Listing 7-4. Exercising the Parallel Debugger

```
using System;
using System.Diagnostics;
using System.Threading;
using System.Threading.Tasks;

namespace Listing_04 {

    class Listing_04 {
        static CountdownEvent cdEvent;
        static SemaphoreSlim semA, semB;

        static void Main(string[] args) {
            // initialize the semaphores
            semA = new SemaphoreSlim(2);
            semB = new SemaphoreSlim(2);

            // define the number of tasks we will use
            int taskCount = 10;

            // initialize the barrier
            cdEvent = new CountdownEvent(taskCount);

            Task[] tasks = new Task[10];
            for (int i = 0; i < taskCount; i++) {
                tasks[i] = Task.Factory.StartNew((stateObject) => {
                    InitialMethod((int)stateObject);
                }, i);
            }

            // wait for all of the tasks to have reached a terminal method
            cdEvent.Wait();
```

```
        // throw an exception to force the debugger to break
        throw new Exception();
    }

    static void InitialMethod(int argument) {
        if (argument % 2 == 0) {
            MethodA(argument);
        } else {
            MethodB(argument);
        }
    }

    static void MethodA(int argument) {
        if (argument < 5) {
            TerminalMethodA();
        } else {
            TerminalMethodB();
        }
    }

    static void MethodB(int argument) {
        if (argument < 5) {
            TerminalMethodA();
        } else {
            TerminalMethodB();
        }
    }

    static void TerminalMethodA() {
        // signal the countdown event
        cdEvent.Signal();
        // acquire the lock for this method
        semA.Wait();
        // perform some work
        for (int i = 0; i < 500000000; i++) {
            Math.Pow(i, 2);
        }
        // release the semaphore
        semA.Release();
    }

    static void TerminalMethodB() {
        // signal the countdown event
        cdEvent.Signal();
        // acquire the lock for this method
        semB.Wait();
        // perform some work
        for (int i = 0; i < 500000000; i++) {
            Math.Pow(i, 3);
        }
```

```
        // release the semaphore
        semB.Release();
    }
  }
}
```

To see the parallel debugging features, compile the code in Listing 7-4, and select Start Debugging from the Debug menu. Once the Tasks have been created and reached the required point, the main application threads will throw an exception, and the debugger will break.

The first new feature to look at is the Parallel Tasks window, which you can display by selecting Parallel Tasks from the Debug ➤ Windows menu. This window shows all of the Tasks in your code, as illustrated in Figure 7-7.

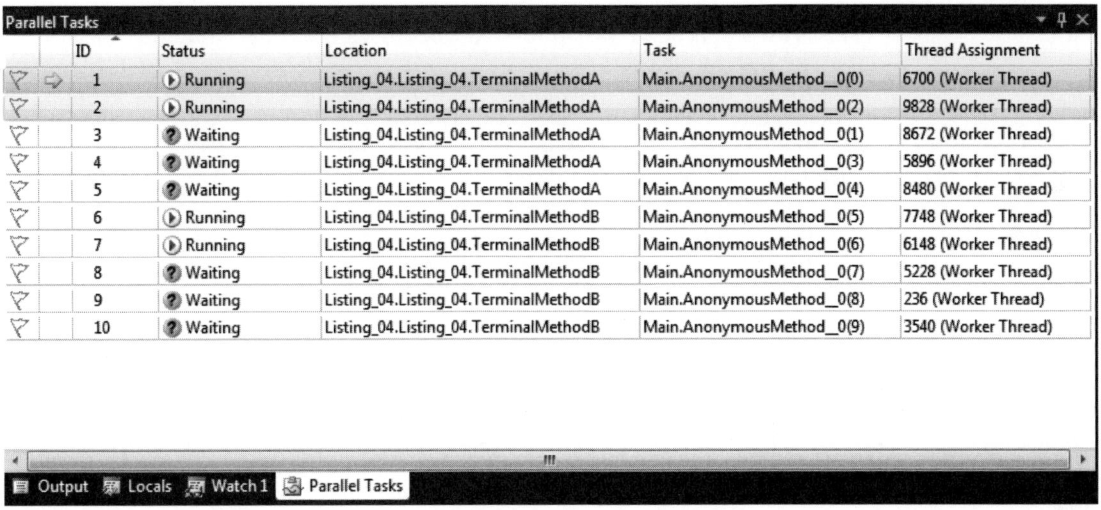

	ID	Status	Location	Task	Thread Assignment
⇨	1	▶ Running	Listing_04.Listing_04.TerminalMethodA	Main.AnonymousMethod__0(0)	6700 (Worker Thread)
	2	▶ Running	Listing_04.Listing_04.TerminalMethodA	Main.AnonymousMethod__0(2)	9828 (Worker Thread)
	3	❔ Waiting	Listing_04.Listing_04.TerminalMethodA	Main.AnonymousMethod__0(1)	8672 (Worker Thread)
	4	❔ Waiting	Listing_04.Listing_04.TerminalMethodA	Main.AnonymousMethod__0(3)	5896 (Worker Thread)
	5	❔ Waiting	Listing_04.Listing_04.TerminalMethodA	Main.AnonymousMethod__0(4)	8480 (Worker Thread)
	6	▶ Running	Listing_04.Listing_04.TerminalMethodB	Main.AnonymousMethod__0(5)	7748 (Worker Thread)
	7	▶ Running	Listing_04.Listing_04.TerminalMethodB	Main.AnonymousMethod__0(6)	6148 (Worker Thread)
	8	❔ Waiting	Listing_04.Listing_04.TerminalMethodB	Main.AnonymousMethod__0(7)	5228 (Worker Thread)
	9	❔ Waiting	Listing_04.Listing_04.TerminalMethodB	Main.AnonymousMethod__0(8)	236 (Worker Thread)
	10	❔ Waiting	Listing_04.Listing_04.TerminalMethodB	Main.AnonymousMethod__0(9)	3540 (Worker Thread)

Output   Locals   Watch 1   Parallel Tasks

Figure 7-7. *The Parallel Tasks debugger window*

For Listing 7-4, all ten Tasks are listed in Figure 7-7, and the Task ID, the current status and other information is displayed for each. The currenly viewed Task is indicated by the yellow arrow (if you don't see a yellow arrow, double-click the first task in the list); double-clicking a Task in the list makes that the current Task. The currently viewed Task's call stack is displayed in the Call Stack debugger window and is also highlighted in the Parallel Stacks window, as you'll see in a moment.

You can select columns to display diferent Task information by right-clicking the column headers. Table 7-2 describes the available columns.

Table 7-2. Parallel Tasks Columns

Column	Description
Flags	Right-clicking the flag icon allows you to flag or unflag a Task. The Parallel Stacks window allows you to view only flagged Tasks to simplify the display.
Icons	A yellow arrow shows the currently viewed Task. A white arrow shows the Task that caused the debugger to break. A pause icon shows that a Task is frozen.
ID	This is the Task ID, which is equivalent to the result from the Task.CurrentId property.
Status	This is the status of the Task prior to the debugger breaking. "Running" means that the Task was executing. "Waiting" means that the Task was waiting to acquire a synchronization primitive or waiting for another Task to complete. A scheduled Task has been created and is awaiting execution. A deadlocked Task is one that is engaged in a deadlock with another Task; see the "Detecting Deadlocks" section later in this chapter for details.
Location	This is the location in the call stack of the Task. You can see the entire call stack by hovering over this field with the mouse.
Task	The initial method and arguments that were used to create the Task.
Parent	This is the ID of the parent Task if there is one.
Thread Assignment	This is the name of the classic thread that is executing the Task. Note that a thread can be used to perform more than one Task and that a Task may be performed inline (see Chapter 4 for details of inline execution).

You can group the Tasks in the list by any of the columns, so you can see all of the Tasks with a given status or were executing a given method when the debugger broke. As you step through the code with a debugger, you can switch from Task to Task.

You can freeze a Task by right-clicking and selecting Freeze Thread. The Task will no longer execute when you step through the code. However, it is the classic thread executing the Task that is frozen, not just the Task, so some care should be taken when using this feature.

The other new window is the Parallel Stacks display, which you can select from the Debug ➤ Windows menu. Figure 7-8 shows this window for Listing 7-4.

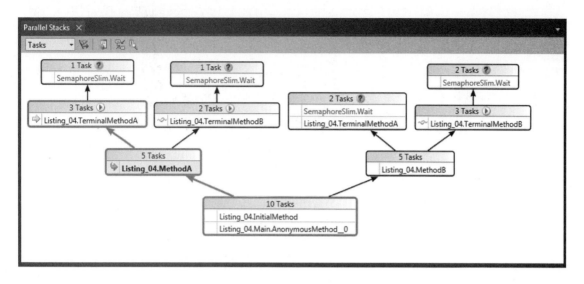

Figure 7-8. *The Parallel Stacks debugger window*

Make sure that you have selected `Tasks` from the drop-down list at the top-left of the window. This debugger window shows you a graphical representation of all of your `Tasks` that is focused on the methods that they have called. You can see that of the ten `Tasks` created in Listing 7-4, five have called `MethodA()`, five have called `MethodB()`, and so on down through the call stack. The buttons across the top of the window allow you to display only `Tasks` you have flagged in the Parallel Tasks window and to focus on one specific method, rather than showing the entire call tree. If you hover over the title of each box, you will see details of the `Tasks` that have called it, and you can switch to any of them.

As you switch from `Task` to `Task`, the code window will show the source statements for the current `Task`. The Call Stack switches to the calls made by that `Task`; the Locals window shows the data for the current `Task`, and so on.

By using the new parallel windows, you can drive the debugger from `Task` to `Task` effortlessly. You can see what each `Task` was doing when the debugger broke, see the local data for each `Task`, and walk through `Task`-by-`Task` as the code executes. Unlike the Concurrency Visualizer, which is an awkward tool, the parallel debugger features are fast and elegant, and they allow you to dig deep into the detail of your parallel program.

Handling Exceptions

There is a minor wrinkle when debugging code where you have handled exceptions thrown by `Tasks` in your code. For an example, see Listing 7-5.

Listing 7-5. A Program That Handles Task Exceptions

```
using System;
using System.Threading.Tasks;

namespace Listing_05 {

    class Listing_05 {

        static void Main(string[] args) {

            Task[] tasks = new Task[2];
            for (int i = 0; i < tasks.Length; i++) {
                tasks[i] = Task.Factory.StartNew(() => {
                    for (int j = 0; j < 5000000; j++) {
                        if (j == 500) {
                            throw new Exception("Value is 500");
                        }
                        Math.Pow(j, 2);
                    }
                });
            }

            // wait for the tasks and catch any exceptions
            try {
                Task.WaitAll(tasks);
            } catch (AggregateException ex) {
                ex.Handle(innerEx => {
                    Console.WriteLine("Exception message is {0}", innerEx.Message);
                    return true;
                });
            }
        }
    }
}
```

When you run this code normally, each `Task` throws an exception, and these exceptions are wrapped in an instance of `System.AggregateException`, which is handled by the `try. . .catch` code block around the `Task.WaitAll()` method.

However, when you run this code in the debugger, the debugger will break and flag the exceptions as unhandled. To fix this, select "Options and Settings" from the Debug menu in Visual Studio, and uncheck the Enable Just My Code option, as shown in Figure 7-9. This allows for `Task` exception handling to be handled properly in the debugger.

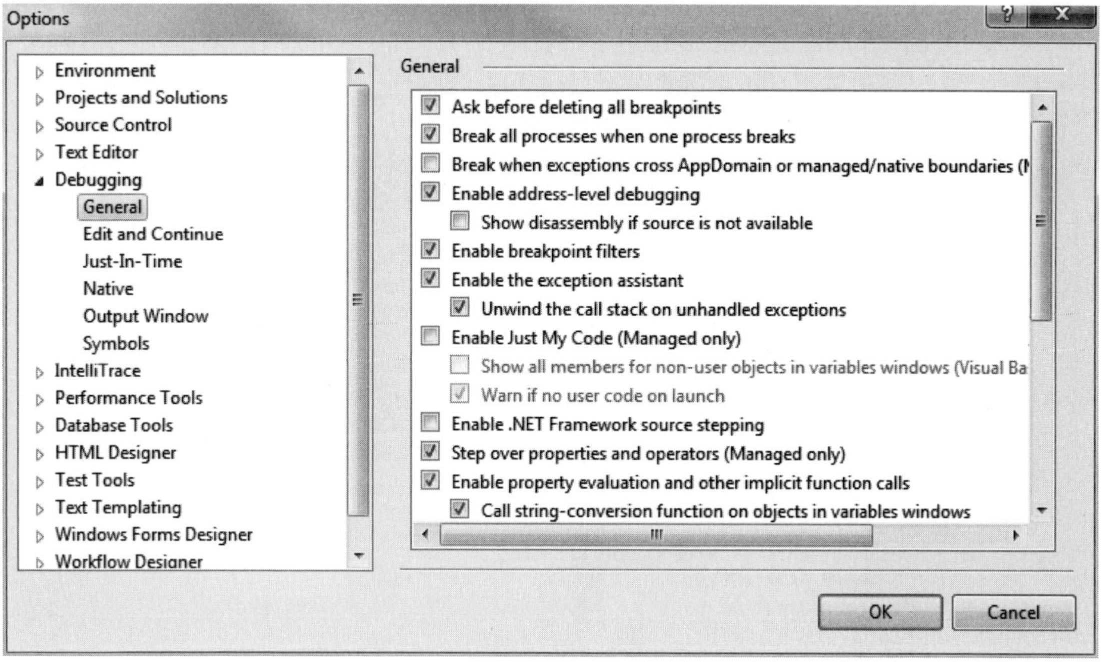

Figure 7-9. Unchecking the Enable Just My Code debugger option

Detecting Deadlocks

One of the most useful features of the debugger is the ability to detect deadlocks in your application. Deadlocks occur when two or more Tasks are waiting on each other to finish or are otherwise holding resources, such as a lock on a primitive, that the other Task needs before it can move forward. The ability of the debugger to find and report deadlocks is impressive. Listing 7-6 shows a simple program that creates a number of Tasks that collectively represent a deadlock, because each Task in the array waits for the next Task to finish.

Listing 7-6. A Circular Deadlock

```
using System.Diagnostics;
using System.Threading;
using System.Threading.Tasks;

namespace Listing_06 {

    class Listing_06 {
```

```
static void Main(string[] args) {
    // specify the number of tasks
    int taskCount = 10;
    // create a countdown event so that
    // we can wait until all of the tasks
    // have been created before breaking
    CountdownEvent cdEvent = new CountdownEvent(taskCount);
    // create the set of tasks
    Task[] tasks = new Task[taskCount];
    for (int i = 0; i < taskCount; i++) {
        tasks[i] = Task.Factory.StartNew((stateObj) => {
            // signalthe countdown event
            cdEvent.Signal();
            // wait on the next task in the array
            tasks[(((int)stateObj) + 1) % taskCount].Wait();
        }, i);
    }

    // wait for the count down event
    cdEvent.Wait();
    // break if there is a debugger attached
    if (Debugger.IsAttached) {
        Debugger.Break();
    }
}
```

As with the previous example, Listing 7-5 uses CountDownEvent to ensure that the Tasks have all been created and scheduled. This time, we break the debugger in the code using the System.Diagnostics. Debugger class. Figure 7-10 shows the Parallel Tasks debugger window when Listing 7-5 breaks.

	ID	Status	Location	Task
⌃ ▾	**Listing_05.Listing_05.Main.AnonymousMethod_0 (10)**			
▽	1	⬤ Waiting-Deadlock	Listing_05.Listing_05.Main.AnonymousMetł	Main.AnonymousMethod_0(1)
▽	2	⬤ Waiting-Deadlock	Listing_05.Listing_05.Main.AnonymousMetł	Main.AnonymousMethod_0(0)
▽	3	⬤ Waiting-Deadlock	Listing_05.Listing_05.Main.AnonymousMetł	Main.AnonymousMethod_0(2)
▽	4	⬤ Waiting-Deadlc	"Task 3" is waiting on object: ousMetł	Main.AnonymousMethod_0(3)
▽	5	⬤ Waiting-Deadlc	"Task 4" (Owned by thread 7672). ousMetł	Main.AnonymousMethod_0(4)
▽	6	⬤ Waiting-Deadlock	Listing_05.Listing_05.Main.AnonymousMetł	Main.AnonymousMethod_0(5)
▽	7	⬤ Waiting-Deadlock	Listing_05.Listing_05.Main.AnonymousMetł	Main.AnonymousMethod_0(6)
▽	8	⬤ Waiting-Deadlock	Listing_05.Listing_05.Main.AnonymousMetł	Main.AnonymousMethod_0(7)
▽	9	⬤ Waiting-Deadlock	Listing_05.Listing_05.Main.AnonymousMetł	Main.AnonymousMethod_0(8)
▽	10	⬤ Waiting-Deadlock	Listing_05.Listing_05.Main.AnonymousMetł	Main.AnonymousMethod_0(9)

■ Output ▦ Locals ▦ Watch 1 ▣ Parallel Tasks

Figure 7-10. Detecting deadlocks

You can see that all of the Tasks have been identified as being deadlocked. If you hover over each Task, you can see what the Task is waiting for. The debugger doesn't always manage to detect complex deadlocks, but it does a pretty good job most of the time.

Summary

In this chapter, you have seen how to measure performance and track down parallel bugs. The Visual Studio 2010 tools can be very helpful, but to get the best from them, you need to have a good understanding of the kinds of problems that can arise. I have listed some of the most common problems in each chapter as we have moved through this book, but you will find that your personal coding style leads you to create patterns of problems that you will have to track down and fix. The best advice I can give you is not to give up. Spending hours chasing down an intermittent issue can be exceptionally painful, but you will learn a huge amount as you do so. Over time, you will get a feel for what lies behind the problems are you looking for and your ability to locate and fix parallel defects will become much better—and, on occasion, you will find that hunting down a particularly elusive error can even be enjoyable.

CHAPTER 8

■ ■ ■

Common Parallel Algorithms

In this chapter are 11 common parallel algorithms implemented using the TPL. You can download all of the source code for all of the algorithms from www.Apress.com.

These are some of the most widely used building blocks in parallel programming, and I have included them as a reference for when you are facing a problem, a time-saver for when you need a quick answer, and a demonstration of how the TPL abstractions we covered throughout this book allow complex and rich functions to be developed with relatively few lines of code.

There are lots of variations in parallel algorithms. I have chosen those that I think have the broadest application and in which the core ideas are easily seen. I have kept the implementations as simple as possible, so you'll need to deal with exceptions, cancellations, and degrees of parallelization yourself; you'll find all you need to do so in earlier chapters.

Sorting, Searching, and Caching

The following sections offer solutions for challenges faced in sorting and caching.

Using Parallel Quicksort

Quicksort is a sorting algorithm that is well suited to parallelization. It has three steps:

1.   Pick an element, called a pivot, from the data to be sorted

2.   Reorder the data so that all of the elements that are less than the pivot come before the pivot in the data and all the elements that are greater than the pivot come after the pivot.

3.   Recursively process the subset of lesser elements and the subset of greater elements.

Quicksort is ideal for parallel execution because the sets of data elements are processed independently, which means we don't have to worry about data races. This implementation sorts arrays and uses an IComparer for item comparison. We will use an *in-place* Quicksort, meaning that we move elements around inside the array, rather than creating new arrays to hold the subsets.

To avoid the overhead of parallelization for small amounts of work, we add support for using the sequential Quicksort implementation available in the System.Array.Sort() method when a given level of recursion is reached or where the number of elements to sort in a subset is less than a given number. I set these values based on some simple testing on my development system, which is a four-core machine. Using these values, the parallel implementation is around twice as fast as the sequential implementation.

The Code

The following code illustrates the use of an in-place Quicksort:

```
using System;
using System.Collections.Generic;
using System.Threading.Tasks;

namespace Parallel_Sort {

    class Parallel_Sort<T> {

        public static void ParallelQuickSort(T[] data, IComparer<T> comparer,
            int maxDepth = 16, int minBlockSize = 10000) {
            // call the internal method
            doSort(data, 0, data.Length - 1, comparer, 0, maxDepth, minBlockSize);
        }

        internal static void doSort(T[] data, int startIndex, int endIndex,
            IComparer<T> comparer, int depth, int maxDepth, int minBlockSize) {

            if (startIndex < endIndex) {
                // if we have exceeded the depth threshold or there are
                // fewer items than we would like, then use sequential sort
                if (depth > maxDepth || endIndex - startIndex < minBlockSize) {
                    Array.Sort(data, startIndex, endIndex - startIndex + 1, comparer);
                } else {
                    // we need to parallelize
                    int pivotIndex = partitionBlock(data, startIndex, endIndex, comparer);
                    // recurse on the left and right blocks
                    Task leftTask = Task.Factory.StartNew(() => {
                        doSort(data, startIndex, pivotIndex - 1, comparer,
                            depth + 1, maxDepth, minBlockSize);
                    });
                    Task rightTask = Task.Factory.StartNew(() => {
                        doSort(data, pivotIndex + 1, endIndex, comparer,
                            depth + 1, maxDepth, minBlockSize);
                    });
```

```
                // wait for the tasks to complete
                Task.WaitAll(leftTask, rightTask);
            }
        }
    }

    internal static int partitionBlock(T[] data, int startIndex, int endIndex,
        IComparer<T> comparer) {

        // get the pivot value - we will be comparing all
        // of the other items against this value
        T pivot = data[startIndex];
        // put the pivot value at the end of block
        swapValues(data, startIndex, endIndex);
        // index used to store values smaller than the pivot
        int storeIndex = startIndex;
        // iterate through the items in the block
        for (int i = startIndex; i < endIndex; i++) {
            // look for items that are smaller or equal to the pivot
            if (comparer.Compare(data[i], pivot) <= 0) {
                // move the value and increment the index
                swapValues(data, i, storeIndex);
                storeIndex++;
            }
        }
        swapValues(data, storeIndex, endIndex);
        return storeIndex;
    }

    internal static void swapValues(T[] data, int firstIndex, int secondIndex) {
        T holder = data[firstIndex];
        data[firstIndex] = data[secondIndex];
        data[secondIndex] = holder;
    }
    }
}
}
```

Using the Code

To use the algorithm, you must have an array to sort and an implementation of **IComparer** that will compare instances of the array type. The following code shows a simple example using an **int** array:

```
using System;
using System.Collections.Generic;

namespace Parallel_Sort {

    class Use_Parallel_Sort {
```

273

```
        static void Main(string[] args) {
            // generate some random source data
            Random rnd = new Random();
            int[] sourceData = new int[5000000];
            for (int i = 0; i < sourceData.Length; i++) {
                sourceData[i] = rnd.Next(1, 100);
            }

            // perform the parallel sort
            Parallel_Sort<int>.ParallelQuickSort(sourceData, new IntComparer());
        }

        public class IntComparer : IComparer<int> {
            public int Compare(int first, int second) {
                return first.CompareTo(second);
            }
        }
    }
}
```

Traversing a Parallel Tree

There is no standard Tree structure in the .NET Framework class library, in part because there are so many different ways of implementing them.

The Code

This example creates a very simple Tree type, which has a data value and two child nodes. For each node in the tree, a user-supplied System.Action() is invoked on the data value and Tasks are created to parallel process the child nodes.

```
using System;
using System.Threading.Tasks;

namespace Parallel_Tree_Traverse {

    public class Tree<T> {
        public Tree<T> LeftNode, RightNode;
        public T Data;
    }

    class TreeTraverser {
        public static void TraverseTree<T>(Tree<T> tree, Action<T> action) {
            if (tree != null) {
                // invoke the action for the data
                action.Invoke(tree.Data);
```

```
                    // start tasks to process the left and right nodes if they exist
                    if (tree.LeftNode != null && tree.RightNode != null) {
                        Task leftTask = Task.Factory.StartNew(
                            () => TraverseTree(tree.LeftNode, action));
                        Task rightTask = Task.Factory.StartNew(
                            () => TraverseTree(tree.RightNode, action));
                        // wait for the tasks to complete
                        Task.WaitAll(leftTask, rightTask);
                    }
                }
            }
        }
    }
}
```

Using the Code

The following example creates a Tree<int> and populates it with random values. The System.Action
prints out even values as they are encountered during tree traversal.

```
using System;

namespace Parallel_Tree_Traverse {
    class Use_Parallel_Tree_Traverse {

        static void Main(string[] args) {

            // create and populate a simple tree
            Tree<int> tree = populateTree(new Tree<int>(), new Random());

            // traverse the tree, print out the even values
            TreeTraverser.TraverseTree(tree, item => {
                if (item % 2 == 0) {
                    Console.WriteLine("Item {0}", item);
                }
            });

            // wait for input before exiting
            Console.WriteLine("Press enter to finish");
            Console.ReadLine();
        }

        internal static Tree<int> populateTree(Tree<int> parentNode,
            Random rnd, int depth = 0) {

            parentNode.Data = rnd.Next(1, 1000);
            if (depth < 10) {
                parentNode.LeftNode = new Tree<int>();
                parentNode.RightNode = new Tree<int>();
```

```
            populateTree(parentNode.LeftNode, rnd, depth + 1);
            populateTree(parentNode.RightNode, rnd, depth + 1);
        }
        return parentNode;
    }
  }
}
```

Searching a Parallel Tree

The parallel tree traversal example can be easily modified to become a parallel tree search. This implementation uses a `CancellationToken` to reduce the number of `Task`s that are started after a result has been found. Searches are performed using a function and the first tree node that causes the function to return true is considered to be the result; subsequent matches are not sought. We use a wrapper around the search result in order to avoid complications with the C# generic type support.

The Code

This code searches a parallel tree:

```
using System;
using System.Threading;
using System.Threading.Tasks;

namespace Parallel_Tree_Search {

    public class Tree<T> {
        public Tree<T> LeftNode, RightNode;
        public T Data;
    }

    class TreeSearch {

        public static T SearchTree<T>(Tree<T> tree, Func<T, bool> searchFunction) {
            // create the cancellation token source
            CancellationTokenSource tokenSource = new CancellationTokenSource();
            // search the tree
            TWrapper<T> result = performSearch(tree, searchFunction, tokenSource);
            return result == null ? default(T) : result.Value;
        }

        class TWrapper<T> {
            public T Value;
        }

        private static TWrapper<T> performSearch<T>(Tree<T> tree,
            Func<T, bool> searchFunction,
            CancellationTokenSource tokenSource) {
```

```
        // define the result
        TWrapper<T> result = null;
        // only proceed if we have something to search
        if (tree != null) {
            // apply the search function to the current tree
            if (searchFunction(tree.Data)) {
                //cancel the token source
                tokenSource.Cancel();
                // set the result
                result = new TWrapper<T>() { Value = tree.Data };
            } else {
                // we have not found a result - continue the search
                if (tree.LeftNode != null && tree.RightNode != null) {
                    // start the task for the left node
                    Task<TWrapper<T>> leftTask = Task<TWrapper<T>>.Factory.StartNew(
                        () => performSearch(tree.LeftNode, searchFunction, tokenSource),
                        tokenSource.Token);
                    // start the task for the right node
                    Task<TWrapper<T>> rightTask = Task<TWrapper<T>>.Factory.StartNew(
                        () => performSearch(tree.RightNode, searchFunction,
                        tokenSource), tokenSource.Token);

                    try {
                        // set the result based on the tasks
                        result = leftTask.Result != null ?
                        leftTask.Result : rightTask.Result != null ?
                        rightTask.Result : null;
                    } catch (AggregateException) { }
                }
            }
        }
        // return the result
        return result;
    }
  }
}
```

Using the Code

The following example creates and populates a tree of integer values and then searches for the first instance of the value 183. I have cheated here somewhat and supplied a seed value for the random number generator so that I know that 183 will exist in the tree.

```
using System;

namespace Parallel_Tree_Search {
    class Use_TreeSearch {

        static void Main(string[] args) {
```

```
        // create and populate a simple tree
        Tree<int> tree = populateTree(new Tree<int>(), new Random(2));

        // traverse the tree, print out the even values
        int result = TreeSearch.SearchTree(tree, item => {
            if (item == 183) Console.WriteLine("Value : {0}", item);
            return item == 183;
        });

        Console.WriteLine("Search match ? {0}", result);

        // wait for input before exiting
        Console.WriteLine("Press enter to finish");
        Console.ReadLine();
    }

    private static Tree<int> populateTree(Tree<int> parentNode,
        Random rnd, int depth = 0) {

        parentNode.Data = rnd.Next(1, 1000);
        if (depth < 10) {
            parentNode.LeftNode = new Tree<int>();
            parentNode.RightNode = new Tree<int>();
            populateTree(parentNode.LeftNode, rnd, depth + 1);
            populateTree(parentNode.RightNode, rnd, depth + 1);
        }
        return parentNode;
    }
  }
}
```

Using a Parallel Cache

A *cache* is an optimization that reuses the results from an expensive function. The function can be expensive in any number of ways—raw computation, network bandwidth, time, and so on. This cache is very simple but demonstrates how you can combine parallel features to make something that can be surprisingly useful.

The constructor for the cache takes a factory function as an argument that is called to create new values when calls are made to the GetValue() method for keys for which no key-value pair presently exists.

All of the hard work in this class is performed by the underlying ConcurrentDictionary class, which takes care of synchronization and data management. But, ConcurrentDictionary only cares about ensuring the integrity of the key-value pairs it is managing and does not consider the cost of using the factory function, which gives rise to a problem.

The problem is the GetOrAdd() method in the ConcurrentDictionary class, which tries to retrieve the value for a given key. If no key-value pair exists, the factory function is called to create a value, which is added to the collection and returned as the result of the method call. Unfortunately, the ConcurrentDictionary class calls the factory function before acquiring an internal synchronization primitive, which can lead to the factory function being called more than once to create values for a given key if one Task requests a key before another Task's request has finished creating the corresponding value. Given that the whole point of the cache is to minimize the use of the function, this result can be undesirable.

The problem exists during the period from when a request for a nonexistent key-value pair is made to when an entry for that key-value pair exists in the collection. The use of Lazy<TValue> is a sleight-of-hand that reduces (but does not eliminate) the likelihood of duplicated factory function calls. Rather than invoke the expensive factory function directly, a Lazy value is created that will invoke the expensive factory function after the key-value pair has been added to the collection. This has the effect of limiting the amount of time for which no key-value pair exists. Lazy values are safe for parallel use and will only be initialized once irrespective of how many times the Value property is read.

The Code

The following code implements the Lazy value solution:

```
using System;
using System.Collections.Concurrent;

namespace Parallel_Cache {

    class Parallel_Cache<TKey,TValue> {
        private ConcurrentDictionary<TKey, Lazy<TValue>> dictionary;
        private Func<TKey, TValue> valueFactory;

        public Parallel_Cache(Func<TKey, TValue> factory) {
            // set the factory instance variable
            valueFactory = factory;
            // initialize the dictionary
            dictionary = new ConcurrentDictionary<TKey,Lazy<TValue>>();
        }

        public TValue GetValue(TKey key) {
            return dictionary.GetOrAdd(key,
                new Lazy<TValue>(() => valueFactory(key))).Value;
        }
    }
}
```

Using the Code

The following code creates a set of Tasks, each of which requests the same set of values from the cache. The factory function simply squares the values of the key.

```
using System;
using System.Threading.Tasks;

namespace Parallel_Cache {

    class Use_Parallel_Cache {
        static void Main(string[] args) {
```

```
            // create the cache
            Parallel_Cache<int, double> cache
                = new Parallel_Cache<int, double>(key => {
                    Console.WriteLine("Created value for key {0}", key);
                    return Math.Pow(key, 2);
                });

            for (int i = 0; i < 10; i++) {
                Task.Factory.StartNew(() => {
                    for (int j = 0; j < 20; j++) {
                        Console.WriteLine(
                            "Task {0} got value {1} for key {2}",
                            Task.CurrentId, cache.GetValue(j), j);
                    }
                });
            }

            // wait for input before exiting
            Console.WriteLine("Press enter to finish");
            Console.ReadLine();
        }
    }
}
```

Using Parallel Map and Reductions

The solutions in this section address common situations in mapping and reduction.

Using a Parallel Map

Mapping is the same thing as projection, which you saw in Chapter 6. Each of a set of source values is mapped (or projected) to a result value—something that is very easily performed using PLINQ.

The Code

There are countless variations of the basic map operation, and one of the most common is where each source value is mapped to multiple result values. This can be achieved by replacing the Select() method in the following code below with SelectMany().

```
using System;
using System.Linq;

namespace Parallel_Map {

    class Parallel_Map {
```

```
public static TOutput[] ParallelMap<TInput, TOutput>(
    Func<TInput, TOutput> mapFunction,
    TInput[] input) {

    return input
        .AsParallel()
        .AsOrdered()
        .Select(value => mapFunction(value))
        .ToArray();
    }
  }
}
```

Using the Code

The following example maps an array of integers to their squares:

```
using System;
using System.Linq;

namespace Parallel_Map {

    class Use_Parallel_Map {

        static void Main(string[] args) {

            // create the source data
            int[] sourceData = Enumerable.Range(0, 100).ToArray();

            // define the mapping function
            Func<int, double> mapFunction = value => Math.Pow(value, 2);

            // map the source data
            double[] resultData
                = Parallel_Map.ParallelMap<int, double>(
                        mapFunction,
                        sourceData);

            // run through the results
            for (int i = 0; i < sourceData.Length; i++) {
                Console.WriteLine("Value {0} mapped to {1}",
                    sourceData[i],
                    resultData[i]);
            }
        }
    }
}
```

Using a Parallel Reduction

Mapping is never far from its companion *reduction*. In reductions, a sequence of source values is reduced to a single value using a function. Another term for reduction is aggregation – which we saw in Chapter 6 and which is a key PLINQ feature.

The Code

The following example creates a parallel reduction:

```
using System;
using System.Linq;

namespace Parallel_Reduce {

    class Parallel_Reduce {

        public static TValue Reduce<TValue>(
            TValue[] sourceData,
            TValue seedValue,
            Func<TValue, TValue, TValue> reduceFunction) {

            // perform the reduction
            return sourceData
                .AsParallel()
                .Aggregate(
                    seedValue,
                    (localResult, value) =>
                        reduceFunction(localResult, value),
                    (overallResult, localResult) =>
                        reduceFunction(overallResult, localResult),
                    overallResult => overallResult);
        }
    }
}
```

Using the Code

The following reduces a sequence of integers using addition:

```
using System;
using System.Linq;

namespace Parallel_Reduce {

    class Use_Parallel_Reduce {

        static void Main(string[] args) {
```

```
        // create some source data
        int[] sourceData = Enumerable.Range(0, 10).ToArray();

        // create the aggregation function
        Func<int, int, int> reduceFunction = (value1, value2) => value1 + value2;

        // perform the reduction
        int result = Parallel_Reduce.Reduce<int>(sourceData, 0, reduceFunction);

        // write out the result
        Console.WriteLine("Result: {0}", result);

        // wait for input before exiting
        Console.WriteLine("Press enter to finish");
        Console.ReadLine();
    }
  }
}
```

Using Parallel MapReduce

The final piece in the mapping and reduction set is where a Map algorithm and a Reduce algorithm are combined to create a MapReduce algorithm. There are three stages to MapReduce. First, a sequence of values is mapped to a sequence of intermediate results; typically, each source value is mapped to multiple intermediate values, but this is not always the case. Second, the intermediate values are grouped together using a key. Finally, each group of intermediate values is reduced to a result value.

The Code

This implementation of MapReduce uses four data types: the type of the source data, intermediate result, grouping key, and final result data. Many implementations only use three, omitting the separation between the key and the final result types. I find the four-type approach more useful because it allows separation of the reduction type from the grouping type. You can see an example of this here, where I return a KeyValuePair that allows me to associate the intermediate result with the final result value:

```
using System;
using System.Collections.Generic;
using System.Linq;

namespace Parallel_MapReduce {
    class Parallel_MapReduce {

        public static IEnumerable<TOutput>
            MapReduce<TInput, TIntermediate, TKey, TOutput>(
                IEnumerable<TInput> sourceData,
                Func<TInput, IEnumerable<TIntermediate>> mapFunction,
                Func<TIntermediate, TKey> groupFunction,
                Func<IGrouping<TKey, TIntermediate>, TOutput> reduceFunction) {
```

```
                    return sourceData
                        .AsParallel()
                        .SelectMany(mapFunction)
                        .GroupBy(groupFunction)
                        .Select(reduceFunction);
            }
        }
}
```

Using the Code

The following code calculates the frequency of factors for a sequence of integers. The map function takes an `int` value and returns an `IEnumerable<int>` containing the factors for that source value; this means that the source and intermediate data types are both `int` for this MapReduce.

Because we want to determine the frequency of a result, the group function selects the value itself—that is to say, all instances of a given intermediate result are grouped together. This means that the key type for this MapReduce is also `int`.

The reduce function creates a `KeyValuePair` which uses the factor value as the key and the result of `Count()` applied to the grouping, which gives the frequency that this intermediate result occurred. This means that the result type is `KeyValuePair<int, int>` for this MapReduce.

```
using System;
using System.Collections.Generic;
using System.Linq;

namespace Parallel_MapReduce {

    class Use_Parallel_MapReduce {

        static void Main(string[] args) {

            // create a function that lists the factors
            Func<int, IEnumerable<int>> map = value => {
                IList<int> factors = new List<int>();
                for (int i = 1; i < value; i++) {
                    if (value % i == 0) {
                        factors.Add(i);
                    }
                }
                return factors;
            };

            // create the group function - in this example
            // we want to group the same results together,
            // so we select the value itself
            Func<int, int> group = value => value;

            // create the reduce function - this simply
            // counts the number of elements in the grouping
            // and returns a Key/Value pair with the result as the
```

```
            // key and the count as the value
            Func<IGrouping<int, int>,
                KeyValuePair<int, int>> reduce =
                grouping => {
                    return new KeyValuePair<int, int>(
                        grouping.Key, grouping.Count());
            };

            // create some source data
            IEnumerable<int> sourceData = Enumerable.Range(1, 50);

            // use parallel map reduce with the source data
            // and the map, group and reduce functions
            IEnumerable<KeyValuePair<int, int>> result =
                Parallel_MapReduce.MapReduce(
                    sourceData,
                    map,
                    group,
                    reduce);

            // process the results
            foreach (KeyValuePair<int, int> kvp in result) {
                Console.WriteLine("{0} is a factor {1} times",
                    kvp.Key,
                    kvp.Value);
            }
        }
    }
}
```

Speculative Processing

The examples in this section illustrate speculative selection and caching.

Selection

Speculative selection performs several different functions that yield the same result value and returns a result as soon as one of the functions "wins". Typically, this technique is used if there is a quick algorithm that works for only certain values and a slower algorithm that works for all values.

Imagine, for example, trying to guess a password. One algorithm randomly tries values from a dictionary, while another tries variations on the user's name. In some cases, the second function will return a result quickly. In speculative selection, you perform both functions in parallel and take the result from whichever gives a result first.

The Code

This implementation takes any number of functions. The maximum number that will be performed in parallel will be limited by the task scheduler used by the `Parallel.ForEach()` loop, so if you have lots of functions to choose from, you should either write a custom scheduler (see Chapter 4) or, better still, order the functions so that ones that take the least time to execute but which have the highest likelihood of success are at the start of the arguments.

```
using System;
using System.Threading;
using System.Threading.Tasks;

namespace Speculative_Selection {

    static class Speculative_Selection {

        public static void Compute<TInput, TOutput>(
            TInput value,
            Action<long, TOutput> callback,
            params Func<TInput, TOutput>[] functions) {

            // define a counter to indicate the results produced
            int resultCounter = 0;

            // start a task to perform the parallel loop, otherwise
            // this method will block until a result has been found
            // and the functions running at that time have finished,
            // even if they are unsuccessful
            Task.Factory.StartNew(() => {
                // perform the parallel foreach
                Parallel.ForEach(functions,
                    (Func<TInput, TOutput> func,
                    ParallelLoopState loopState,
                    long iterationIndex) => {
                        // compute the result
                        TOutput localResult = func(value);
                        // increment the counter
                        if (Interlocked.Increment(ref resultCounter) == 1) {
                            // we are the first iteration to produce the result
                            // stop the loop
                            loopState.Stop();
                            // invoke the callback
                            callback(iterationIndex, localResult);
                        }
                    }
                );
            });
        }
    }
}
```

Using the Code

The following code defines two functions that compute the same result; the only difference is the period that the function waits before returning the result value. A callback Action is defined that writes out the result and the index of the winning function and the computation is performed for ten sequential integer values.

```
using System;
using System.Threading;
using System.Threading.Tasks;

namespace Speculative_Selection {

    class Use_Speculative_Suggestion {

        static void Main(string[] args) {

            // create some sample functions
            Func<int, double> pFunction = value => {
                Random rnd = new Random();
                Thread.Sleep(rnd.Next(1, 2000));
                return Math.Pow(value, 2);
            };

            // create some sample functions
            Func<int, double> pFunction2 = value => {
                Random rnd = new Random();
                Thread.Sleep(rnd.Next(1, 1000));
                return Math.Pow(value, 2);
            };

            // define the callback
            Action<long, double> callback = (index, result) => {
                Console.WriteLine("Received result of {0} from function {1}",
                    result, index);
            };

            // speculative compute for some values
            for (int i = 0; i < 10; i++) {
                Speculative_Selection.Compute<int, double>(
                    i,
                    callback,
                    pFunction, pFunction2);
            }

            // wait for input before exiting
            Console.WriteLine("Press enter to finish");
            Console.ReadLine();
        }
    }
}
```

Speculative Caching

A *speculative cache* is an adaption of the parallel cache from earlier in the chapter that speculates on what keys are likely to be requested in the future based on a given request now. When accurately anticipating later requests, the cache can improve performance by building up a stock of precomputed values. Values that are computed but never requested are wasted effort.

The Code

The following implementation takes a speculator function and a factory function as constructor arguments. When a request is made for a key that does not presently exist in the cache, the key is placed in a queue for background processing in a `Parallel.ForEach` loop. When processed, the speculator generates an array of values that should be precomputed, and these are passed to the factory function if they are not already in cache.

You will notice the use of the `Lazy` type again; this is to minimize duplicative calls to the factory function, just as in the original parallel cache.

```
using System;
using System.Collections.Concurrent;
using System.Threading.Tasks;

namespace Speculative_Cache {

    class Speculative_Cache<TKey, TValue> {
        private ConcurrentDictionary<TKey, Lazy<TValue>> dictionary;
        private BlockingCollection<TKey> queue;
        private Func<TKey, TKey[]> speculatorFunction;
        private Func<TKey, TValue> factoryFunction;

        public Speculative_Cache(Func<TKey, TValue> factory,
                                 Func<TKey, TKey[]> speculator) {

            // set the speculator instance variable
            speculatorFunction = speculator;
            // initialize the dictionary
            dictionary = new ConcurrentDictionary<TKey, Lazy<TValue>>();
            // initialize the queue
            queue = new BlockingCollection<TKey>();

            // create the wrapper function
            factoryFunction = (key => {
                // call the factory function
                TValue value = factory(key);
                // add the key to the speculative queue
                queue.Add(key);
                // return the results
                return value;
            });
        }
```

```
            // start the task that will handle speculation
            Task.Factory.StartNew(() => {
                Parallel.ForEach(queue.GetConsumingEnumerable(),
                    new ParallelOptions { MaxDegreeOfParallelism = 2 },
                    key => {
                        // enumerate the keys to speculate
                        foreach (TKey specKey in speculatorFunction(key)) {
                            TValue res = dictionary.GetOrAdd(
                                specKey,
                                new Lazy<TValue>(() => factory(specKey))).Value;
                        }
                    });
            });
        }

        public TValue GetValue(TKey key) {
            return  dictionary.GetOrAdd(key,
                new Lazy<TValue>(() => factoryFunction(key))).Value;
        }
    }
}
```

Using the Code

In the following code, the speculator function generates the next five sequential values for a given key. The factory function returns the square of the key value. An instance of the speculative cache is created and values are requested for the first 100 integer values.

```
using System;
using System.Linq;

namespace Speculative_Cache {

    class Use_Speculative_Cache {
        static void Main(string[] args) {

            // create a new instance of the cache
            Speculative_Cache<int, double> cache
                = new Speculative_Cache<int, double>(
                    key1 => {
                        Console.WriteLine("Created value for key {0}", key1);
                        return Math.Pow(key1, 2);
                    },
                    key2 => Enumerable.Range(key2 + 1, 5).ToArray());

            // request some values from the cache
            for (int i = 0; i < 100; i++) {
                double value = cache.GetValue(i);
                Console.WriteLine("Got result {0} for key {1}", value, i);
            }
```

```
                  // wait for input before exiting
                  Console.WriteLine("Press enter to finish");
                  Console.ReadLine();
              }
          }
      }
```

Using Producers and Consumers

The examples in this section cover decoupling the Console class and pipelining functions.

Decoupling the Console Class

The previous chapter mentioned that you should avoid using the System.Console class in parallel programs. The synchronization in the Console class affects the overall performance of your application, and adding Console.WriteLine() calls when trying to fix a problem can actually change the interaction between the tasks in your program enough that you may not be able to recreate the issue.

That said, everyone still uses System.Console —myself included. And, having admitted and accepted that fact, the best compromise is to use a decoupled console class, which is a simple Producer/Consumer pattern that allows Tasks to put messages destined for the console into a queue with minimal delay and for a single consumer Task to take those messages and write them out.

The Code

The following implementation is a little more general than it needs to be. The items in the queue are System.Actions that write messages to the Console class. You could easily adapt this model to perform other types of Action as required.

```
using System;
using System.Collections.Concurrent;
using System.Threading.Tasks;

namespace Decoupled_Console {
    class Decoupled_Console {
        // queue-based blocking collection
        private static BlockingCollection<Action> blockingQueue;
        // task that processes messages to the console
        private static Task messageWorker;

        static Decoupled_Console() {
            // create the blocking collection
            blockingQueue = new BlockingCollection<Action>();
```

```
            // create and start the worker task
            messageWorker = Task.Factory.StartNew(() => {
                foreach (Action action in blockingQueue.GetConsumingEnumerable()) {
                    // invoke the action
                    action.Invoke();
                }
            }, TaskCreationOptions.LongRunning);
        }

        public static void WriteLine(object value) {
            blockingQueue.Add(new Action(() =>
                Console.WriteLine(value)));
        }

        public static void WriteLine(string format, params object[] values) {
            blockingQueue.Add(new Action(() =>
                Console.WriteLine(format, values)));
        }
    }
}
```

Using the Code

Using the decoupled console is just like using the regular Console class. The following code starts a number of Tasks, each of which writes a number of messages:

```
using System;
using System.Threading.Tasks;

namespace Decoupled_Console {
    class Using_Decoupled_Console {

        static void Main(string[] args) {
            // create a set of tasks that each writes messages
            for (int i = 0; i < 10; i++) {
                Task.Factory.StartNew(state => {
                    for (int j = 0; j < 10; j++) {
                        Decoupled_Console.WriteLine("Message from task {0}",
                            Task.CurrentId);
                    }
                }, i);
            }

            // wait for input before exiting
            Console.WriteLine("Press enter to finish");
            Console.ReadLine();
        }
    }
}
```

Creating a Pipeline

A *pipeline* chains together a number of functions that are used to process data values. The result of one function is used as the input to the next in the pipeline—the result of the final function is the result of the pipeline as a whole.

You could simple write one function that encompassed all of the transformations represented by the individual functions, but the benefit of using a pipeline like the one included here is flexibility. You can easily change the functions that are used, change the order in which they are applied, and reuse the basic logic as required.

The Code

This version is a *decoupled, long-lived pipeline. Long-lived* meaning that once we have created an instance and started it off, we can feed values in over a period of time, and those values will be processed using the chained functions. *Decoupled* means that when we add a value, we also supply a callback that will be invoked when the value has been processed by all of the functions—the AddValue() method doesn't block while the functions are applied.

We create a new instance by providing the first function you want in the pipeline. Additional functions are added by calling the AddFunction() method. This implementation is strongly-typed, such that when we add a new function to the pipeline, the input type must match the output type of the last function we added.

Once we have added all of the functions we require, we must call the StartProcessing() method. This creates the underlying collection and the Task and Parallel.ForEach loop that collect and push values through the function chain. We close down the pipeline by calling the StopProcessing() method.

```
using System;
using System.Collections.Concurrent;
using System.Threading.Tasks;

namespace Pipeline {

    class Pipeline <TInput, TOutput> {
        // queue based blocking collection
        private BlockingCollection<ValueCallBackWrapper> valueQueue;
        // the function to use
        Func<TInput, TOutput> pipelineFunction;


        public Pipeline(Func<TInput, TOutput> function) {
            // assign the function
            pipelineFunction = function;
        }

        public Pipeline<TInput, TNewOutput>
            AddFunction<TNewOutput>(Func<TOutput, TNewOutput> newfunction) {

            // create a composite function
            Func<TInput, TNewOutput> compositeFunction = (inputValue => {
                return newfunction(pipelineFunction(inputValue));
            });
```

```
            // return a new pipeline around the composite function
            return new Pipeline<TInput, TNewOutput>(compositeFunction);
        }

        public void AddValue(TInput value, Action<TInput, TOutput> callback) {
            // add the value to the queue for processing
            valueQueue.Add(new ValueCallBackWrapper {
                Value = value, Callback = callback
            });
        }

        public void StartProcessing() {
            // initialize the collection
            valueQueue = new BlockingCollection<ValueCallBackWrapper>();
            // create a parallel loop to consume
            // items from the collection
            Task.Factory.StartNew(() => {
                Parallel.ForEach(
                    valueQueue.GetConsumingEnumerable(),
                    wrapper => {
                        wrapper.Callback(
                            wrapper.Value,
                            pipelineFunction(wrapper.Value));
                    });
            });
        }

        public void StopProcessing() {
            // signal to the collection that no
            // further values will be added
            valueQueue.CompleteAdding();
        }

        private class ValueCallBackWrapper {
            public TInput Value;
            public Action<TInput, TOutput> Callback;
        }

    }
}
```

Using the Code

The following code defines three very simple functions and chains them together with a Pipeline.
Sequential values are generated and put into the pipeline, along with a callback that filters the results
and prints out selected values to the Console.

```csharp
using System;

namespace Pipeline {

    class Use_Pipleline {
        static void Main(string[] args) {

            // create a set of functions that we want to pipleline together
            Func<int, double> func1 = (input => Math.Pow(input, 2));
            Func<double, double> func2 = (input => input / 2);
            Func<double, bool> func3 = (input => input % 2 == 0 && input > 100);

            // define a callback
            Action<int, bool> callback = (input, output) => {
                if (output) {
                    Console.WriteLine("Found value {0} with result {1}", input, output);
                }
            };

            // create the pipeline
            Pipeline<int, bool> pipe = new Pipeline<int, double>(func1)
                .AddFunction(func2)
                .AddFunction(func3);

            // start the pipeline
            pipe.StartProcessing();

            // generate values and push them into the pipeline
            for (int i = 0; i < 1000; i++) {
                Console.WriteLine("Added value {0}", i);
                pipe.AddValue(i, callback);
            }

            // stop the pipeline
            pipe.StopProcessing();

            // wait for input before exiting
            Console.WriteLine("Press enter to finish");
            Console.ReadLine();
        }
    }
}
```

Index

■T

You Need the Companion eBook

Your purchase of this book entitles you to buy the companion PDF-version eBook for only $10. Take the weightless companion with you anywhere.

We believe this Apress title will prove so indispensable that you'll want to carry it with you everywhere, which is why we are offering the companion eBook (in PDF format) for $10 to customers who purchase this book now. Convenient and fully searchable, the PDF version of any content-rich, page-heavy Apress book makes a valuable addition to your programming library. You can easily find and copy code—or perform examples by quickly toggling between instructions and the application. Even simultaneously tackling a donut, diet soda, and complex code becomes simplified with hands-free eBooks!

Once you purchase your book, getting the $10 companion eBook is simple:

❶ Visit **www.apress.com/promo/tendollars/**.

❷ Complete a basic registration form to receive a randomly generated question about this title.

❸ Answer the question correctly in 60 seconds, and you will receive a promotional code to redeem for the $10.00 eBook.

233 Spring Street, New York, NY 10013

Offer valid through 11/10.